The Short and Snarky Guide to Coxing & Rowing:
Straight Talk on Coxing and Rowing from Real Coxswains

ACKNOWLEDGMENTS

This book is dedicated to Joseph "Okie" O'Connor who was the cox we aspire to be. Okie lived and breathed rowing, and we miss him daily. This book is also dedicated to Jake Poinier and Christine Getzler-Vaughan, who simultaneous fed and starved our egos. To our two favorite Reading '92s—Hilary Schneider, who started it all when she promised the rowing coach she would bring someone "little and loud" to practice the next day, and Amy Smack, who not only tolerated rowing a 2x on the treacherous waters of the James River with a coxswain, she joined in enough bone-headed, near death experiences to ensure that safety is never far from the forefront when we're out on the water. To the incomparable Patti Hucks, who in her own subtle and very funny way helped turn an intolerable 22-year old brat into a halfway decent masters cox. If there is anyone who appreciates good rowing snark, it would be Patti. Thanks also to Jessica Nigri, who always pushes us to be better.

Thanks to our editors, Diane Ingalsbe, Claudia Kalinoski and Janet Mrazek. Our thanks also go out to the many fine people we have had the pleasure of coxing, rowing with, being coached by, and coaching over the decades. Thanks especially to all of the rowers, coxswains, coaches, staff, and volunteers with TTLR, RSRC, TJC, XCP, BCP, ASU, and TRA over the last decade, many of whom began their international modeling careers on these very pages. It is a true testament to the community spirit of the sport that all of these clubs manage to thrive, and sometimes co-exist, in a place that really is the backwaters of rowing. We'd like to single out: Alicia Jerger, Ryan Allison, Emily Burkett, Melanie Kaupke, Ali Mettler, Ryan Adler, Bonnie Willis, Nancy Tran, Alex Oryal, Reinhold Povilaitis, Helen Griffin, Lisa Galow, Kristine Malcolm, Denise Lee, Kris Bliss, Sarah Crago, Kelly Irwin Adu'Elohiym, Lance Matheson, Nola Isla, Terry Santiago, Julie Galvin, Ryan Gilliam, Nora Cera, Jennifer Blatt, John Kloos, Sarah Stone, Bob Rosen, Barb Backes, Steve Miller, John Sands, Cindy Carver, John Hobbs, Dottie Turiano, Todd Templeton, Janice Eng, Wendy Benz, Christina Mencuccini, Elizabeth Jordan, and Lisa Zima for all of their enthusiasm and support in helping this project along, and especially Jan Miller, who perhaps unwittingly created the monster that is Short and Snarky.

Thanks ladies and gentlemen. You all deserve a power ten.

Cover Photo Credits: Jack Baney, Lindsay Desroches, and Short and Snarky Coxswains

TABLE OF CONTENTS

Acknowledgements 3
Introduction 9

Chapter 1 Coxswain Expectations
    A. The Job 11
    B. The Reality 11
    C. What Everyone Expects of You 11
    D. Attributes of a Great Cox 13
    E. What Makes a Bad Cox 14

Chapter 2 Coxswain Learning Curve
    A. Your First Practice 15
    B. After Your First Practice 16
    C. Your First Month of Coxing 17
    D. Your First Year of Coxing 17
    E. Your Second Year and Beyond 18

Chapter 3 The Rowing Stroke & Rowing Equipment
    A. The Basic Rowing Stroke 19
    B. The Parts of a Boat 22
    C. Types of Boats 23
    D. Rower Position/Seats in an 8+ 24
    E. Parts of an Oar 25
    F. Parts of an Oarlock 25
    G. The Coxswain Seat and How to Sit in It 25
    H. Cox-Box and How to Use It 28
    I. Care of Your Cox-Box and Mic 29
    J. Ergometers and How to Use Them 29
    K. Other Equipment and Basic Data 30
    L. Keeping Your Equipment in Good Working Order 30

Chapter 4 Basic Boat Handling on Land and Docks for Coxswains
    A. Giving Commands on Land 31
    B. Moving Boats on Land 32
    C. Walking a Boat Down to the Dock (Or Anywhere Else) 42
    D. Getting a Boat Into the Water and Launching 43
    E. Putting a Boat Into the Water from a Dock 44
    F. Launching from a Dock 46
    G. Landing at a Dock 47
    H. Taking a Boat Out of the Water from a Dock 48
    I. Putting a Boat In the Water with a Water Launch 49
    J. Taking a Boat Out of the Water from a Water Launch Situation ... 51
    K. Docking Tips and Tricks 52

Chapter 5 Steering Like a Champion in Practices and Races
    A. Steering to Safety 55
    B. Steering, Safety, and Traffic Patterns 56
    C. Steering a Line Versus Steering a Point 57

    D. How to Grip the Steering 58
    E. Ways to Steer a Boat 61
    F. How to Actually Steer 62
    G. When to Steer 62
    H. Steering Tips for the Real World. 64
    I. How to Get a Point from a Stationary Position—What Your Coach Really Wants!. 64
    J. Basic Steering Maneuvers—How to Back, Spin and Turn Your Crew. 65
    K. Steering Maneuvers with the Coaching Launch 67
    L. Steering on the Water With Other Coxswains/Other Boat Traffic 67
    M. Steering in Bad Weather Conditions 68
    N. How to Steer a Bowloader 4+ 69

Chapter 6 How to Run a Great Practice and Keep on Your Coach's Good Side
    A. The Start of Practice—Getting Organized 71
    B. Typical Practice Components 72
    C. Learning How to Measure Distance Accurately 73
    D. Right Place, Right Time 74
    E. Steering and Communicating with other Coxswains. 74
    F. Not Wasting Time 75
    G. How to Cox a Seat Race 75
    H. How to Run a Land-based Captain's Practice 76
    I. Practices During the Off Season 76

Chapter 7 How to Make Yourself Better
    A. The Simple Formula for Getting Better Faster 77
    B. Honestly Assess Your Skill Level—The Coxswain Evaluation Form. 78
    C. Write Down Your Goals 78
    D. Research Resources. 79
    E. Asking Your Rowers for Feedback 80
    F. Asking Your Coaches for Feedback and Help. 81
    G. Working with Experienced Coxswains on Your Team 82
    H. Setting Up Your Recording/Review System 82
    I. Review Your Notes/Recordings—Practice Logistics, Tone, Rhythm and Technical Calls . . 83
    J. Self-Analysis—Assessing How Annoying You Are. 85
    K. Self-Analysis—Assessing How Boring You Are 87
    L. How to Conquer Self-Analysis 87
    M. Preparation—Writing it Down and Saying it Out Loud. 88
    N. The Big Notebook 88
    O. The Mini Notebook.. 89
    P. Practicing Your Calls and Commands Off the Water 91
    Q. Checking in—Evaluating Your Improvement 91

Chapter 8 Basic Technique and Technical Fixes
    A. What to Look for at Each Point in the Stroke 93
    B. How to Fix an Unset Boat. 95
    C. How to Fix Timing Problems and Other Stuff 100
    D. Finding and Fixing Miscellaneous Issues. 104

Chapter 9 What to Say, How to Say it, What Not to Say, When to Shut Up
    A. Categories of Things Coxswains Say 109

  B. What to Actually Say... 110
  C. Positive Versus Negative and Follow Ups.. 111
  D. Long List of Boring Phrases Your Coach Probably Thinks You Should Say 111
  E. How to Speak into a Cox-Box... 115
  F. How to Count... 115
  G. Enunciating 115
  H. Rhythm 116
  I. Intensity... 116
  J. Fixing the Sound of Your Voice—learning to Speak from the Diaphragm 118
  K. What to Avoid Saying 119
  L. Signs That You Might Be Boring and Annoying.. 120
  M. The Lost Art of Silence—Strategically Timed Silences... 120

Chapter 10 Pre-Race Day—Logistics, Race Plans and Racing Strategies
  A. All About Sprint Races 123
  B. All About Head Races.. 123
  C. Developing a Race Plan.. 124
  D. Racing Strategies 124
  E. Derigging and Loading the Trailer 126
  F. Coxswain's Role During Travel 127
  G. Weigh Ins... 127
  H. Sportsmanship and Rules of Rowing.. 128
  I. The Night Before the Regatta 129

Chapter 11 Race Day—All Things Racing from the Dock to the Finish Line
  A. Your Race Day Gear 131
  B. Writing it Down 132
  C. The Coaches and Coxswains Meeting 132
  D. Your Role on Race Day 133
  E. Pre-race Checklist 133
  F. Launching 134
  G Race Warm Ups 134
  H. Navigating the Marshalling Area.. 135
  I. Sprint Race Starts 135
  J. Step by Step Tips for Coxing a Sprint Race 138
  K. Step by Step Tips for Coxing a Head Race 141
  L. After the Finish 147
  M. Protests.. 147
  N. Accuracy and Misinformation During Races.. 148

Chapter 12 Getting to Know Your Crew and What Makes Them Tick
  A. How to Get Inside the Heads of Your Crew 149
  B. Close But Not Too Close.. 150
  C. Get to Know Other People's Motivations 150
  D. Sappy or Effective? 150
  E. What Really Motivates People? 151

Chapter 13 Coxswain Culture—Establishing Your Authority
  A. Getting the Respect You Deserve from Your Coach and Your Rowers 153
  B. It's OK to Be a Coxswain.. 154

    C. Learning the Trade 154
    D. Confidence Can't be Bought 154
    E. Owning It—Developing Your Own Style 155
    F. Etiquette in Practice. 155
    G. Working with Other Coxswains 155
    H. Sportsmanship 156

Chapter 14 Avoiding the Garbage and Becoming a Team Leader
    A. Leaving the Drama at the Dock 159
    B. Keeping Your Ego in Check 160
    C. Becoming a Team Leader. 160
    D. Sports Psychology Basics 162
    E. Visualization 163

Chapter 15 What Coxswains Wish They Could Say to Coaches and Rowers
    A. The Short and Snarky Coxing Manifesto. 165
    B. Notes to Coaches on Coaching Coxswains 166

Chapter 16 Coxing Straight Talk: Stuff Nobody Else Will Tell You
    A. How to Earn the Top Spot at 1V Coxswain 169
    B. How to Get Into a (Better) College by Coxing (Maybe) 171
    C. How to Make Yourself More Interesting, Awesome and Entertain an Audience 171
    D. How to Snag Additional Coxing Opportunities—Camps, Clinics, Races. 172
    E. How to Cox Masters When You're Much Younger 173
    F. How to Navigate the Politics of a Masters Rowing Club 174
    G. How to Deal When Your Boat Absolutely Sucks 175
    H. How to Deal with Mean Girl Drama of the Coxing Variety. 175
    I. How to Keep Healthy 177
    J. How to Get Your Coach to Like You Better 178
    K. How to Deal with the Weight Issue 178
    L. How to Deal with a Disorganized Coach or Flaky Rowers 179
    M. Damage Control in the Wake of Totally Blowing It 179
    N. How to Cox for Rowers of the Opposite Sex. 181
    O. When to Hang Up Your Cox-Box Mic for Good 182

Appendix A—Big List of Coxswain Stuff. 183

Appendix B—Big List of Rowing Terms 186

Appendix C—Big List of Rowing Commands and Phrases. 193

Appendix D—Sample Race Plans for 1k Sprints, 2k Sprints, and Head Racing 196

Appendix E—Coxswain Evaluation Form 199

Appendix F—Big List of Rowing Drills. 206

INTRODUCTION

There are many measures of what makes a truly great coxswain. Accolades. National Team experience. Hardware. Ivy pedigree. Global racing cred. Top of the rolodex crew list. Suffice to say we are not truly great coxswains. We didn't beat the Bulgarians at Junior Worlds, we don't get asked to cox the Harvard alumni eight at the Charles every year, and we sure never went to the Olympics except to watch from the back of the stadium. If you are looking for guidance from a world-class coxswain, you might want to consider another book. There are plenty of options out there.

This book is written for people like us. The ones who knock around dilapidated boathouses in the hinterlands, toiling in obscurity for a crew that might strive for a bronze at regionals in the Master's Men's 4+ G category. The ones who wake up in the dark and slog down to a freezing boathouse to stand around trying to convince eight fourteen-year-old girls to pull so hard on the erg that they throw up on their shoes. The ones who from time to time eat an entire pizza by themselves, occasionally drop their tools into the river, and sometimes have buoys sneak under bows. You know who you are. This book is for you. We will help you make your boathouse a happier place by keeping your equipment off the repair list, help you make your mediocre crews a little bit faster, and your faster crews a little better. We will also give you the straight talk about coxing for mere mortals that real coxing books would never dare, and we will have fun doing it.

ABOUT SHORT AND SNARKY COXSWAINS

One of the Short and Snarky Coxswains coxed collegiately at a fine Division III rowing program in the NESCAC conference, where she perfected the art of steering like a champion through eight layers of polar fleece on one of New England's most scenic rivers. She has coxed, rowed, and coached at eleven boathouses in eight different states across the U.S. and has steered crews to medals at Head of the Charles, Dad Vails, New England Championships, Heads of the Schuylkill, Hooch, and Connecticut, Champion International Collegiate Regatta, US Rowing Masters Nationals, and pretty much all of the regional US-Rowing masters regattas. Her greatest sporting achievement of all spans three decades, where she has now medaled in three different sports, including rowing, at the internationally renowned, and hotly contested, Badger State Games, an annual competition for residents of one of America's least fit states, which usually draws at least two entries per event—sometimes. Now that she can barely squeeze herself into a coxswain seat, she coaches for a local masters program. She holds the US Rowing Level I, II, and III coaching certification and occasionally thinks about becoming a referee.

The other Short and Snarky Coxswain had initial aspirations to be a juniors rower, but her coach said if she wasn't going to be growing anymore, she should just get comfortable in the coxswain seat. That's where she's been comfortable for about half of her life. Oh my, has it been that long? After her high school team's heyday—where she and her crews rowed themselves to greatness in numerous West Coast events—she moved on to coaching for a high school club team. Around that time, a local competitive masters team solicited her for her sparkling personality and ability not to hit things. She plugged herself into their speakers (and their hearts). The rest is coxing history, with numerous successful finishes at West Coast events and a gold medal at US Rowing Masters Nationals. Well known for entertaining her crews with many a good story and a bad joke, she sidelines as a comedy writer and stand up comic.

ABOUT THIS BOOK

We're the first to admit that coxing books are incredibly boring, this one included, and there is no real way around it. With that in mind, we designed this book to be read in bits and pieces. It is full of lists, bullet points, and hopefully funny stories to break up the drudgery. Don't feel like you need to read it all at once. We're best in small doses anyway. We also tried to add humor and to increase the fun quotient over normal rowing books. This is the book we wish we had available when we first started coxing and the book we wish our coxswains and coaches would read. Actually, it's the book we wish everyone associated with this great sport would read. Or buy at least.

This book is meant to be combined with the Short and Snarky social media presence. We can be found at @shortandsnarkyrowing on just about all the social media sites you can think of. We use social media to answer your coxing questions, share great coxing photos, commiserate on coxing issues, and help troubleshoot all manner of coxing situations. Email us at shortandsnarky@yahoo.com.

The other thing we should probably mention is that this book was written from a North American perspective with North American rowing terms. You Brits, Aussies, Kiwis, and others have your own, typically more colorful, words for many rowing terms and commands. That doesn't mean you will not enjoy this book, but some of the words and phrases will be different. Consider yourself warned.

CHAPTER 1
COXSWAIN EXPECTATIONS

A. The Job
B. The Reality
C. What Everyone Expects of You
D. Attributes of a Great Cox
E. What Makes a Bad Cox

A. The Job

Ostensibly, a coxswain's role is to steer the boat in a safe and straight direction, help improve rowing technique, and motivate the rowers to pull harder than they would on their own. Seems easy, right? It's really not.

B. The Reality

Here is the reality of the situation—coxing doesn't come naturally to any of us mere mortals. It involves juggling a thousand things at the same time, most of which makes no intuitive sense. Then there is rowing's dirtiest little secret—as a coxswain you will get almost no instructions on how to accomplish the myriad of tasks in front of you. Let us explore, for a moment, why this is the way it is.

First, most coaches are former rowers, not coxswains. They don't know much at all about coxing. Accordingly, you're not going to get much coaching, if any at all. Coaches think they're 'coaching' you or helping you improve by saying things like, "COXSWAIN, STEER STRAIGHT!" or "COXSWAIN, GET YOUR POINT!"

Second, most coaches and rowers completely underestimate the difficulty involved with coxing. Almost all of them think that it's easy, comes naturally, and, also, that as a coxswain you possess superpowers and should be able to read their minds. Coaches and rowers also, especially, fail to realize how hard it is to see a darn thing with eight linebackers blocking out the sunlight and obstructing the view. Because of this, they probably don't automatically have the same level of respect for coxswains that they do for rowers. (Sorry, but it's true!)

So instead of getting coached or respected, new coxswains will instead get blamed, yelled at, and scapegoated. That means if you want to be a successful coxswain, you've got to have a thick skin, and you've got no choice but to teach yourself if you want to get any better. It is not fair, and it is not logical, but it is completely up to you. The good news is that we are on your side. We get how hard coxing is because we have sat hundreds of thousands of meters in your very uncomfortable seat. Somehow we're still here, mostly in one piece, ready to share twenty years of mistakes and what we've learned with you.

C. What Everyone Expects of You

Well, since you asked, what rowers and coaches really expect is to be able to grab a small, confident, quick-thinking, generally responsible person off the street and expect that they'll have a National Team-caliber coxswain in a matter of weeks with no coaching. That will never happen, but there are some general things that just about all coaches and rowers can reasonably expect of coxswains. In order to improve, you need to know what those are and try to master them as soon as possible. The specifics, as we often say, are going to depend on the coach and the crew, as well as how long you've been coxing. The following is a general list:

What a Coach Expects from a Novice Coxswain	What Rowers Expect from a Novice Coxswain
Is thinking about safety all the time. Doesn't hit anything, get near hitting anything, or at least stops before getting close to hitting anything.	Rowers not only expect that the cox won't hit anything, they want to be confident enough that the cox won't hit anything that they stop worrying about the cox's steering or feel like they have to be constantly looking out of the boat.
Knows the workout or race plan.	Knows the workout or race plan. Listens to the coach.
Understands the practice, the traffic pattern of the lake or river, and knows where he or she is supposed to be at least most of the time.	Doesn't scream, blabber, annoy, or whine.
Makes good efforts to implement the practice and be in the right place at the right time.	Can admit mistakes and doesn't repeat mistakes.
Listens to the coach and doesn't talk when the coach is talking.	Only says something when it's meaningful.
Doesn't slow the crew down when racing.	Keeps the crew calm on race day.
No drama, ego, or baggage.	No drama, ego, or baggage.

What a Coach Expects from an Experienced Coxswain	What Rowers Expects from an Experienced Coxswain
Is thinking about safety all of the time.	Steers a good course.
Has an advanced grasp on steering and picks the best course.	Knows the workout or race plan.
Runs an effective practice and makes sound decisions reflecting the coach's practice plans even when the coach is not right next to the boat.	Fixes technical issues.
Fixes and improves rowers' technique.	Is truthful and accurate.
Is always prepared—solves problems.	Delivers critical information at the right time (e.g. time left, distance, rate, position relative to other crews).
Motivates the crew to do better than their abilities.	Can translate what the coach is saying in other ways.
Executes race plans on race day.	Motivates and inspires the crew to exceed their own abilities.
Makes the crew faster in intangible ways.	Responds to conditions and can help the crew prepare.
Is a team leader.	Makes the crew faster in intangible ways.
Manages the crew during travel and practices and helps maximize practice time.	Commands the crew in a confident and non-cocky way.
No drama, ego or baggage.	Did we mention no drama, ego, or baggage?

D. Attributes of a Great Cox

Regardless of your experience coxing, what really makes a great cox is certain personality qualities. We can teach you some of these and others you either have or you don't. Looking back on our own coxing journeys, as long and tortured as they have been, we can dissect some of the personality characteristics that just about every cox has (or needs in a big way).

Confidence. If you're lacking this, you are in trouble. Go immediately to one of about a zillion self-help manuals that purport to teach shy, quiet, diminutive types how to be self-assured. There is always the old saying, 'Fake it 'til ya' make it'—coxing is all about that if you lack natural confidence. All successful coxswains have an abundance of natural confidence in their own abilities or have learned to fake it really well. Now, keep in mind, when you've got a lot of natural confidence, you can come across as being an egomaniac, self-absorbed, arrogant, know-it-all, bossy, and any number of negative traits. So while it is essential for a cox to be really confident, maybe you want to keep it to yourself how awesome you think you are.

Quick decision-making abilities. This is another one of those things that most successful coxswains just naturally have. It is really tough to learn. If you are one of those wishy-washy types, again go directly to the self-help books. A coxswain needs to be able to make a decision and go with it. Those who second-guess themselves will not win the respect of their crews or coaches. For those tentative types, one thing that might help is to envision how you will respond in various situations and rehearse what you would do until you're confident that you can handle what comes your way.

Willingness to self-teach. A great cox is one who seeks out information on rowing, coxing, kinesiology, and other relevant subjects. Learn the rules of rowing, listen to recordings of other coxswains, increase your understanding of rowing technique, practice your calls, and find the ends of the coxing internet. Put in the time to evaluate your own recordings, practice calls, workouts and how your crew responded. We're not above talking to ourselves or coxing our everyday activities. Follow our recipe for self-evaluation in Chapter 7. Whatever it takes. If you want to get better, it is up to you.

Not afraid to take criticism and make themselves better. Most of the time, coxswains get generally yelled at or are given completely unhelpful guidance. If you're not getting feedback as a cox, ask for it. Ask your coaches and rowers what, specifically, you can work on. When you get criticism, try to use it to make yourself better. If it's steering, how can you work on that part? Would a ride-along with another coach help? Would studying maps of the lake help? If it is fixing technique, make a list of the common things your coach says to specific rowers every day. What are the common problems? What drills could be used to help those problems? Think about solutions to problems and go to your coach with a game plan.

Know your coxing developmental stage. In your first year or two of coxing, you should think of yourself as a giant sponge, just trying to soak up everything you can about rowing. During this learning stage, ask as many questions as you can, seek out information, and try to get the basics under control. You have a lot of leeway at this point because you're new, and people will still want to help you. It's important to learn as much as you can now before people expect you to already know it! (Keep in mind, everyone will have an opinion on what a good coxswain 'should' be, but, remember, opinions are like egos, everyone has one!) As you move into years two and three, you've laid the base for success. While you are still spending time learning, you're now able to interpret what the coach is saying to your rowers and bring more of your own personality to the boat. This is the time to really learn about technique, how drills can work to help your crew, and try out different things for races. After three or four years, you should be in the position as a teacher yourself—you should have a good understanding of rowing technique, how to fix problems, advanced steering, and racing strategy. You should be thinking about ways to make your crew better at every step, but still keeping your ego in check. You're never too experienced to learn more. Now is the time to refine your techniques and expand your rowing horizons.

Calm and Ready to Respond Under Pressure. Lots of people think they will be good in a crisis situation. Believe us, rowing is all about preparing for crisis situations! It is hard to say what you will really do when bad things happen, but try to anticipate some common rowing issues based on what you see in the safety video. Examples include storms or fog coming up, boats swamping, rowers falling in the water, crashes with other crews, serious equipment breakage, hitting something stationary like a bridge, being waked or hit by larger watercraft, having a launch stall, a rower with a medical emergency like an asthma attack or heart attack, a bystander falling into the lake, or other serious issue. Hopefully it rarely happens, but a great coxswain will be the one who knows exactly how to respond when something goes wrong.

Problem-Solver. When stuff breaks, you look for a way to fix it. When the boat has problems like rush, check, or set issues, you look for specific fixes. When crazy things happen, you respond not by freaking out, but by looking for a way around. Being a problem-solver is a mindset. Always be thinking about ways to turn the situation around, instead of complaining or throwing up your hands and turning to the coach.

Prepared. Think of the Scouts, except without the badges or cookies. A good cox has the tools to fix the breakage on the water, has extra athletic tape, knows the lineups and the workout, and knows the race plan. Study and plan ahead like crazy, and make it seem effortless.

E. What Makes a Bad Cox

We told you what makes a great cox, but what makes a bad one? It is probably not what you think. By the way, hitting a bridge at full speed is kind of obvious, but that does not automatically make you a bad coxswain. A bad coxswain is:

An arrogant know-it-all.

A bully or picks on people in a personal way. If there is one rower he or she doesn't personally like, all the cox does is criticize that rower's technique.

Poor understanding of the rowers. Doesn't understand his or her audience or what the rowers want to hear.

A devisive force on the team. Blames everyone else for mistakes. Gossips or otherwise divides the team. Undermines or complains about the coach or other rowers.

Does not know his or her own coxing developmental stage. In other words, thinks they are better than they are, and is resistant to feedback and learning.

Is lazy or is not a self-starter. Waits for the coach or the rowers to ask them or tell them before they do something. Doesn't bother to self-evaluate or seek out new information.

Freaks out easily. In other words, someone who cannot handle problems or reacts poorly when things go wrong.

Does not do any preparation off the water. Is fine with the status quo, and does not strive to get better on his or her own. Cannot take criticism.

Unfocused and unreliable. Someone who does not pay attention to the coach or what is going on at practice. Sometimes fails to show up. Flaky.

Easily distracted. This is a self-descriptor. We cannot help it that our ADHD-prone minds find so many cool things going on around us when we are rowing. Yes, this alone officially makes at least one of your authors a terrible coxswain. Terrible, but endearing.

Doesn't understand how to use his or her voice. Screams or talks into the Cox-Box in stream-of-consciousness talking or monotone. In other words, doesn't understand the importance of deliberately choosing words or calls, doesn't understand the importance of tone of voice or rhythm.

Doesn't listen to the coach. Talks over the coach, doesn't take direction from the coach, or otherwise does the opposite of what the coach says.

CHAPTER 2
COXSWAIN LEARNING CURVE

A. Your First Practice
B. After Your First Practice
C. Your First Month of Coxing
D. Your First Year of Coxing
E. Your Second Year and Beyond

A. Your First Practice

One of your authors remembers her first rowing practice. She was utterly consumed for a good 24 hours in advance with what kind of shoes to wear. Nobody bothered to mention that the boats come with shoes attached. We do not pretend to understand your own particular form of irrational fear associated with your first rowing practice, but if you are reading this, we can assume you are already stressing a little bit. You may or may not be aware at this point that you will have full responsibility for tens of thousands of dollars worth of equipment and up to eight human lives, with little or no margin for error, and be given zero instruction. They probably will make you get up before dawn. We're not sure what you were thinking, but you're here, and you're already in too deep to get out now. This chapter will help you get off the ground running, hopefully keeping equipment and your rowers in one piece from day one.

Here are the instructions you'll get from your coach: Welcome to rowing. It's a 55-foot long boat. You sit at the back. Those little cords crammed up next to your body? You steer with those. Push your right hand forward on the cord to go right, also known as starboard. Push your left hand forward to go left, also known as port. Oh, and don't steer too much or hit anything. That's about it.

A few tips for your first day:

Calm down. Anybody can do this. OK, almost anybody. Well, some people. But we're sure you are going to be great.

Don't crash. Know that the equipment is expensive. Your biggest goal today is not to hit anything. When in doubt, yell 'WEIGH ENOUGH,' and your rowers should stop. If your boat is about to make direct impact with something, yell 'HOLD WATER HARD!' in the loudest voice you can muster. If your coach gets annoyed, he or she needs to get over it. (Although you should definitely keep that thought to yourself.) At the end of the day, you're probably in the junkiest boat in the club. Really, if any coach lets a brand new coxswain in a new $40,000 boat, the club can obviously afford to crash a few. Bad on them.

Don't hurt people. Know that people can die while rowing. They fall out of boats and drown; they hit things and get seriously injured, and if you're coxing masters, they sometimes have heart attacks. They even sometimes file lawsuits, which are possibly scarier. By the way, did we mention that you are in charge of the safety of your crew? Good luck with that. No, seriously, good luck with that. But also know that rowing accidents are rare, and unless your coach is a complete bonehead, you should have a coaching launch with you. If you have not watched a rowing safety video, remind your coach at the end of practice. You need to see it as soon as possible. Your big job today is to keep your rowers safe. As in don't hit anything and watch for medical problems.

Play with the steering. It's going to take a while to figure it out, so push on those cords up and back. See how the boat responds. You've got to just do it. Forget about all the instructions flying around. You figure it out. That should be your first hour on the water. You'll hear your coach yelling to, "Steer as little as possible." Sure. Whatever that means. Trust us, you need to figure out what that means by doing it.

Look far. An 8+ steers like driving a school bus towing a trailer if you were perched on the back bumper. Given your complete unfamiliarity with steering, figure the boat will take at least two boat lengths to respond. So keep looking at what's coming up ahead.

Watch where you're going. Try to look over and around the eight people sitting in front of you to see where you're going. It is OK to stick your head and torso out to the right or left, but try to keep your weight and your body 'inside the boat.' In other words, don't lean out more than you absolutely need to. However, not hitting anything is your first priority. Everything else, including the balance of the boat, is unimportant today. Pop your body up and out to see if you have to.

Shut up. Stay silent unless told to say something. Today is not the day to worry about what to say.

Listen. Your new name is 'coxswain.' As in 'COXSWAIN, STEER STRAIGHT!' or 'COXSWAIN, GET YOUR POINT!' or 'COXSWAIN, WATCH YOUR STEERING!' or 'COXSWAIN, GET AWAY FROM THE OIL TANKER/OTHER CREWS/CHANNEL MARKER/WALL!' This will be the extent of your coach's instructions to you. Maybe forever. This is mostly his or her way of saying, "DON'T HIT ANYTHING, OR YOU'RE NEVER COMING BACK!"

Raise your hand. Acknowledge when the coach says something to you, even if you have no idea what he or she means. It means you understand that your coach is talking to you. Ask your stroke for translation—your stroke is the person sitting directly in front of you with the sour look on his or her face. If you are in a bow-loader, you are lucky because you will not be able to see how annoyed your rowers are right now.

Listen more. Try to pick up as many terms as possible. You're going to hear so much obscure foreign jargon flying around, you'll think you rowed across the border and into Latvia. Don't worry about it. Read up on the terms at the back of this book later.

Don't get discouraged. It's your first day. This isn't easy. Everything you do the first day is going to be wrong. If you really want to cox, you've got to be a tough cookie.

B. After Your First Practice

Congratulations! You survived your first practice. You probably got yelled at a lot. Your rowers were talking in the boat, giving you contradictory and confusing guidance, and are almost certainly visibly irritated with your performance. You're feeling not so great, but the good news is you didn't hit anything. (If you did, read the steering chapter immediately!) Nobody died. (If they did, this was definitely your first and last practice, and you should go hire a good lawyer).

Now what?

Celebrate. Marvel at your bad self for being brave enough to do something new. We congratulate you because nobody else is going to. You survived! Go you!

Go buy a big notebook/binder and mini-notebook. For more on what to write in these, see Chapter 7.

Read the rowing terms. Again and again. If you've got time at the boathouse, ask a rower to walk you through all the parts of the boat on a real boat. Have them quiz you, ask what each means, and write that down in your new rowing notebook.

Look at the traffic pattern for the lake or river you're rowing on. Use overhead maps. Stare at them often. Get to know them well.

Go read the steering chapter. Again and again.

Watch the safety video. Maybe twice. If you don't laugh at the ridiculous ejector crab every time you see that video, you either have no soul or you're taking yourself way too seriously. Maybe both.

C. Your First Month of Coxing

After the first practice, you will start to gain confidence. The coxswains who don't are not really cut out for this gig and might want to consider something safer like competitive lawn darts or swallowing fire. If you're one of the few strong ones, here is what you should strive for in the first month or so of coxing:

Learn the equipment. Master the Cox-Box, Speed Coach, or similar apps if your club or team uses them. See Chapter 3 for more information on the equipment.

Learn the jargon. Make sure you have 100% familiarity with the basic rowing terms. Read the Glossary at Appendix B at the back of this book for more information. Learn them now. It is going to be pretty embarrassing to ask what 'bow' means a few weeks from now. This is your big chance to ask questions and make sure you have an understanding of what everyone is talking about.

Figure out where to go. Make sure you have 100% familiarity with your lake or river's traffic pattern.

Get to know your crew. Start to get to know what makes your crew tick. Erg days and off-the-water workouts are the best time to get to know your crew.

Master on-land boat maneuvering. You should strive to master being able to safely get a boat into and out of the boathouse from any rack, into slings, and into and out of the water.

D. Your First Year of Coxing

Well, you made it this far. The first few months of coxing (and in all reality the first few years!) are a humbling experience. You might have mastered the Cox-Box and a few rowing terms, but we won't assume anything at this point. Your big focus from months 2-12 will be working on your steering and increasing your depth and breadth of rowing vocabulary, terms, phrases, and calls. As you gain familiarity with these basics, start placing more effort into learning about rowing technique and fixing basic technical issues. Here is your priority list for the first year:

Read the steering chapter, again and again. Keep working on it. This is still job number one. What you say is much less important than perfecting your steering in the initial months. Self-evaluate after each practice, and think about ways you can improve steering.

Read the 'What to Say' chapter. Multiple times.

Start the recording and review process. See Chapter 7 for more information on how to self-evaluate.

Start to learn technique. Become a student of rowing technique and how to fix basic problems in the boat. Read real books on rowing technique (not this one!).

Use the off-season to your advantage. If you row in a cold-weather place, make the winter break an opportunity to work out with your team and familiarize yourself with all things rowing. Teach yourself to erg, and see if you can aim for non-embarrassing splits. Challenge the other coxswains to a 2k competition on the ergs, but don't go overboard on working out with the team—you should primarily use your winter training time to expand your expertise of rowing technique, drills, and self-analysis. Trust us, your coach and your rowers would rather see you watching You Tube clips of starts than bench pressing your body weight.

E. Your Second Year and Beyond

With a year of coxing under your belt, we might point out that coxing is now officially your thing. Don't you want to be good at your thing? Anyone can get to the one-year or even the two-year mark with mediocre steering and calls, but you will really start to plateau as cox at about this point unless you put significant effort in. Coxswains who do not put in the off-the-water effort will see themselves slipping into or languishing in the lower division boats, while other coxswains who started at the same time are getting the top boats. If you were wondering why that is, it is probably because those other coxswains are putting in the off-the-water time and effort. It is also possible that they have some good blackmail-worthy dirt on the coach, are prone to lavish gifts, or have families that do things like donate boats. You can't do much about that, but if you are ready to take it to the next level in year two and beyond, we have a few things to recommend:

Perfect your steering. At this point you should be well on your way to understanding the difference between steering toward a point and steering a line. Your goals in year two and beyond should be maneuvering your boat using the two finger method, developing a good sense of when to use different levels of pressure from your rowers versus rudder, and understanding how to get your boat to respond with a minimal amount of drag with the rudder. At races you should aspire to use the best possible course in head races, and stay in the middle of your lane with zero drag in sprint races. Self-evaluate after each practice, and constantly think about ways you can improve steering.

Go beyond the 'What to Say' chapter. It is now time that you're ready to start improving on your stock calls and go-to sayings. Think about new ways to say things, and study what works well and what works slightly less well. Put your creativity into play with a good sense of what works for your crew. At this point you should be experimenting with tone, rhythm, and deep calls from your diaphragm.

Master technique fixes. Continue to work hard to understand technique and how to fix technique problems. Read real books on rowing technique and ask your coach about technical fixes.

Refine the recording and review process. See Chapter 7 for information on how to do this. Recording your practices is the single best way to improve your coxing skills faster. By year two, you should be in the habit of regularly recording your practices, regularly reviewing, and highlighting your best clips. Put together a highlight reel of the best clips for each situation—drills, long practice pieces, short practice pieces, race pieces, etc… This will help you when you get stuck. If you have a particularly bad practice, you can always go home and watch/listen to the highlight reel to convince yourself that you are not completely terrible.

Really give some thought to motivation. Motivating your crew depends on the crew. By year two you should be well acquainted with your rowers (or at least well acquainted with the process for getting acquainted with an ever-evolving cast of rowers) and well on your way to figuring out what makes them tick.

CHAPTER 3
THE ROWING STROKE & ROWING EQUIPMENT

A. The Basic Rowing Stroke
B. The Parts of a Boat
C. Types of Boats
D. Rower Position/Seats in an 8+
E. Parts of an Oar
F. Parts of an Oarlock
G. The Coxswain Seat and How to Sit in It
H. Cox-Box and How to Use It
I. Care of Your Cox-Box and Mic
J. Ergometers and How to Use Them
K. Other Equipment and Basic Data
L. Keeping Your Equipment in Good Working Order

A. The Basic Rowing Stroke

Get cozy because we warn you, this chapter is not the most interesting in this book. Additionally, there are plenty of rowing books far better, and far more boring, than this one if you are looking for information on the rowing stroke. We strongly encourage you to seek those out. The best thing we can tell you as a coxswain is that you should learn how to row YOURSELF. That means not by watching other people doing it, but by actually doing it yourself until you have the basics down.

The stroke has two basic parts, the drive and the recovery. Here is what you should remind your rowers about at each part of the stroke:

The Drive

The drive is the part of the stroke where oars are in the water. The drive begins at the catch, continues as rowers push their legs down, swing their backs open, and pull their arms in, and ends at the release as blades exit the water.

The catch. The catch is where the oars are placed in the water. Bodies should be at full compression. This means that the shins should be straight up and down, perpendicular to the water. Heels should be off the footplate, and rowers should be on the balls of their feet. The back is straight with a lean forward, with a slight arch of the lower back; shoulders should be up and relaxed. The arms should be fully extended, not dropped down on the knees or broken at the elbows, and wrists should be flat. Hands should be relaxed, and rowers should let the blades fall to the water by a slight release of the oar with the arm hinging from the outside shoulder. There is a natural tendency in lower skill-level crews for rowers to dive forward at the catch. Remind your rowers to keep their hands up at the catch, keep their heads and chins up, and eyes forward. Remind rowers to have their bodies over at the start of the recovery, not reaching out for extra length by diving into the catch.

Leg drive. The leg drive portion of the drive begins as the oar enters the water at the catch. The body should remain in a forward leaning position, and arms should remain straight until legs are at least about half way pushed down. Remind your rowers to connect their feet with the foot stretchers, move from pushing off the balls of their feet to pushing their heels down to the plate.

Back swing. As rowers are more than half way through with the leg drive, they should begin to start to open up their backs. Arms should continue to be outstretched straight and forward, with shoulders tall and relaxed. As the seat moves to the back of the tracks, the rowers are swinging their backs open toward the bow of the boat. This position is called the 'layback.' If done well as a crew, the momentum will move the boat forward, and the rowers will experience an almost zen-like state called 'swing.' As a coxswain you will notice that the boat feels like it is floating forward. This rarely happens, so if you have yet to experience it, do not worry. Newer rowers have a tendency to open their backs up too early or yank with the back. During the drive, remind your rowers not to open their backs up early. Instead they should focus on pushing with the legs, adding the backs as an "add on" to the legs. If done right, the bulk of the stroke is done primarily with the legs (60%+) while the back is secondary (~15-20%).

Arms in. The last part of the drive is the arms coming in. The arms should start to break as the rower begins his or her layback and should start to break at the elbows. Elbows should be drawn at a comfortable position beyond the sides of the body, and the oar should continue toward the rowers' chests until just before the body. Remind your rowers to relax their shoulders, keep the wrists flat, and maintain the connection between their feet and the foot stretchers. There is a natural tendency in newer rowers to break their wrists, drop the oar toward their laps, or otherwise 'crank' on the oar in a downward motion. Remind your rowers to continue to pull the oar in toward the middle of their chests to their marks, following the arc of the oar through the water.

The finish. The end of the stroke is called 'the finish' or 'the release.' At this point the oar is taken out of the water by the rowers tapping their oar handles down toward their laps about an inch or two. As the oar is taken out of the water, rowers are flipping their wrists back to feather the blades. Remind your rowers to take their blades out of the water square and then feather the blades as soon as the lower part of the blade leaves the water.

The Recovery

The recovery is the part of the stroke where the blades are not in the water. Rowers are moving back toward the stern of the boat and preparing to take another catch. The recovery starts at the finish as blades exit the water. The recovery, like the drive, has three major parts and is basically the same as the drive but done in reverse order.

Arms away. As rowers feather their blades, they push the hands forward from the body. The back stays where it is, essentially in a layback position. A common problem in newer crews is getting their hands 'stuck' or stopping at the finish. Remind rowers to push their hands away at the same speed they brought them in. Hands should be moved quickly away from the body and be moved at a consistent speed throughout the crew. Remind the rowers to push their hands away together, which helps set the boat.

Body over. As soon as the hands come away from the body, the rowers will swing their backs over, pivoting forward from the hips. This is often called 'body preparation.' Rowers should maintain this body angle throughout the rest of the recovery.

21

Legs up. As the body comes over, rowers will start to compress their legs forward, drawing nearer to the stern as they come up the tracks. Knees will start to compress until rowers reach their full compression. A common problem in crews of all levels is coming forward too quickly, known as "rushing the slide" or "rush." Remind your rowers to control their slides, thinking about engaging the hamstrings and decelerating as they come up. Crews who rush will generally throw all of their collective body weight toward the stern, throwing off the set of the boat and generally slowing the run of the boat down (not to mention giving their coxswain a nice little bruise in the center of their back, known as a 'check bruise'). When rowers are at about 3/4 of the way compressed, they should start squaring up their blades in preparation for the next catch. Common problems with the square up include inconsistent square timing, 'flip catches' (essentially waiting until the very last minute to square), and 'washing in' where the blade enters the water not fully square. Remind your rowers to square early, following the stroke's blade.

B. The Parts of a Boat

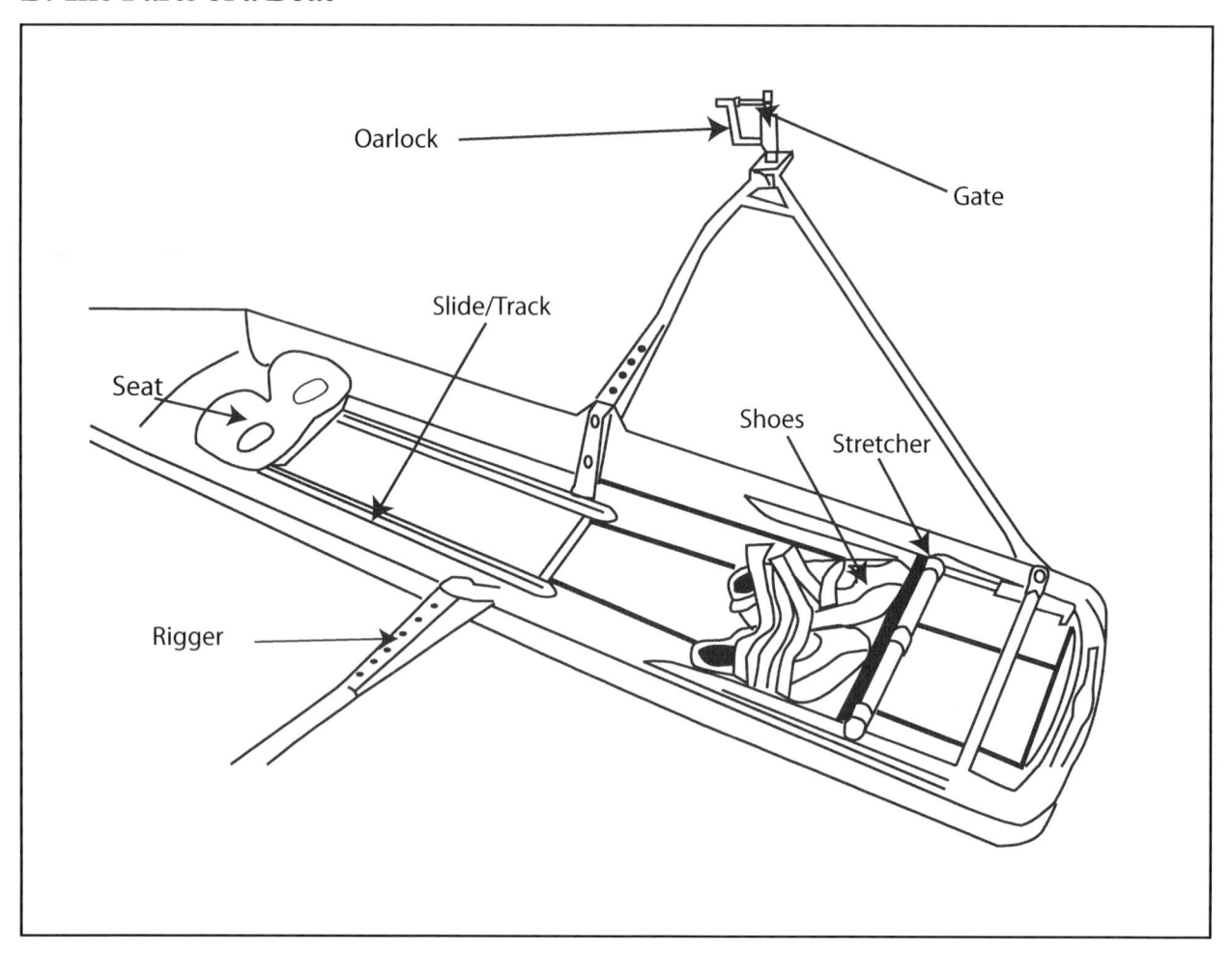

C. Types of Boats
Boats without Coxswains

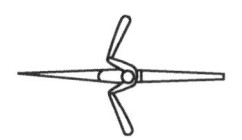

SINGLE (1x): The smallest boat used in rowing, where one rower uses two sculling oars.

PAIR (2-): A boat rowed by two rowers, each with one sweep oar.

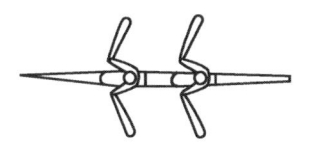

DOUBLE (2x): A boat rowed by two rowers, each with two sculling oars.

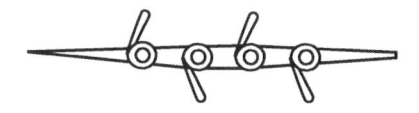

STRAIGHT FOUR (4-): A rowing shell with four rowers, each with a sweep oar. This boat does not have a coxswain.

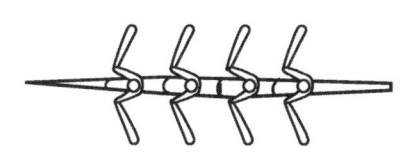

QUAD (4x): A boat with four rowers, each with two sculling oars. This boat does not have a coxswain and is instead steered by the rowers.

Boats with Coxswains

COXED PAIR (2+): A boat with two rowers, each with a sweep oar, and a coxswain. This boat configuration was formerly rowed in the Olympics, but is uncommon in North America, and is not raced on the junior, college, or masters level.

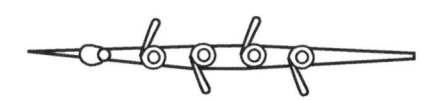

FOUR (4+): A boat with four rowers, each with one sweep oar, steered by a coxswain.

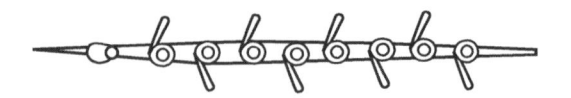

EIGHT: A boat with eight rowers, each with one sweep oar, and a coxswain.

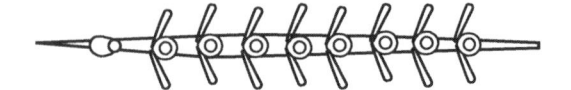

OCTUPLE: A boat with eight rowers, each with two sculling oars, and a coxswain. This configuration is very rare in North America and is not raced at the junior, college, or masters level.

D. Rower Position/Seats in an 8+

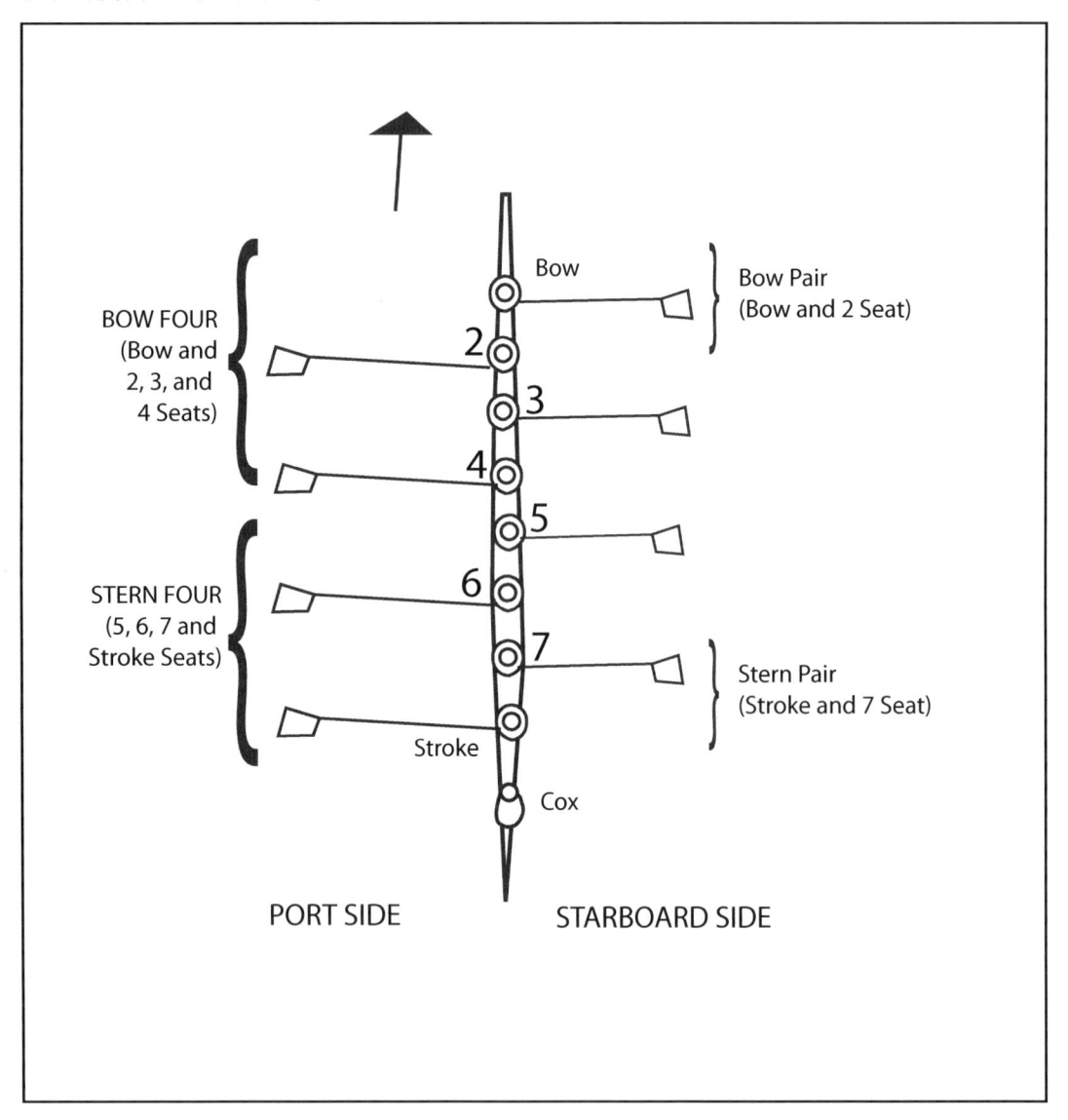

E. Parts of an Oar

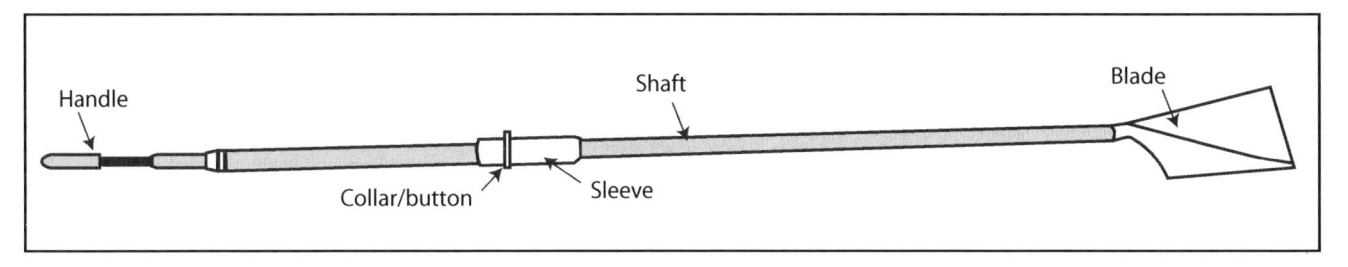

Handle · Shaft · Blade · Collar/button · Sleeve

F. Parts of an Oarlock

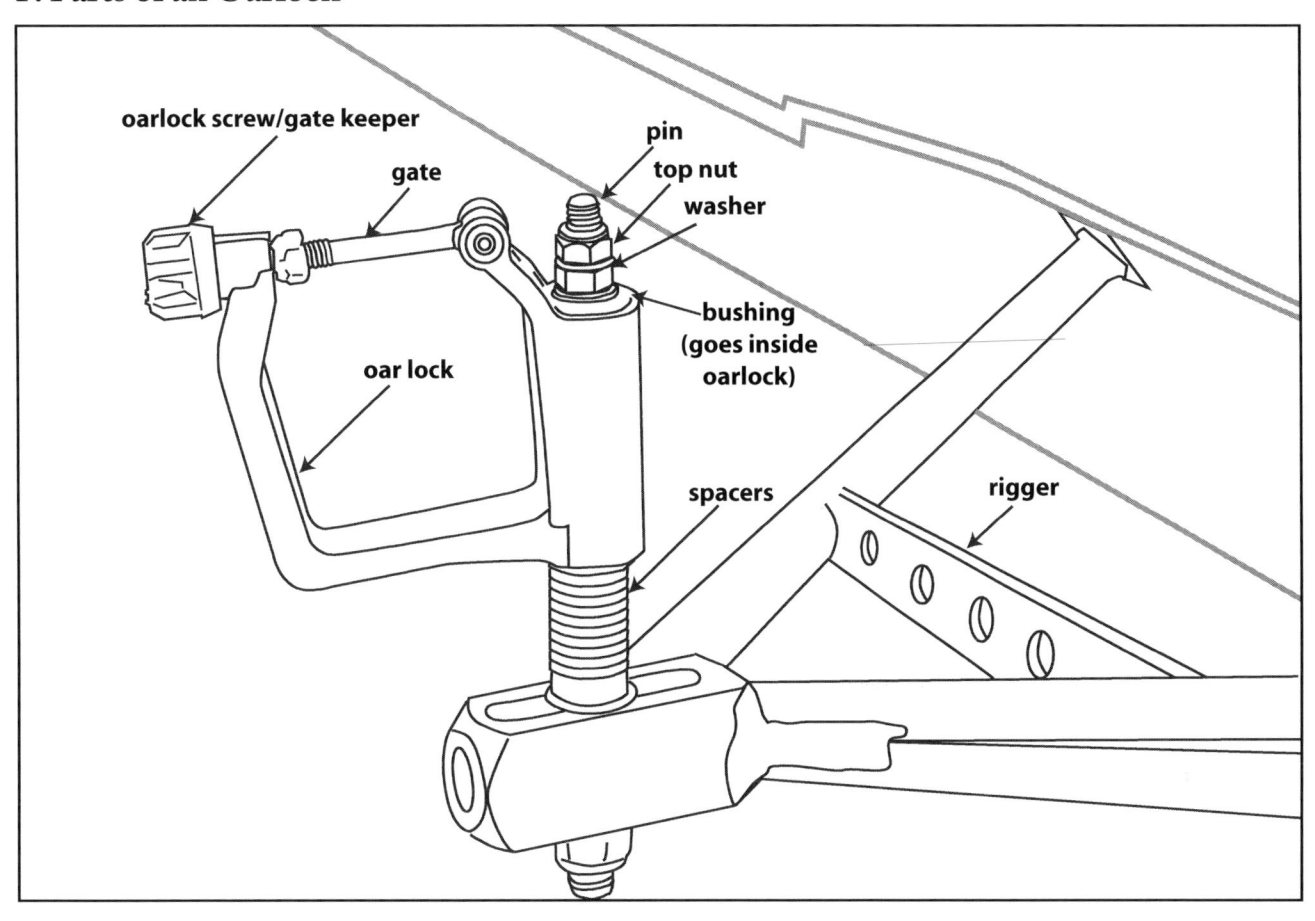

oarlock screw/gate keeper
gate
pin
top nut
washer
oar lock
bushing (goes inside oarlock)
spacers
rigger

G. The Coxswain Seat and How to Sit in It

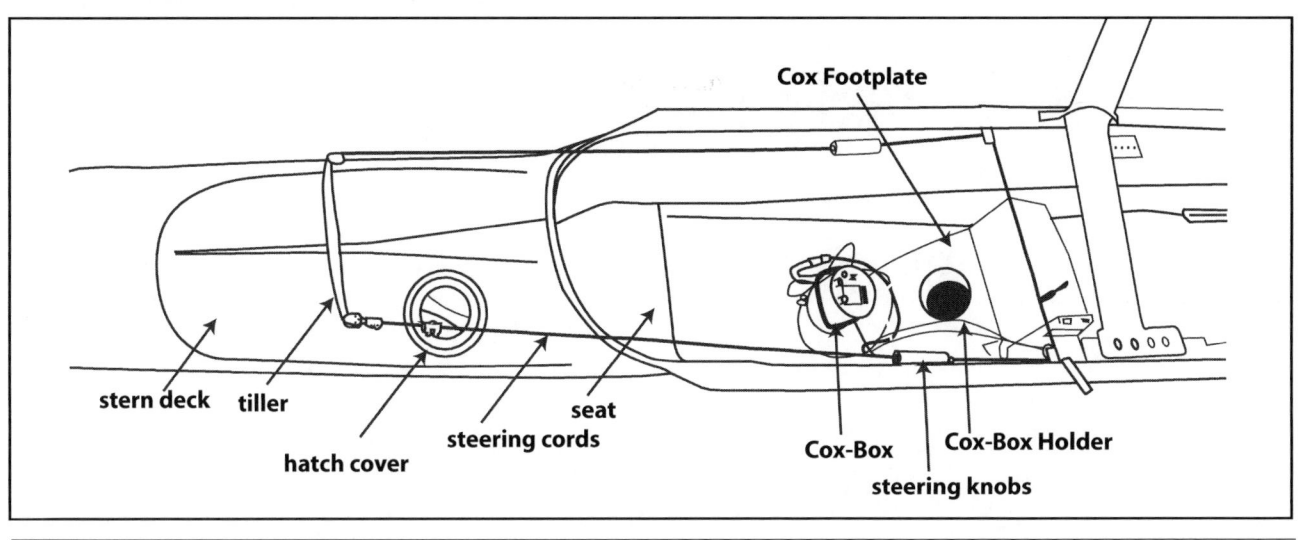

Cox Footplate
stern deck
tiller
hatch cover
steering cords
seat
Cox-Box
Cox-Box Holder
steering knobs

Stern-loaded Boats

Telling someone how to sit in a coxswain's seat seems a little obvious. However, as hard to believe as it might seem, we have seen people do it wrong, so we've added this section. Generally the coxswain seat is in the stern of the boat. It is several inches below the deck. Most coxswain seats have a back strap, which can be adjusted to comfortably lean back into. When you get in, you want to sit directly on the seat, with your rear end as far back as possible, feet on the foot plate, with the Cox-Box positioned between your feet. Brace yourself against the gunwales with your elbows. Most rowing shells have a holder for the Cox-Box, but if your boat does not have one, you should hold it between your feet. During practices it is appropriate to sit in an upright position, or lean slightly forward, with your rear end back in the seat as far as it will go. Adjust the back strap so that it comfortably holds you in position. You should never lean back, as in an easy chair, or you will screw up your back, possibly permanently. Plus, it looks like you have no idea what you are doing. In races, you should be bent over forward in a compressed position. For more information on how to position the steering cords and how to hold them, see Chapter 5.

Basic Practice Posture for Stern-loaded Boat:

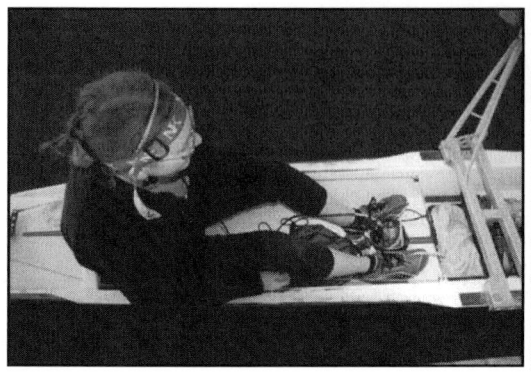

Top View   *Side View*   *Front View*

Basic Racing Posture Stern-loaded Boat:

Bow-loaders

Bow-loaded rowing shells only come in 4+ varieties, not 8+ varieties. In a bow-loader, the coxswain does not have a seat, but instead puts his or her legs and torso down below the bow deck. For bow-loader 4+ boats, you should sit up in practices, bracing yourself against the gunwales with your elbows, just as you would in a stern-loaded 4+ boat, and keep your head and shoulders up and out of the boat. Turn around frequently, so you can see what is going on in the boat. Racing a bow-loader boat requires you to lie down, keeping all but your head inside of the boat. Many bow-loaders come with a very uncomfortable neck/

head rest. Use it while racing, but otherwise sit up in the boat on the warm up and return to the dock, so you can see and alleviate the (literal!) pain in your neck. For more information on sitting in and especially steering bow-loaders, see Chapter 5.

Basic Practice Posture for a Bowloader 4+:

Basic Posture for Racing in a Bowloader 4+:

H. Cox-Box and How to Use It

The Cox-Box is a voice amplification system used in rowing shells. We should note that 'Cox-Box' is a proprietary trademark of NK Electronics. You will see the classic blue-and-white NK logo on the headbands of coxswains globally. NK maintains a tidy monopoly on rowing electronics in North America and elsewhere. Australian brand Cox-Mate and other systems are also used by rowing clubs and teams. For the purposes of this book, we use the term 'Cox-Box' to refer to all voice amplification systems.

The Cox-Box headband is attached to a mic which positions near the wearer's face, allowing what the coxswain says to be amplified. The Cox-Box not only projects your voice to speakers inside of the boat, but also gives you some important data including elapsed time, stroke count, and strokes per minute. Let us examine how to read your Cox-Box.

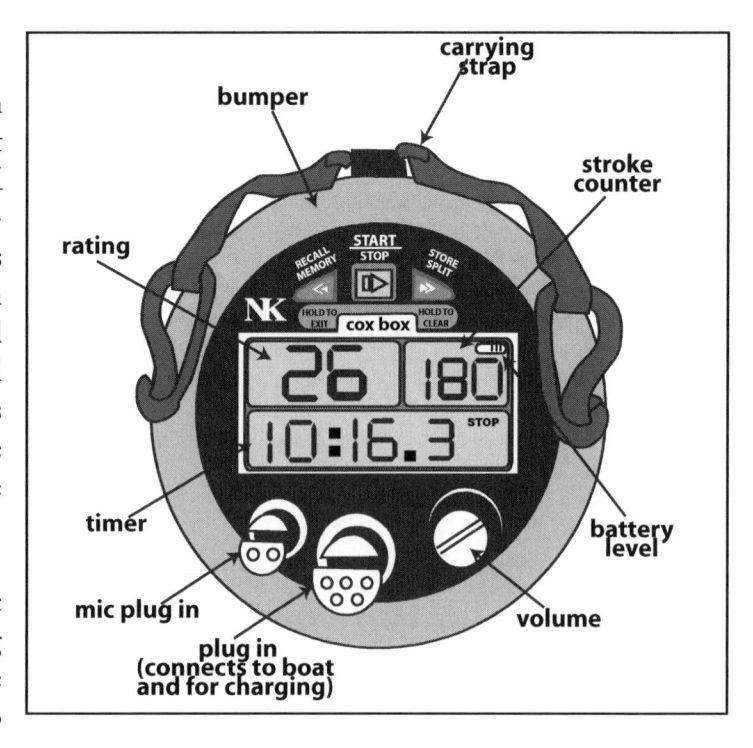

Rating. The big number at the top left is your strokes per minute, also known as your 'stroke rate,' 'stroke rating,' 'rate,' or 'rating.' (All of these terms mean essentially the same thing and are used interchangeably. We have seen certain clubs favor one term over the other, but any of these are correct to use.) This means just what you think it means—the rate is the number of strokes per minute taken by your crew. For example, if your crew is pulling 28 strokes per minute, the stroke rating is 28. This data is generated by a small magnet on the bottom of the stroke seat, which passes over a magnetized sensor attached to the hull. Your Cox-Box plugin contains a wire attached to this sensor. Note that it usually takes three strokes to get an accurate rate reading on the Cox-Box.

Stroke Counter. The number in the top left corner of the Cox-Box is the number of strokes taken since the Cox-Box was last zeroed out. You can clear it by holding down the clear button or, on older models of Cox-Boxes, holding down the silver lever for several seconds.

Timer. This number in the bottom part of your Cox-Box screen is the elapsed time since the Cox-Box was last zeroed out. Like the stroke counter, it can be reset by zeroing the Cox-Box out.

Volume. All Cox-Boxes have a volume knob. The natural tendency for some coxswains is to turn the volume up to maximum and blast the crew out. We do not recommend this. Each crew will have a different volume tolerance. We encourage you to ask your crew what works for them. Older speaker systems will require higher volume (as will senior masters rowers). Turning down your volume strategically can make your rowers listen more closely. Often the most effective coxswain is not the loudest one.

Plug in. Cox-Boxes are equipped with a plug in system, unlike any you have ever seen before, where several tiny prongs on the boat connector will be inserted into the Cox-Box. Each tiny prong has a corresponding wire in the boat. Some connect to speakers and others to the stroke counter. As a result, you should be very careful to plug in the Cox-Box correctly.

I. Care of Your Cox-Box and Mic

Cox-Boxes are a pretty amazing invention and can last for decades if cared for correctly. They float (sort of), are waterproof, and work even in the worst downpour, blazing heat, and freezing temperatures. During the season, you should plug in your Cox-Box when you are not using it. A fully charged Cox-Box will last for about 4+ hours of use. We highly recommend following the directions on the NK website for charging and off-season storage, cleaning, and servicing advice. We learned the hard way that you should not store them in an outdoor space where the temperatures roast in the summer or freeze in the winter. Cox-Boxes can only be serviced by NK and should be sent in regularly for maintenance. As far as the mics go, they should be stored over hooks or loosely coiled. Curling or rolling up the mic cords in tight coils will lead to wires breaking, resulting over time in a bad crackling over your speakers. Whatever you do, never carry the Cox-Box by the mic cord. Also note that on the older Cox-Box mics, the metal connector that plugs the mic into the box is the weakest part of the system—take good care of it or you will be buying a new mic in short order.

J. Ergometers and How to Use Them

Ergometers, more commonly known as ergs (or in Europe ergos), are the premier off-the-water training tool for rowers. The rowing stroke on an erg is basically the same as in a rowing shell. Rowers pull on the handles of the erg, which drives a flywheel. While there are a number of manufacturers, ergs manufactured by Concept2 are by far the most popular worldwide. Concept2 comes out with new models periodically, so rowing clubs and teams will likely have a diversity of models. Screens are slightly different among the models, but all will share the same data, just in slightly different configurations.

Coxswains should not be scared of ergs. Do your best to familiarize yourself with them, including learning how to row on them. Learn what the data means and how you can use the ergs as a teaching and training tool for your rowers. The four major numbers on any erg screen will be time, rating, split, and meters (shown either as elapsed meters or as meters left in the piece). Here we cover these in a bit more detail:

Rating. The number at the top right is your strokes per minute, also known as 'stroke rate,' 'stroke rating,' 'rate,' or 'rating.' (See Cox-Box information above.) This is the number of strokes taken by a rower in one minute. Generally this number will be between 18 and 40.

Time. This timer can be set to show either elapsed time or time remaining in the workout. This is typically easy to spot because it looks like a stopwatch and is generally in the top left part of the screen.

Split. This is the largest number in the middle of the screen. Split is shown in time, so 2:05 would equate to two minutes and five seconds. Split is the amount of time it takes for the rower to pull 500 meters.

Meters. This can be set to show either meters that the rower has already pulled or meters left to pull in the workout.

We highly recommend that you visit Concept2's website for more information on using, maintaining, and storing ergs.

K. Other Equipment and Basic Data

Tools like the SpeedCoach, also made by NK Electronics, are slowly going by the wayside as better and better rowing apps for mobile devices have been introduced. SpeedCoach and apps like it generally provide the same type of data as an erg. Most will show splits, ratings, time, and other data and also have recall functions so you can go back and track progress. We have found that the rowing apps are highly accurate especially for measuring meters and splits because they rely on pin-point satellite data from your mobile device. These apps are lifesavers in the event that your Cox-Box fails you. There are many other free or inexpensive apps that function as stroke rating counters or help you organize your lineups, take notes, or record your calls. If you are going to rely heavily on your mobile device, make sure to invest in a good waterproof case with a lanyard that goes around your neck.

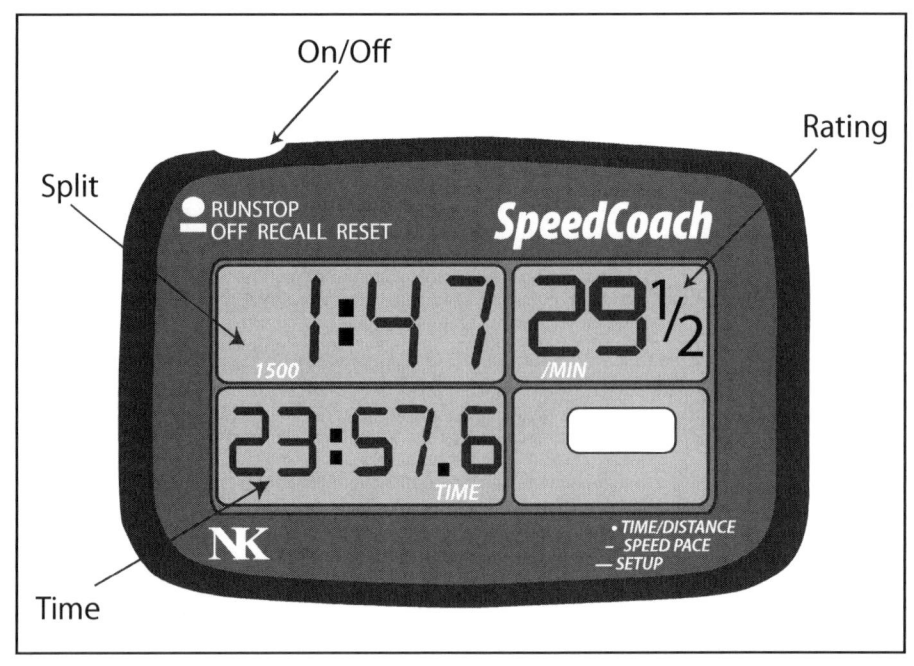

Speed Coach

L. Keeping Your Equipment in Good Working Order

As a coxswain, it is very important for you to make sure your equipment is in good working order at all times. You should routinely remind your crew to check for function and report all breakage to coaches. Before every practice, check for loose skegs, bowballs, and top nuts especially. Rowers should be checking that foot stretchers are in proper working order, that seats, wheels, and tracks function properly, and that oar collars are in the right place and tightened. Even more importantly, as a coxswain, you should be keeping an eye out for how your rowers treat the equipment. For newer crews, this means not banging the equipment around, dropping boats or oars, or stepping into the wrong spot in the boats. For more experienced crews, this means not adjusting equipment without checking with the coach or getting sloppy about maintenance. Keep in mind that this stuff is expensive, and when something does break, you can't always just run down to the hardware store for a replacement.

CHAPTER 4
BASIC BOAT HANDLING ON LAND AND DOCKS FOR COXSWAINS

A. Giving Commands on Land
B. Moving Boats on Land
C. Walking a Boat Down to the Dock (Or Anywhere Else)
D. Getting a Boat Into the Water and Launching
E. Putting a Boat Into the Water from a Dock
F. Launching from a Dock
G. Landing at a Dock
H. Taking a Boat Out of the Water from a Dock
I. Putting a Boat in the Water from a Water launch
J. Taking a Boat Out of the Water from a Water launch Situation
K. Docking Tips and Tricks

A. Giving Commands on Land

Whether you are giving commands on land or on the water, your primary goal is to protect people from injury and keep the equipment from getting damaged. (Both are expensive!) When you are moving equipment on land, the following are critical to success:

- You are doing things that are safe and that make sense.

- You have the attention of your entire crew before you start moving anything.

- Your rowers are focused on you and are not talking or offering divergent opinions. (If they are routinely not listening, consider enforcing penalties like extra erg pieces or squat jumps to get their attention.)

- Everyone knows the plan before getting hands on.

As a newer coxswain, the best thing you can do is watch and listen to experienced coxswains moving boats on land. Listen to what they say and how things are done at your boathouse. Every boathouse has its own little quirks, procedures, and rules related to moving boats. Ask questions, and write down appropriate sequences. Ask about typical obstacles like the rogue lamppost by the dock, boat-eating trees, tight corners, and the one rack that doesn't quite fit a certain boat. Every boathouse has something. If your boathouse straps down its boats on the racks, make sure someone shows you how to do this properly, and after your crew stores a boat, you check to make sure it is strapped correctly. (If they do it wrong, you will be the one who gets yelled at!)

B. Moving Boats on Land
Getting a Boat off a Shoulder Height Rack

"Hands on, reach across"

"Up an inch, READY, UP"

"Take it out of the rack, slowly, READY OUT"

"Up and over heads, READY UP"

"Split to Shoulders, READY SPLIT"

"Walk it out of house, READY GO"

Putting a Boat Back into a Shoulder Height Rack

"Walk it forward into the house, READY GO"
[as soon as you get lined up, say…]

"WEIGH ENOUGH and reach across"

"Up to low overheads, READY UP"

"Walk it into the rack, slowly, READY IN"

"Set it on racks together, READY DOWN"

Getting a Boat off a Waist High Rack

"Hands on and reach across"

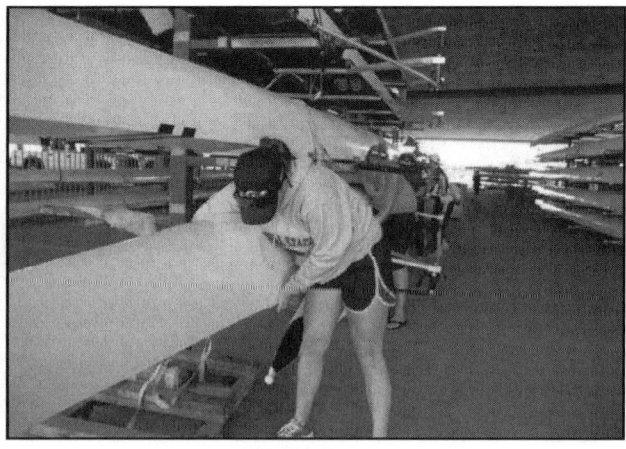

"Up an inch, READY UP"

"Out of the racks, READY OUT"

[indicate which rowers are going around, and do it one or two at a time] For example: "Starboards HOLD, Ports go under"

"Everyone holding on their own sides"

"Up to shoulders, READY UP"

"Walk it out of house, READY OUT"

Putting a Boat Back into a Waist High Rack

"Walk it forward into the house, WEIGH ENOUGH"

"Down to waists, READY DOWN"

"Ports reach across, Starboards come under one at a time"

"Everyone reaching across"

"Walk it into the rack, slowly, READY IN"

"Set it on racks together, READY DOWN"

Getting a Boat Off High Rack or Boat Trailer.

To move boats off high racks, you need two sets of sturdy stairs and tall, strong rowers. If you are dealing with crews other than young, strong, tall, capable rowers, or moving heavy, older boats, you should have as many extra people on hand to help as possible. If you have extra people around, ask a few tall, strong rowers to climb up on the racks or boat trailer to help guide the boat. Send your four tallest rowers up to the top step (two on each end of the boat), and your four remaining rowers on the ground.

"Hands on"

"Up an inch, READY UP"

"Take it off the racks, READY OUT"

"Start angling down, rowers on the ground, arms up, ready to grab"

"Down a step together, READY DOWN"

"Next step down together, READY DOWN"
"Everyone on the ground, READY TO GRAB"

"Last step, READY DOWN"

Getting a Boat Back Up to a High Rack or Boat Trailer

Again, designate your four tallest, strongest rowers (two on each end of the boat) to go up the stairs first. Those rowers should start on the side of the boat closest to the rack, with the boat at shoulder height. The other four rowers will go up the steps just below. If you have extra people around, ask a few tall, strong rowers to climb up on the racks or boat trailer to help guide the boat.

"Up and overheads, taller rowers up the first step together, READY UP"

"Next step up, READY UP"

"Next step, READY UP"

"Onto the racks, READY UP"

37

"Set it on"

Getting a Boat off Ground Rollers

"Hands on"

"Roll it out slowly, READY OUT"

"Four (or two) people walk around" (you can specify which rowers)

"Hands on"

"Up to waists, READY UP"  *"Up to shoulders, READY UP"*

"Walk it out of house, READY OUT"

Putting a Boat Back Onto Ground Rollers

"Walk it forward into the house, READY GO"
[as soon as you get lined up, say…]

"WEIGH ENOUGH"
[as a cox you should get the rollers lined up]

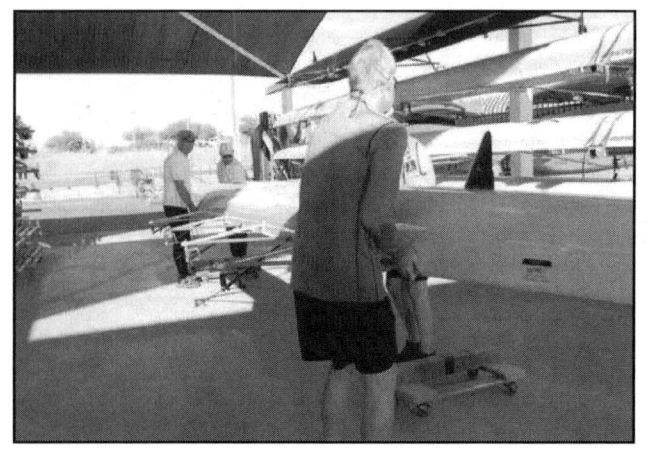

"Down to waists, READY DOWN"

"Down to an inch above rollers, READY DOWN"
[make sure you are not on riggers]

"Set it on rollers together, READY DOWN"

"Everyone come around to the outside"

"Push it in to racks together, READY IN"

Putting a Boat into Slings (starting at carrying on shoulders)

"Walk it forward to slings, READY GO"

"WEIGH ENOUGH" "Reach one hand across"

"Up and over heads, READY UP"

"Roll it to waists, READY DOWN"

"Down to slings, READY DOWN"

Getting a Boat Up Off Slings (With Inside Facing Upwards)
(Remind all rowers to get on one side of the boat)

"Hands on, reaching across"

"Up to waists, READY UP"

"Roll up and over heads, READY UP"

"Split to shoulders, READY SPLIT"
"Walk it forward, READY GO"

C. Walking a Boat Down to the Dock (Or Anywhere Else)

Your job here is to again be the eyes and ears of the crew. As you walk a boat forward, you want to be on one end of the boat or the other, not in the middle. Generally the coxswain should be leading and keep looking back for obstacles behind, especially when swinging the boat out or moving around corners. Posts, signs, trees, riggers from other boats, and people are typical obstacles. Do not assume bystanders, especially rowers from other crews, see you or know you are coming through with a boat. Do not hesitate to tap people on shoulders and LOUDLY ask them to move. Try to be polite, but it is better to be loud and obnoxious than to hit someone's grandmother in the head with a rigger.

Some general calls are as follows:

To move sideways:
"Side step toward [give a specific and non-confusing location], READY SIDESTEP IT"

To move backwards/change direction:
"WEIGH ENOUGH"
"Turn and face the stern/bow"
"Walk it forward, READY GO"

To stop:
"WEIGH ENOUGH"

To move the stern one direction
"WEIGH ENOUGH"
"Bow stay put, swing the stern toward [give a specific and non-confusing location], STERN READY GO"

To move the bow one direction:
"WEIGH ENOUGH"
"Stern stay put, swing the bow toward [give a specific and non-confusing location], BOW READY GO"

Moving boats when bystanders are around:
"Coming through behind you with a boat, WATCH YOUR HEADS"

D. Getting a Boat Into the Water and Launching

No two rowing venues are exactly alike. Some lucky crews have floating docks (generally interlocking plastic cubes that fit together) or fixed docks. These are the easiest to navigate. In tidal areas, docks may be attached with ramps that rise and fall with the tides or currents and can be quite steep and slippery at times. In some places, you will be launching off a fixed pier situation, where the water is several inches or even feet below the dock. In other places, you will be walking the boat directly into the water. It is important for coxswains to learn how their local club does things and what to be looking for safety wise. Here we provide you with some general scenarios.

E. Putting a Boat Into the Water from a Dock

Here we are going to assume that you are launching off a floating dock, which sits on the water's surface, without obstacles around. As a coxswain, you should be standing at the skeg with your hands on the boat as it is rolled down and in, guiding the skeg away from the dock. Your big job is to ensure that the skeg does not get ripped off while the boat is being put into the water. As you walk the boat onto the dock, if you have an option of which side to put the boat in, indicate to your crew which side they will be using.

"WEIGH ENOUGH. Up and over heads, READY UP"

"Lay hold"/"reach across" (whichever)

"Toes to the edge of the dock"

"Roll to waists, READY ROLL"

44

"Lean it away and set it in the water, READY DOWN"

Make sure someone is standing at the dock holding the boat, and you are attaching your Cox-Box and getting your gear set up.

"Ports get oars, Starboard unlock"

"Run the blades out"

Ports will each carry two oars down to the dock while starboards are unlocking the oarlocks. Each rower will place his or her own oar in the oarlock and lock it down. As the coxswain, your job should be to supervise, making sure all oars are locked in correctly and all of the blades are shipped out correctly.

"Hold for cox!" You should then get into the boat.

"One foot in (pause for the rowers to get their feet in), AND DOWN"

"Tie in and count down from bow when ready" You should be getting your Cox-Box, mic, tool kit, and mobile device into the boat and set up at this point.

F. Launching from a Dock

Your crew is in the boat, tied in, and ready to go; you are in the boat with Cox-Box attached and working. Now you have to get off of the dock. Keep an eye on wind and weather patterns. If unusual conditions are present, let your rowers know before you leave the dock. For example, if there is a heavy head wind or current is pushing you toward the shore, they will have to compensate. Explain the plan of action before you leave the dock and ask your rowers if they have any questions about what is about to happen. Here are the basic commands:

"Lean away from the dock"    *"One hand out for the dock"*

"Ready to walk it down" (or "Ready to shove it"), "READY GO"

As soon as you are clear of the end of the dock, assuming you are facing forward, your bow pair will row you off the dock. If you put the boat in backwards, or have an unusual set up, your stern pair will be backing your boat off the dock.

Continue to row/add in rowers until you are comfortably clear of the dock and the shore. "WEIGH ENOUGH" "Final adjustments, count down from bow when ready"

G. Landing at a Dock

To the un-indoctrinated, a coxswain's worth can be gaged by his or her docking skills. To return to a dock, you want to completely STOP your crew well over two boat lengths off the dock. As you stop, take a moment to gage wind and weather conditions and communicate with other coxswains about the order of docking for your respective crews. Adjust your point, and proceed rowing by your stern pair or stern four only. As you approach the dock:

"Stern 4/Stern Pair only rowing"

Coast in, adjusting steering as needed. "Dock side oars up and lean away"

"Get a hand out for the dock"

"Hold for cox" (You should then get out.)

"One foot up....AND OUT!"
Rowers will put one foot up. Give them enough time to get their feet out, and then tell them to get out.

H. Taking a Boat Out of the Water from a Dock

"Hands on"

"Up to waists...READY UP"

"Up and over heads...READY UP"  *"Split to shoulders...READY DOWN"*

I. Putting a Boat In the Water with a Water Launch

Crews in warm-weather places like Southern California and Florida are more likely to encounter the dreaded water launch (also known as a beach launch or wet launch) at their home rowing venues. Water launches are also common at regattas where dock space is short and in cold weather places during the shoulder seasons when crews have to travel to other venues to row due to ice or docks have been taken out for the winter. No matter the situation, a water launch is a drag for coxswains. If it is cold out, your feet will be frozen for the duration of the practice or race. The other option, having your crew carry you into the coxswain seat without touching the water, is kind of wimpy and embarrassing. We will admit that we have been carried in more than a few times, but it is not something we are proud of. If it is really cold, we might even demand it. We will also recount not so fondly having been dropped by rowers on several occasions, resulting in a truly miserable practice or race. If you are going to walk in, remember to bring a small towel and a really warm pair of socks or boots with you for the boat. If it is cold, you should wear shorts as you wade in, and put pants on when you get into the boat. The biggest thing to watch out for with water launches is the skeg. You need to be in deep enough water that the skeg will clear when the weight of the rowers are all in the boat. If you are a normal-sized coxswain, say 5'3" or less, this means you will be wading in to above your knees to mid-thigh level. You should hold the boat for the rowers. Make sure all of the oars are locked in, and then let your crew know you will be getting in first. (Do not apologize for getting in first if it is cold out. The rowers will be moving to warm up, and you will be sitting there with your lower extremities encased in blocks of ice.) Unless your crew is very skilled and used to water launches, load your boat by pairs. Remember to connect your Cox-Box, so they can hear you. We like to load bow pair, then stern pair, then 3 and 4 seat, then 5 and 6 seat.

Commands for Putting a Boat Into the Water from a Water Launch Situation

Stop at the edge of the water, and allow them to kick shoes off, if that is how your team does it. "WEIGH ENOUGH" *"Walk it in to knees, READY IN" Make sure they are in deep enough to be well clear of the skeg*

"Up and over heads...READY UP"    *"Roll to waists...AND DOWN"*

"Set it in"    *"Ports get oars; Starboards unlock and hold the boat" (or vice versa)*

Get your coxswain equipment set up    *"Run the oars out ... Hold for Cox." [Cox gets in.]*

"One foot in....    *AND SHOVE!"*

50

Then immediately have your rowers (e.g. the side closest to the shore) start rowing to make sure you are clear of ripping the skeg off and move into deeper water before having them tie in.

J. Taking a Boat Out of the Water from a Water Launch Situation

Slowly approach your beach or landing spot. Floating or drifting in is appropriate in most situations. If you come in too fast, you are in danger of ripping the skeg off of the bottom of the boat. Watch until you can see the bottom of the lake. You will be warning your crew that the tallest person will be getting out to guide the crew in. You want to be in about 1.5 feet of water when you ask that person to get out. The designated rower who hops out should do so on the side of the boat nearest to the beach and pull the boat into the appropriate amount of water. We like to hop out soon after and run to the shore immediately in anticipation of getting our frozen feet into a hot shower. So long as you are in shouting distance of your crew, it is fine to cox the boat out from the shore. With experienced crews, it is fine to have everyone disembark at the same time. With newer crews, you can unload by pairs. The big thing to remind your rowers is that they should not take any oars out until everyone is out of the boat.

Here are some general commands:

"One foot out…

and UP"

Unplug your Cox-Box mic and get out of the boat "Starboards take oars up; Ports hold the boat"

"Hands on"

51

"Up to waists, READY UP"

"Up over heads, READY UP"

"Sidestep it toward the shore together, READY GO"

"Split to shoulders, READY SPLIT"
Give them time to scramble to stuff their feet into shoes if this is customary for your team.

"Swing the bow toward the boathouse, pivoting in the stern, READY SWING"

"Walk it up, READY GO"

K. Docking Tips and Tricks

Stop first. Stop at least two boat lengths off the dock to assess wind condition, current, and communicate docking order with other coxswains.

Take it easy. Go SLOWLY as you approach the dock, rowing with the minimum amount of rowers possible. Rowing by pairs or by single person is usually the way to go. If you're going slow, you will never have a situation where you crush the bow or push the bow up on the end of the dock.

Consider the weather. In bad or unusual weather or wind conditions, think about what you are going to do, explain it to your rowers, and stick with the plan. Move quickly and decisively. This is a situation where the expression, 'He who hesitates, is lost,' really rings true. If you get into trouble, back it, come up with a new strategy, and implement that, also quickly and decisively. There may be occasions where you will have to make a circle and come in again. Safety trumps docking order.

Go with the flow. If wind or current is blowing you toward the dock, you want to let it take you there with minimal rowing by your rowers. Point your bow slightly into the wind, and coast in.

Cross the current. If wind or current is blowing you away from the dock, steer straight at the end of the dock, and approach as slowly as possible (Warn rowers that they may have to hold water if you gage it wrong). This is where your rowers need to be listening to you!

Hold water. If you are pointed at the dock at a bad angle, you might be able to save the landing by having your stroke and six seats or seven and five seats (depending on which side you are coming in on) jam their oars in and hold water.

Chop. If you are too far off the dock, you might be able to save the landing by having your bow and three seats or two and four seats (depending on which side you are coming in on) take a few quick, short, 'chop' strokes.

Lean out. When in a pinch, it is OK to lean your body weight out one side or the other to move the boat into the right spot. Your steering will not do much with only one or two people rowing.

Start over. If you are at a terrible angle, and it is too late to save the landing, have your stern four back it and start again. We have all been there. If you remain confident and authoritative, none of your rowers will question you.

CHAPTER 5
STEERING LIKE A CHAMPION IN PRACTICES AND RACES

A. Steering to Safety
B. Steering, Safety, and Traffic Patterns
C. Steering a Line Versus Steering a Point
D. How to Grip the Steering
E. Ways to Steer a Boat
F. How to Actually Steer
G. When to Steer
H. Steering Tips for the Real World
I. How to Get a Point from a Stationary Position—What Your Coach Really Wants!
J. Basic Steering Maneuvers—How to Back, Spin, and Turn Your Crew
K. Steering Maneuvers with the Coaching Launch
L. Steering on the Water With Other Coxswains and Other Boat Traffic
M. Steering in Bad Weather Conditions
N. How to Steer a Bowloader 4+

A. Steering to Safety

In this book we talk a lot about safety. You might think we are being overly dramatic. We wish that were the case. When we were starting out in rowing, we did not give much thought to safety. Unfortunately, we've had some close calls over the years. We've seen people fall out of boats into cold water, had close calls in the dark with other boats and obstacles much larger than a rowing shell, seen crews crash into things injuring people and equipment, and had a very unfortunate situation where a friend and coach drowned after falling from a launch. We cannot stress it enough—as a coxswain, your number one job is safety. Your second job is steering. (Followed a distant third by what you actually say!) Getting up to speed with steering is the easiest way to ensure that your crew is safe. Being aware of the situation, the other traffic, and obstacles on the place where you row is key to successful steering. Here are a few tips on steering to safety:

The Thirty-Second Check. Most coaches and coxing books will tell you that you should be looking around at all times. That is totally unrealistic. You have to watch your rowers' technique, your Cox-Box, and other equipment. You also have eight large individuals blocking your view at all times. Our general rule of thumb is that you should do a check, looking ahead about 50 meters, at least once every thirty seconds. That is the minimum. During that check, you're going to be looking around for other crews on the water, other boat traffic large and small, any fixed obstacles around like buoys, channel markers, and bridges, and any weather or wakes ahead. During this check, you should adjust your steering accordingly.

The 360-Degree Check. Every minute or two you should be doing a complete 360-degree check of everything around you, including on the sides and behind you. Watch for boat traffic coming up behind you, your coaching launch, and other surprises from the back. (Your stroke seat should be keeping you informed as well.) Realistically it probably will not happen that often, but it is a really good thing to get in the habit of doing, especially if you cox a crew that is slower than other boat traffic on the water. This is particularly important if you row in a high traffic area with lots of powerboats and areas without a clear traffic pattern. We can recall a situation, rowing very near the shoreline of a small urban lake, where a large black Labrador retriever launched from the bank, nearly jumping on our bow deck. Luckily, we were used to looking 360-degrees around and knew it was coming, enough to move over just in time.

When in Doubt, Weigh Enough. We said it before, and we will say it again, you should always make the smart choice and stop before you hit something. Your coach will be more mad at you for crashing than for stopping the practice unnecessarily.

B. Steering, Safety, and Traffic Patterns

The most essential step before executing any maneuver is to think about safety and how your turning, backing, or moving fits in with the big picture of the lake or river you row on. If you row on a body of water with lots of other boat traffic (rowing or otherwise), it is almost like an airport without a control tower. Sure, everybody might know the traffic pattern, but they are moving at different speeds to different places. Some busy lakes and bays have absolutely no traffic pattern, or one that recreational power boaters regularly disobey. Here are a few general tips:

Know your traffic pattern before you go out. This is a no-brainer. If you don't know it, ask, and if the explanation does not make sense, keep asking until you understand. Maps are great tools to help you figure out the course you are rowing on.

Be smart. Know where your coach wants you to stop, but use your head. If a massive coal barge is barreling toward you, perhaps you should not stop exactly where the coach told you to stop.

Look around—all around. Before you stop, do a 360-degree check of where you are and what other boats are around you. Watch especially for the kind of traffic that can sneak up on you without much advance warning, such as small powerboats or sailboats. If you are going to be overtaken shortly, wait for the overtaking boats to pass.

Don't sit in the middle of the traffic pattern. If you are moving across a river from one side to the other, as a general rule, you should do so as quickly and safely as possible. Unless your local conditions require otherwise, this means rowing by all eight at full slide.

Get in position for your next piece before you take a break. When you finish a piece and need to turn before starting the next one, do your turn, move back into the traffic pattern on the other side of the lake or river, and THEN let your crew take a break and drink water. You want to be in the right spot to start the next piece before your coach has to remind you. (They WILL remind you!)

Don't stop or turn in dangerous places. Do not stop or sit under bridges or in other spots where you are hidden from oncoming traffic or are likely to get in the way of other boats. Avoid dumb stuff like turning right before or after a bridge, stopping under a bridge, stopping and doing a river turn in front of crews coming up behind you, or running right through popular fishing or diving spots.

Be considerate of other boaters if you row in a high traffic area. This means giving the ferry boat captains a wide berth and doing what you can to avoid running over the fishing lines of nearby fishing boats, as well as communicating with your coach and other coxswains from your own team.

C. Steering a Line Versus Steering a Point

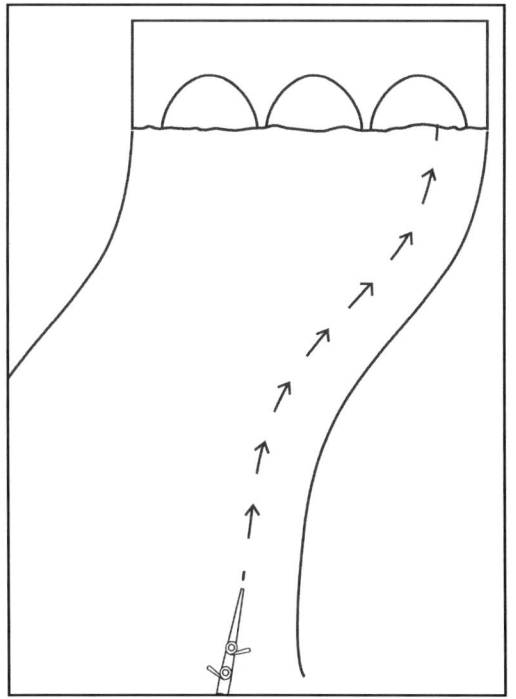

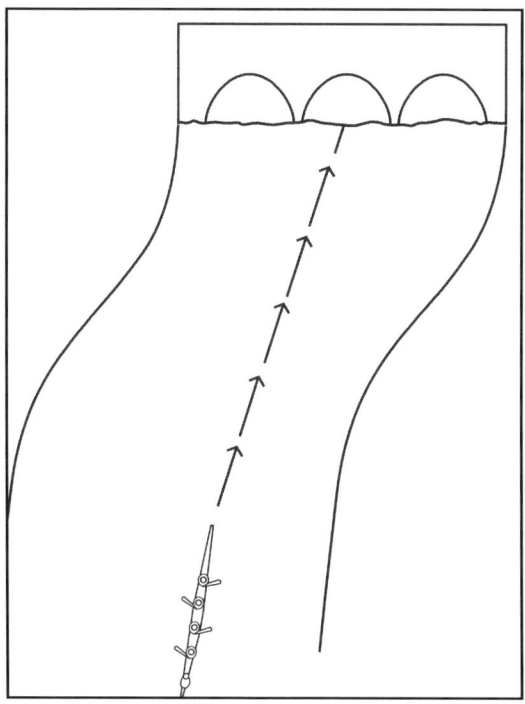

Steering a line

Steering a point

Most coxswains are instructed, if they are given any steering instructions at all, to steer toward a point. With steering a point, a coxswain finds some distant object on the horizon (a tree, a utility tower, the arch of a bridge) and heads toward that object. The coxswain lines that object up, looking over the stroke's left shoulder. If the boat gets off from that point, the coxswain adjusts the steering. Easy, right? Wrong. It's difficult and takes at least a few months to master. Plus, it totally ignores the reality of the curvature of most bodies of water.

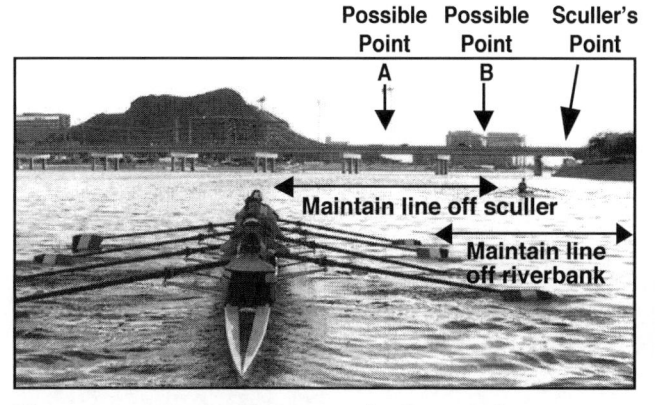

You can steer using a point and a line at the same time. The photo illustrates a number of points and lines you can use for steering

When you are out with your team and there are boats on both sides it is important to follow your point but maintain a line off crews on both sides

We are big advocates for novice coxswains to start out steering a line instead of steering a point, or at least some combination of the two. So, what is the difference? With steering a line, the coxswain navigates off the edge of the lake or river and keeps his or her shell a set distance from that point. For example, a coxswain steering a line would, say, keep the shoreline of the river 20 feet off his or her starboard side, maintaining that distance as the river curves. So for new coxswains, here is how to steer a line.

Look up ahead and sideways. That means about 45 degrees to your right and left. Try to maintain the spacing with the shore, looking up ahead as you go as well.

Keep a consistent distance with the shore. That means looking—side to side—with the shoreline of the river or lake and the other crews (if any).

Look behind you periodically. You want to know who or what is coming up behind you. You can also ask your stroke to let you know when boat traffic is coming up from the back.

Communicate with other coxswains on your team. Work with each other to hold a set spacing, say 5 or so meters between the boats, by talking to each other. Follow the shoreline together as it curves around. If you are the newer coxswain, take your steering cues from more experienced teammates and work to maintain the positions of the boats from side-to-side.

D. How to Grip the Steering

There are a few ways to grip the steering cords.

The Hand-Wrap Technique

We had to illustrate the less than optimal way to steer first, so you know what not to do. The less than optimal way to steer is to wrap both of your hands around the steering cords, pushing or pulling them forward or backward simultaneously. Hands are wrapped completely around the steering cords, and the back of your hand/knuckles will pass against the inside of the boat. Steering with your hands wrapped completely around the cords ensures that you will oversteer consistently, zigging and zagging down the river. We see this typically with rowers who think they can cox and novice coxswains who do not know any better. Avoid it, if you know what is good for you. If you're in older model boats with wide gunwales, you don't have much choice but to steer this way.

Steering Held Between Thumb and Forefinger

This is the better way to hold the steering. You can control the steering and make fine movements using your thumb and forefinger only. Your other fingers can be used to help brace your body.

Once you've got the proper grip with the steering between your thumb and forefinger, there are several variations on holding the steering:

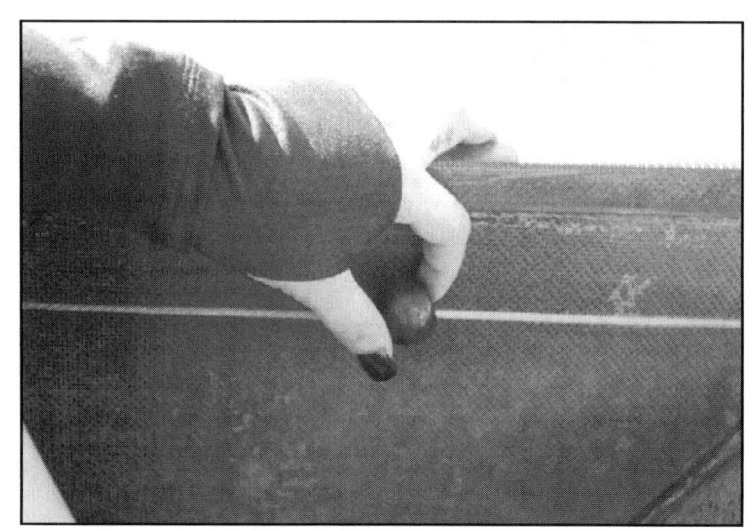

One-handed technique

To steer with one hand, follow these simple steps. First, get into the coxswain seat. Get your Cox-Box and other equipment set up. Now, grasp the gunwales with both hands, with palms of your hands wrapped around the top of each. Depending on the make and model of your boat, your pinkie finger and probably your ring finger should be on the outside of the gunwale, and your thumb and index finger should be on the inside of the boat. We are not going to tell you what to do with your middle finger. That is your choice, inside or out. (So long as you do not point it at the coach or stroke seat.) You want to then take the steering cord (ideally just behind the steering knobs, assuming your boat has them) and grasp it between your thumb and at least your index finger, although we like to grasp it between our thumb, index, and middle finger of your dominant hand. If you are right-handed, you would be steering predominantly with your right hand. Leftie coxswains can predominantly steer with their left hands. Your non-dominant hand should be wrapped around the gunwale on the other side, with the palm on the outside of the boat and the thumb on the inside. The steering cord should be between the thumb of the non-dominant hand and the inside of the boat with enough room to slide freely. To steer, you will make subtle adjustments forward and backward with your dominant hand. You should not be moving the cord up or back more than an inch or so, and remember to set your steering back to dead center after your adjustment. Keep in mind that the fingers on the outside of the boat should be pressing against the gunwales, keeping your body in place.

Why steer with one hand at a time and not two? We think that it makes you steer less (which is a good thing). Plus, with your non-dominant hand firmly wrapped around the gunwale, you can brace your body, keeping your weight from flailing around, and keeping you from getting your back slammed into the back of the coxswain seat. Another reason to steer using one hand is you may have other things going on in the boat that require the use of your other hand. These include fooling around with your recording device, indicating to your coach that you are not ready to go, flagging down a race official, and waving at attractive fishermen.

Two-handed Technique

The two-handed technique is also popular. Assuming that you are already in the boat with your Cox-Box and other equipment set up, grasp the gunwales with both hands, with palms of your hands wrapped around the top of each. Depending on the make and model of your boat and where the steering cords are positioned, your pinkie finger should be on the outside of the gunwale, and your thumb and index finger should be on the inside of the boat. Again, your ring finger and middle finger can be inside or out. You want to then take the steering cord just behind the steering knobs and grasp it between your thumb and at least your index finger with both hands. When you need to adjust toward starboard, you will push your right hand forward. When you need to adjust to port, you will push your left hand forward. Again, the finger or fingers on the outside of the boat should be pressed against the gunwales, keeping your body in place. With the two-handed technique, all of the steering is done by pushing (as opposed to pulling). Many people think this makes for smoother, more controlled steering and does not affect the balance and response of the boat. We especially like to use this technique when coxing sprint races, where motion needs to be especially subtle and controlled.

Two hands inside the boat
(Boats with wide gunwales)

Two hands, fingers outside gunwale

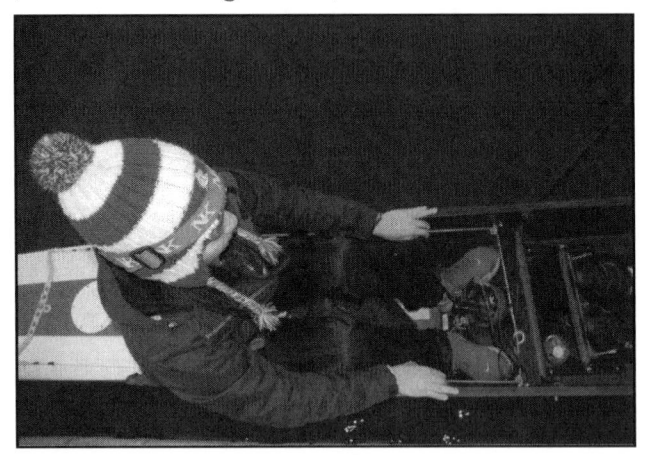

Two hands, fingers on top of the gunwale

The Hybrid Technique

We may have mentioned a time or two that we live in the real world, where things are not always perfect. From that real world comes the hybrid technique, a.k.a. how real coxswains actually steer. We admit to often using a hybrid alternating back and forth from one-handed and two-handed technique depending on the situation. Sometimes we wrap our fingers around the outside of the boat, and sometimes we keep our hands inside the boat. We especially like to grip by wrapping our right hand's pinkie and ring finger around the outside of the boat and using our middle, index, and thumb to grip the cord. On the left hand (our non-dominant hand), we wrap the pinkie, ring, and middle finger on the outside and pinch the steering cord between our index finger and thumb or just loop our thumb on the non-dominant hand around the steering. Then we predominantly use our dominant hand (our right) to push cords up under the steering knob and usually pull slightly back (also with the right hand) pinching the steering cord on the right between our thumb and index finger while slightly (or occasionally) pushing up with our left hand, depending on the adjustment. We are right handed, so we predominantly steer the hybrid technique with our right hands. We use our left hand as needed for things like adjusting the volume of the Cox-Box, fiddling with our timing devices, mobile phone, and other assorted technology in the boat. Sometimes we alternate to our left hand exclusively. Leftie coxswains would predominantly steer with their left hands. Also, sometimes when we pull back with our right hands, we dig our fingernails in above the knot on the steering knob, which no doubt causes excess wear. (Please do not tell our equipment manager!) We are not experts on how other coxswains do things, but we suspect that this is probably typical for most experienced coxswains who adjust grips to fit the situation.

Note that if you are a rower who got thrown in the coxswain seat or a fatty coxswain, you need to pick the cords up as much as possible (where there is play in the cords) above the sides of your legs. This will keep the cords from getting wedged between your body and the inside of the boat, making steering possible.

E. Ways to Steer a Boat

At the end of the day, there are two ways to steer a boat. Either you do it with your steering cords, or you have your rowers pull harder on one side. Or you can use both simultaneously. You can always lean out of a boat to the side you want to go, although we do not really recommend that except in very few circumstances. But how do you know when to do what? As a general rule, if you are in practice, and are not at race pace, you can ask your rowers to pull harder on one side and back off on the other side. In head races and around sharp turns, you should ask your rowers to pull harder on one side, and you should use your steering as well. (You could also consider leaning out, only with experienced crews, and should let your rowers know to expect it!) Otherwise, you should use your steering, making subtle adjustments.

F. How to Actually Steer

This is the reason you bought this book, isn't it? It is pretty simple. Sorry it took us five chapters to get to this point. First of all, in general circumstances, all steering should be subtle and controlled. In other words, it should be minor. Push your steering knob toward the direction you want to go, no more than an inch or so on the cords. Move the cords back to dead center when you are done. Try to avoid creating resistance or drag under the boat with the rudder. More detail on steering in specific circumstances is discussed below. It doesn't sound very hard, does it?

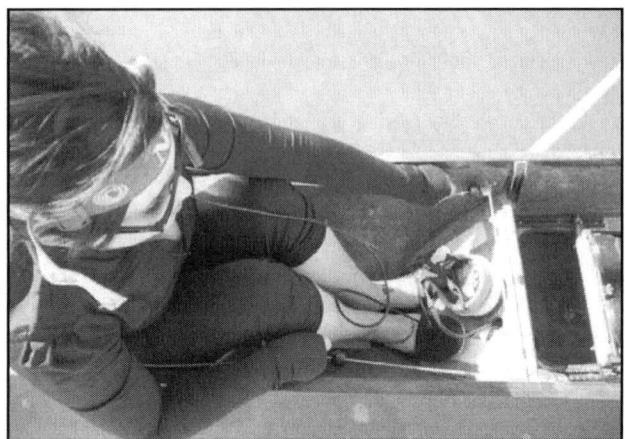

Rudder hard to Starboard   *Rudder hard to Port*

G. When to Steer

Like a lot of things in rowing, there is a ton of conflicting information out there on when to steer. Some coaches claim that you should only steer on the recovery. The thought is that steering on the recovery creates less drag and affects the run of the boat less. Then there is the conventional wisdom that you should only steer when the blades are in the water. The thinking goes that steering with the blades in the water on the drive makes the boat respond faster and is more stable for the rowers. Then again, steering on the drive tends to make the boat 'fall off' to one side at the release as you move the steering back. While we think that steering on the recovery is the better way to go for small adjustments (and if you have an experienced crew, if you are on a straight course, and if you want to be going in a straight line), but for the most part, you will be steering on both the drive and the recovery.

Again, we live in the real world. Minor adjustments just do not exist, especially as you are starting out, coxing any novice crew, in many head race situations, when rowing on water that doesn't go in a straight line (which is most of the world), or when you have any kind of wind or current to contend with during your practice or race. Here are some situations and when you should steer for each:

Steering When You Get Off Course in Normal Conditions. A typical situation is when you were doing other things instead of watching your steering. Or perhaps your crew is comprised of rowers with inconsistent power or a few stronger rowers on one side. Or maybe the wind or current is taking you off course. No matter the reason, you need to get back on track and in the right place. If appropriate (e.g. you are not already at full pressure or doing anything complicated or technical), you can ask rowers on one side to pull harder for a few strokes, reminding them to return to even pressure when you get back on course. You can also gradually push your steering forward in the direction you wish to go on the recovery and hold it there for a short while (a few strokes or less) and then gradually ease the steering cords back to dead center. Let your crew know you are making adjustments by saying thinks like, "I'm moving to port" or "I'm straightening us out." It is not rocket science. Keep it smooth, gradual, and not too jerky. Please do not be one of those coxswains who is so dedicated to following the letter of the conventional wisdom that you only steer on the drive or on the recovery, that you make the boat flop around going back and forth with the steering cords.

Steering with a Strong Wind or Current. There are going to be practices when you go out on the water even in strong weather conditions. In these types of situations, particularly when rowing on tidal rivers, in ocean bays, or where you have strong cross-winds, you may have to set your tiller and hold it to keep from constantly getting blown around by the conditions. Your crew will inevitably feel drag from the rudder. Keep in mind that is better than being blown out to sea.

Steering At Low Speed. Your boat will not respond well when the crew is moving at very low speeds. For example, during warm-ups when rowing by arms only. In these situations, make sure your boat is pointed before you start moving. You can ideally use differential pressure by your rowers to maneuver the boat. If this is not possible, make a more deliberate steering motion on the drive, warning your crew that you will be on the rudder for several strokes. Keep the rudder in place for several strokes. Bigger steering motions during the drive are not so bad when only four or pairs are rowing, such as during a pic drill.

Steering Around Turns in Head Races or River Bends. Steering around corners requires you to push the steering cords forward and hold them there (on both the drive and the recovery) for a few strokes or more. You obviously want to avoid over-steering, but sometimes the situation calls for bigger adjustments. Ease the cords smoothly and steadily forward into the turn and hold it as far as it will go for as long as necessary. Then gradually ease the cords back to dead center at the top of the turn. Repeat as necessary. Your rowers should be actively helping you move around the turn (e.g. by starboards lengthening out and ports shortening up). Let your rowers know that you will be steering and that they can expect to feel the rudder. You should warn your rowers in advance about turns, reminding them to adjust their length and power accordingly at critical times. If you are making big changes, keep them aware, but keep in mind that you should appear confident and matter-of-fact while doing so. If you make a big deal about a turn, indicate that you misjudged, or otherwise hesitate, they will lose confidence in you and will not navigate the turn well. If you normally row on a straight course, make sure you are practicing turns before head racing at other venues.

Steering Crews With Low Skill Level. Steering just on the recovery or making minor, controlled adjustments is unrealistic for crews with low skill levels. You are going to make primary adjustments during the drive when your crew is more stable. You can move the steering at the catch, and move it back to center at the release. If you need to make big adjustments, repeat over multiple strokes, ad nauseum, until the end of practice. Keep in mind that the boat is probably not moving all that fast such that a little bit of rudder will make much of a difference. Novice crews lurch from side to side. Novice crews are comprised of rowers with different levels of fitness and power. Novice crews do not yet know how to apply pressure, properly set a boat, or control their recoveries. Regardless of what the coxswain does, all of this weight thrashing around will cause the boat to move in an unpredictable and meandering direction. Especially in your first few months of coxing, the bottom line is that you should steer in a way that you avoid hitting things, and go in the straightest path forward possible. Do not worry so much about steering on the drive or the recovery. Instead, spend your time focused on making (relatively) small adjustments and avoiding oversteering. Gage how long it takes the boat to respond to corrections (both when you steer on the drive and when you steer on the recovery), and try to get a good feel for how much (really how little!) you have to steer to get the boat to respond how you need it to. Remember, as your rowers improve, your steering will improve, too. Both will take time, so be patient.

Making Minor Adjustments While Steering a Buoyed Race Course or Straight Line. If you are in the perfect situation, on a buoyed race course, with an experienced crew, moving at a brisk speed, and you only need to make a tiny adjustment, you should steer only on the recovery. As the blades release, make adjustments of an inch or less on your steering cords, moving the cords back to center just before the next catch. This is tough to do at high ratings, so your adjustments should be subtle and swift. A light touch is all it takes. (It's a good thing you have such an experienced group of racers!) Use the buoy lines as your guide for steering a line, especially as you watch the crews in other lanes. Brace yourself firmly with fingers pressed against the outside of the boat, and make sure you are steering with two hands.

H. Steering Tips for the Real World

Here are a few steering tips for coxswains who are not perfect. That includes us.

Keep the big picture in mind. Visualize the Googlemaps version of your rowing venue. Steer with the aerial map in mind, avoiding the trouble spots.

Seeing where you are going is job number one. OK, steering is actually job number two after safety, but it is hard to be safe if you cannot see what is in front of you. Go ahead and pop your torso up on the stern deck periodically if you need to see at critical junctures.

Keep thinking twenty strokes ahead. It will take a while for your boat to respond. Give the boat time to adjust. It will take 1-3 strokes before a 4+ responds and even longer in a big, 20-year-old tank of an 8+. Assume at least fifty meters for the boat to start heading where you want it to go.

Avoid over-steering. Because you are assuming at least 50 meters for the boat to respond, you don't need to yank the cords and hold them in order to get to the right place. If the first small adjustment does not work, go back to center and try it again.

Balance your weight inside the boat. Sure it is sometimes fun to lean out. Sometimes it helps you go around the turn better, too. But believe us, your rowers are not going to want to have you throwing off the set by leaning out on a regular basis.

Consider your posture. If you are coxing a race, your body should be hunched forward, and you should be pressing with your pinkie and ring fingers to brace yourself in the boat. If you are coxing a practice, you can relax and sit up a little bit, but you should NEVER be leaning way backwards. Leave that to rowers who get stuck coxing and 200-lb coaches who think they are helping by getting in the boat.

Check your tiller periodically. The tiller is the bar behind you in a stern-coxed boat. Make sure you have a good sense of where dead center is, and verify it until you know exactly where the mid-point really is. If your boat doesn't have a marking or tape at the middle, make sure to ask your coach or equipment manager to add it.

Relax. It's OK to sit easy when your rowers are sitting easy. Really, pop up onto the stern deck, and ease up your grip on the steering. You are only human. No human should sit in a coxswain seat for more than an hour without stretching.

I. How to Get a Point From a Stationary Position—What Your Coach REALLY Wants!

If you have been coxing for any length of time, you have heard the line, stated repeatedly, by all rowing coaches, in all rowing practices, all over the world. (We say it all the time when we coach, and then we want to punch ourselves in the faces.). That would be, "COXSWAIN, GET YOUR POINT!" Said when stopped, your coach means your boat is headed a bit (or a lot) sideways. Here are a few tips on pointing from a stopped position, typically between pieces in practice:

Adjust before every piece. If you really want to be an all-star cox, or even a one-star cox, you want to understand what makes your coach tick. If your coach is like 99.9% of rowing coaches, before any piece starts, he or she wants your boat pointing down river, in a mostly straight direction, not headed toward the river bank or another crew or a large stationary object. Anticipate what your coach wants in advance by 'getting your point' between pieces. In other words, get your boat straight and even with the other crews before your coach has to tell you to do it.

Consider your position relative to other crews. Have your bow seat or two seat (or bow and three or two and four seats) take quick, choppy strokes by arms and backs to get the boat straightened out. If you are up ahead of other crews, have your stern pair back it. If you are even with other crews to start a race piece, consider having one of your rowers scull the oar of the rower behind him or her. Select the option that takes the least amount of time and gets your boat in exactly the right position with other crews.

J. Basic Steering Maneuvers—How to Back, Spin, and Turn Your Crew

As coaches, we see some of the same stupid coxswain mistakes over and over again. One of the big ones is steering maneuvers done in the wrong locations; they obstruct the traffic pattern or put crews in the position to pose a danger to on-coming boat traffic. You can help yourself by asking where the coach wants you to turn and clarifying which of the maneuvers (discussed in more detail below) are appropriate for the place you row and in what situations. Show this list to your coach, preferably with a map of your rowing venue, and discuss this. The off-season or before the season starts is a great time to talk about these kinds of things. Basic maneuvering may seem unimportant to the coach, so don't be surprised if they brush you off, but turning in the right place makes the practice go smoother and keeps you on your coach's good side.

Backing. To appropriately back the boat, you will ask the rowers to turn their blades over, so the front of the blade is turned around. Rowers should typically back by pairs to go in a straight line unless you are in an experienced crew.

Basic River Turns. Basic river turns either spin the boat 180 degrees or 90 degrees, depending on where you want to go. It is amazing to us how few crews know how to do a proper basic river turn. Your job as coxswain is to make sure they understand how to properly execute the turn and then lead them through it. Experienced crews will need zero assistance from the cox while novices will need help every step of the way. If you are dealing with a novice crew, instruct your crew to sit at the finish with hands by the body. Remind them they will be turning using only arms and backs. All eight (or four) members of the crew will be swinging their arms away and bodies over AT THE SAME TIME, REGARDLESS OF WHAT SIDE THEY ARE ON. For example, if you want to go to port, ports will be backing, and starboards will be rowing regularly. Have your crew sit at the finish with hands by the body. Tell ports to turn their blades over and bury their blades in the water, and starboards to have their blades feathered and out of the water, skimming the surface. Everyone will push their arms away and swing their bodies forward (Ports will be pushing back against the water; starboards will just be skimming their feathered blades along the surface). When bodies are fully over, tell your ports to take their blades out and feather them on the surface, and tell your starboards to bury their blades. Then tell all the rowers to open their backs up and bring their arms in. (Starboards will be rowing while ports will be skimming their feathered blades on the surface.) Repeat until turned. All eight (or four) bodies will continue to move together throughout, even though odd and even rowers are doing different things with their oars. Do the reverse if you want to go toward starboard. Note that there are many variations on this, but this is the easiest way to spin a boat with the least amount of time in an unset position.

Basic 90-degree Turn. To go to port, have your port rowers hold water, and your starboard rowers row you around. Or alternate starboards rowing and ports backing. Do the reverse if you want to go to starboard.

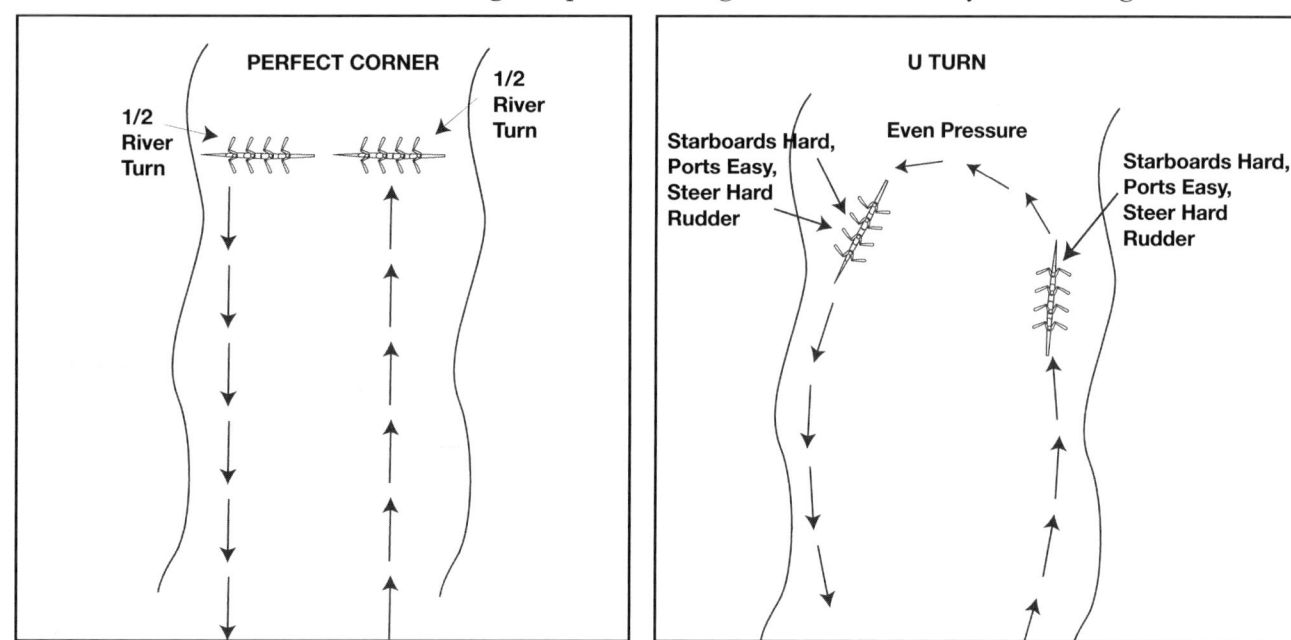

The Perfect Corner. Even if you have miles of big, uninterrupted water to row on, you will have to turn around at some point. We like to use what we call "The Perfect Corner." You will steer up to the first corner, stop, and do a basic river turn, rotating the boat 90-degrees. The row across the river by all eight (or less depending on your situation), stop, and do another basic river turn, rotating the boat another 90-degrees, and then continue toward the direction you started from.

The U-Turn We have spent recent years rowing on a small, urban lake with about 3,000m of rowable water, so we are especially aware of the need to maximize rowable distance in each and every practice. Sometimes practices call for longer pieces, so we have no choice but to row through long, moving corners at the ends of our lake. Here is how to do a moving 'U-Turn' turn for those situations. Let your crew know when you are on hard rudder or leaning out. Corners of 'U-Turns' are one of the few situations where we think it is OK for a coxswain to lean out. Others might beg to differ, but sometimes you have to use what you have to get the job done. Your heaviest steering will come on the corners, but the bulk of the work is done by your rowers (generally on starboard side unless your river or lake uses a clockwise traffic pattern). In a typical situation, steering toward port, remind your starboards to lengthen out and ports to shorten up. Depending on the size of the arc, as you come across the top of the 'U,' you can call for even pressure for a few strokes, but you are going to be on the steering and hard rudder pretty much the entire time if the corner is tight. As you come into the last 'corner' again, remind the starboards to hit it hard and long while your ports should be shortening up and backing off.

K. Steering Maneuvers with the Coaching Launch

Coaching launch working with 8+ *Switching rowers out*

We talk a lot in this book about getting on your coach's good side. (Perhaps it is because we are often on the other side of the gunwale these days.) Working effectively with the coaching launch is one of the best ways to stay in your coach's good graces. There will be plenty of situations when you need to interact with the coaching launch. It could be getting tools, moving rowers in and out of the boat for seat racing, in situations of breakage or other emergency, or when your coach just plain is not paying attention to driving the launch. Here are a few common scenarios:

The coaching launch needs to approach the rowing shell. This can happen when you need to hand off tools, swap out rowers, or pick up something. Make sure your rowers are paying attention to what is happening. Remind them to hold a good set with their oars. If the coaching launch is approaching at the coxswain's seat, both you and your stroke should be ready to grab the launch. The stroke should be compressed with the oar handle as far forward as possible. Both you and the stroke should hold onto the launch until the swap is done. You can count to three and shove the launch off with your stroke. If the coaching launch is approaching in the middle of the rowing shell, remind the rowers to set the boat and separate the oars to allow the launch enough room. You should direct oars being handed off to other rowers during swaps and count down for shoving off the launch. Overall, you need to be in charge but unobtrusive. If an emergency has occurred, the best thing you can do is not make it worse, dwell on it, or excessively express concerns about the injured rower. Your job is to stay calm and get the rowers back to the dock as quickly and safely as possible. Distract them with funny stories, or just shut up, whatever the situation calls for.

The coach needs to watch rowers on both sides of the rowing shell. Make sure you have enough room between you and the shoreline (and other crews), so the coaching launch can rotate around and pass easily in between you and the shore and you and the other boats. If you row in tight spaces or busy water, make sure you are communicating with your coach. Most coaches are fine if you raise your hand and tell the coach that you are expecting him or her to come up on a certain side; otherwise indicate that you are moving over for them to come up. Other coaches are going to prefer that they dictate where you steer. Gage the situation and the coach. If you are in doubt, ask.

The coaching launch is cutting you off. You are going to have to deal with it. Talk to the coach after practice about your concerns. Some coaches are better multi-taskers than others. Some are plain bad drivers. Never complain about it into your mic to your rowers.

L. Steering on the Water With Other Coxswains/Other Boat Traffic

As coxswains we are social by nature and are used to talking to other people, so we are not sure why coxswains are so hesitant to talk to each other on the water or interact with other boaters and other people around the place they row. Good communication is key to increased safety. How does this fit in with steering? It's not exactly a perfect fit, but this seems to be the best place for it.

Make talking to other coxswains or scullers about steering a normal part of practice for your team. A conversation with another cox does not have to be adversarial. In fact, it should be routine. Here is an example: Coxswain A: "I'm heading toward the mud flats; can you move over about 10 meters to port?" Coxswain B: "Sure, in fact I will move over a little bit more than that, so you have enough room. I'm going to take the second arch of the bridge, and you can have the first one."

If you are talking to third parties about steering, cover your mic. Your crew does not need to hear your conversation with the yachtie or the guys on the drilling rig at magnified volume. You are likely going to be shouting to third parties anyway.

Keep it friendly, and let them know where you are headed. If you need another boater to move, ask nicely, and then thank him or her.

Be specific about where you are steering. Let the kayakers or the drunk fishermen know you are coming up on their right or left side (They probably will not know port or starboard). Let stopped boats know you are moving quickly up toward them. Let scullers know which side you will be overtaking them on, and then stick with it.

It is fine to talk to your coach about steering. Let your coach know when you are making steering changes that affect the launch, or even helpfully remind him or her that you are trying to avoid the launch.

Keep it short and to the point. We are not encouraging you to waste your valuable practice time flirting with the guys on the Coast Guard cutter or talking about the weather with the standup paddle boarders at the marina. You want to talk to other boats for safety reasons, to let them know where you are going, not to socialize.

M. Steering in Bad Weather Conditions

We hope you brought along your waterproof gear because it's going to be a wet ride today. Just thinking about steering in bad conditions makes us reminisce fondly about our time rowing in Northern California, where no matter the month, there could be fog, wind, torrential downpours, and bad current. In inclement weather, a coxswain must consider the weather, wind, current, and conditions and bring along extra safety equipment. We highly recommend a giant sponge or two to bail the boat where necessary, and if you are in an area prone to heavy fog, make sure you have a loud whistle with you.

The first question to ask is whether it is safe to go out. Ultimately this will be up to the coach, but you should head out preparing for the worst. If the coach asks for your opinion, be honest. Keep in mind that it is a coxswain rite of passage to have to go out in terrible weather, only to have the coach realize what a mistake he or she made, and then have to navigate back to the dock.

First, it is really important to accurately gage what the wind and the current are going to do to your shell. Docking and launching require special care. Assess the situation before you leave the dock, and plan your maneuvers accordingly. Warn your rowers that they will have to react strongly and quickly to commands. Remind them that there should be absolutely no talking in the boat, and they must listen to you and respond immediately coming off the dock. Do the same on the way into the dock. Agree to what is going to happen before you even get near the dock, and let your rowers know what you are planning.

During the practice, if the wind or current is coming in from a certain direction across your bow, you will have to over-correct or under-correct to go in a straight line and set your tiller accordingly. If you are stopped, keep your tiller pointed, and make sure you are actively having your bow or two seat making adjustments to keep straight. You will likely have to adjust multiple times while you are waiting for other crews or your coach. Be flexible and let your rowers know that you have heavy conditions that are pushing the boat.

Give yourself a much wider bubble than you would normally around big, heavy objects like bridges and channel markers. When in doubt, make more cautious choices than you would for an average practice.

N. How to Steer a Bowloader 4+

First, let us wax poetic on how amazing it is to cox a bowloader in certain race situations. In sprint races, if you are out front, there is no better feeling in the world than literally having your crew walk your toes out across the line ahead of the pack. In head races, you can steer an absolutely perfect course, the shortest distance possible, without any obstruction to your view. Plus, your crew has a perfect vantage point of other crews coming up behind you, which should, at least in theory, make them pull harder. (Although you need to remind them to let you know when crews are coming up behind you!)

However, coxing a bowloader is problematic in more than a few ways. First, if you are lying down, your field of view is extremely limited—you can only see forward and not behind. The other major problem with a bowloader is that the steering generally utilizes a tiller bar, which is less responsive and requires a more drastic steer than a normal stern-loaded 4+, and fours are notoriously unstable already. Coxing a bowloader can also kill your neck and back.

Ideally, bowloaders are reserved for experienced crews in race situations. However, life is not always ideal. For many crews, particularly high schools and club programs, equipment shortages may mean going out in a bowloader for regular practices. Here are a few tips to make your life a little easier if you have to frequently cox a bowloader:

Know your posture. Sit up for practices unless you're doing race pieces. Lie down for races. Pretty simple.

Practice Posture *Racing Posture*

Get familiar with the lever. Bowloaders typically have a steering lever that can be moved from side to side. The lever doesn't respond as well as the steering cords on a normal boat, so you will have to force it over more. You should start steering on the drive and hold the lever for a few strokes until you have corrected your course. Then gradually ease it back to the middle. Rowers are going to feel more drag with the rudder than they do with a normal 4+. It's just a fact of life, so let them know, but do not dwell on it. A bowloader with a steering lever can be set either true to where you want to go or opposite. Ideally you want your boat to move in the direction that you move the lever. If your lever doesn't move the boat toward port when you push it toward port, and vice versa, ask your coach to swap it out.

Take it easy on your back and neck. Sure this is a chapter on steering, but we live in the real world. Bowloaders can hurt. Find some cushy lifejackets around the boathouse or invest in some foam pads to bring along in the boat. You will want to spend most, if not all, of your time sitting upright in practices anyway.

Turn around frequently. It sucks to have to cox a bowloader in practices, especially because you're going to have to be looking back, especially at the oars, but also for other boat traffic coming up behind you, by turning your body around. Give yourself a break and switch sides periodically. You will see more, and you will avoid hurting your back. Keep your hand on the steering when you are turned around.

CHAPTER 6
HOW TO RUN A GREAT PRACTICE AND KEEP ON YOUR COACH'S GOOD SIDE

A. The Start of Practice—Getting Organized
B. Typical Practice Components
C. Learning How to Measure Distance Accurately
D. Right Place, Right Time
E. Steering and Communicating with Other Coxswains
F. Not Wasting Time
G. How to Cox a Seat Race
H. How to Run a Land-based Captain's Practice
I. Practices During the Off Season

For coxswains, rowing practices are one giant audition for the top seats in the racing boats. If you can figure out how to make your crew move fast during practices, your chances of being able to cox for races is good. Keep that in mind when you are bored, freezing cold, or dead tired in practice. Picture yourself sitting at the start line in the big race in the top boat. That might make it a little less painful when your coach gets on you about your steering or for forgetting the drill for the third time. Here are a few tips to make your practices run more smoothly, better understand your workouts and drills, and increase your chance of securing a racing spot:

A. The Start of Practice—Getting Organized

The best coxswains are either hyper organized by nature, or have learned to fake it really well. It goes without saying that you should be on time to practice, know the workouts, and be paying attention to what your coach tells you. Here are a few tips for going above and beyond:

Get everyone going. Get your crew going on carrying oars down. Get your Cox-Box, safety equipment, lights, tools, and other stuff organized, so you are ready to go when your crew gets hands on. Take slings out. Make it easy on your coach by being proactive.

Start the warm up. After the rowers get the oars down, lead, or at least initiate, the pre-workout stretching, run, or body circuits. Do the exercises with your rowers. Keep it light. One of the benefits of these exercises is team bonding, so you should definitely not go overboard and act like a taskmaster. If joking around is not in your nature, do not reprimand others for doing so. Sometimes your rowers need to bond without you, so know when to back off. Go talk to the coach or the other coxswains, and work on your mini-notebook notes for the day's workout.

Check the weather. Is there any wind or current or other conditions that might impact your launching, docking, or steering?

Check in with your coach. Have your mini-notebook out and ready to go to write down today's workouts.

B. Typical Practice Components

Generally a rowing practice involves the following items: a warm-up, a series of 'pieces' (shorter work periods within the practice), drills, and a cool-down.

Warm Ups. Warm ups vary from crew to crew, but typically involve some drill work and light, steady-state rowing to a certain appointed point on the body of water where you row. Crews are often allowed to run the warm up independently from the coach, so it is important as a coxswain that you have good familiarity with the typical warm up and can execute it without your coach's help. The pic drill is a tried-and-true favorite for warm ups. We also like rowing by 6 on the square, rotating pairs through. Your goal is to get your rowers warm and in the right place to begin the practice. It is appropriate to work on blade work during warm ups, but make sure you don't overwhelm your crew by talking too much.

Pieces. As in many sports, rowing workouts generally fall into two categories—steady state and intervals. As you may have guessed, steady state workouts are long rows at consistent pressure. Intervals can be shorter or longer; they typically involve rowing hard for some time, then paddling/stopping for a short time, then rowing hard for some time, then paddling/stopping for some time, and so on.

Interval Workouts. Interval workouts often involve a mix of different pressure and ratings. During an interval workout, the coxswain will be required to focus on time, rating, and pressure and make sure calls are clear and consistent. Coxswains may also be expected to bring crews of different speeds back together between pieces. You will see workouts written down in seemingly cryptic ways. We are here to help you figure these out.

Example 1: Pyramid

3x19' @20-26 / Rest 3' or more specifically 3x19' 4'-3'-2'-1'-2'-3'-4' @20-26 at 3/4 pressure

Here is the translation of these terms:

3x = three times (Here you will be doing three, 19-minute pieces.)

19' = nineteen minutes (Minutes are indicated by a single quote mark), and likewise, 3' = three minutes, and so on.

@20-26 = at a rating ranging from 20 to 26 (rating is indicated by a @)

3/4 pressure = Rowers should be doing the entire workout at 3/4 of their maximum power.

Rest 3' = You will be resting for three minutes between the pieces.

This means that you will be doing three, 19-minute pieces with ratings ranging from 20 to 26. This pyramid workout goes like this: nineteen minutes of continuous rowing, including four minutes at a 20 rating, three minutes at a 22 rating, two minutes at a 24 rating, one minute at a 26 rating, two minutes at a 24 rating, three minutes at a 22 rating, and one minute at a 20 rating. Then stop and rest for three minutes, and then start your next nineteen minute piece. In other words, you will row for nineteen minutes, rest for three, row for nineteen, rest for three, and row for nineteen.

Here the coxswain is expected to keep track of time and ratings. You should be giving your rowers data on time and ratings as they row and give them plenty of advance warning (3-5 strokes) before they have to shift the rating up or down.

Example 2: Power Pyramid

4x 11' (3' at 1/2 pressure, 2' at 3/4 pressure, 1' at full pressure, 2' at 3/4 pressure, 3' at 1/2 pressure) / Rest 3' @24

Here is the translation of these terms:

4x = four times (Here you will be doing four, 11-minute pieces.)

11' = eleven minutes (Here you are rowing in 11-minute pieces.)

Rest 3' = rest three minutes (Here you will rest for three minutes in between your 11-minute pieces.)

@24 = at a 24 rating (Here the entire piece will be done at the same rating, so you need to make sure your stroke holds the rating.)

In this type of workout the coxswain is expected to keep track of time and pressure and keep a consistent rating. You should be giving your rowers data on time and ratings as they row and give them plenty of advance warning (3-5 strokes) before they have to shift the pressure up or down. Focus only on the part of the pyramid you are doing. Remember, nobody wants to hear things like, "Only ten minutes to go." Instead, focus on shorter, more manageable increments, such as, "Last fifteen seconds at 3/4 pressure." Remind rowers to follow stroke, and hold a consistent rate as the pressure varies.

Drills. This book has a massive list of just about every drill we could think of, for just about every situation we could think of. The more you familiarize yourself with the list, the better prepared you will be for when your coach throws a new drill into the mix. Make sure you know the drills your coach has planned before you go out on the water. If this is not possible (or the coach decides to throw something new in on the fly), it is fine to ask for clarification, so you call the drill correctly. Make sure you understand the purpose for doing the drill and the technical problems that the drill is working to correct and can communicate them to your rowers. If it is a drill that is done every other stroke or every few strokes, make sure you keep the focus on the drill even on the off strokes. As the practice progresses, continue to remind your crew about the technical skill you worked on in the drills. If your coach introduced a new drill, and you were not really sure how or if it worked, it is appropriate to ask for follow up after practice.

Cool Down. After a hard or technical workout, many rowers tend to 'check out' on the way back to the dock. Your goal as coxswain is to keep them engaged and get the heart rates down. Adding in square blade rowing or pause drills as a cool down are favorites. Generally, remind them to sit up and breathe on the cool down.

C. Learning How to Measure Distance Accurately

One important skill you need as a coxswain is the ability to measure distance, particularly to be accurate in estimating how many strokes are left in a race or a piece. You need to 'practice' it in practices, or you won't be able to do it in races. The easiest way to measure distance is to get familiar with what a set distance looks like (e.g. when to start your sprint). If you know the distance between two clearly marked landmarks on your home body of water, you can test yourself elsewhere. If you are lazy like us, the best way to cheat on measuring distance is to use a SpeedCoach or app that accurately measures distance, and test yourself regularly. If you practice regularly, you will be surprised at how good you can get. You can use the 'test' not just in the boat but also while you are running, biking, or even driving. Practice it enough, and you will get much better. We promise.

The other good news is that most sprint race courses are well marked every 250 meters. But let's just say for a moment that you are not Magellan, and, unfortunately, the race course you are on does not have a well-marked landmark to clue you in on where you should start your sprint. You can still estimate distance remaining by having a good understanding of how fast your crew actually goes and your average stroke rating/number of elapsed strokes thus far in the piece or race. This is just additional data and is not a perfect substitute for being a good judge of distance, but if this is all you have, by all means, use it!

Example:

Your crew typically takes 4 minutes (or 240 seconds) to cover 1,000m. If you row at 30 strokes per minute, that is a total of 120 strokes in your 1,000m race.

So using this example in a race situation, if you want to start your sprint at 250 meters left, or with about 30 strokes to go, you ideally want to have a good idea of what 250 meters look like, but you can also use the data on your Cox-Box from the stroke counter and the timer.

You can gage this by (a) measuring the distance based on your estimation skills and (b) looking at your clock, stroke count, and average stroke rating. So in this example, you would start your sprint when the stroke counter on your Cox-Box hits 90 and when you have been rowing for about three minutes.

D. Right Place, Right Time

The number one single best thing a coxswain can do to stay on his or her coach's good side in practices and help the practice run more smoothly is to be in the right place at the right time. This applies on land and on the water. Here are a few tips:

Get off the dock fast. Keep your crew moving by setting high expectations for speed getting off the dock. Get them through their pre-workout rituals, get hands on quickly, and get off the dock quickly. Eliminate unnecessary things that waste practice time. You do not want to be a drill sergeant, especially with masters rowers. Just set the expectations—e.g. practice starts at 5:15am, and the boat is expected to be on the water by 5:30am—and enforce the rules. If people are consistently showing up late or wasting time, work with your coach to enforce penalties.

Get your boat to the right place and on time. If your team always starts practices at the dam, by all means get down to the dam, pointed, and ready to go. If the expectation is that all of the varsity boats stay together on the warm up, do not be the crew that is way ahead or behind. If your coach expects you to end practices by bringing all of the boats back together and lining up, do that every time. Those little things add up. In your post-workout notes, you should note the number of times that your coach calls you up or tells you that you are in the wrong place. Try to get that number down as the season progresses. Ideally you want it to never happen, but some coaches are impossible to please.

Learn your coach's boundaries, likes and dislikes, and hot buttons. If the coach is having a bad day, do not take it personally and back off. Do not use the beginning of practice to approach him or her with a million questions. Be considerate of his or her time, and schedule appointments if you need to talk. If the coach is paid hourly or is part time, remember when the coach talks to you, it is on their own personal time. Listen when he or she talks to you. It also never hurts to make him or her laugh, give a compliment, or just demonstrate a positive attitude at 5:00 am.

E. Steering and Communicating with Other Coxswains

One major time waster in rowing practices is coxswains having the boats too close together (where they interfere with one another) or too far apart for the coach to explain the next piece. A coach does not want to think about the coxswain's steering or keeping the crews together and evenly spaced—the coach expects the coxswains to do that on their own. You can help the overall flow of practice by working well with the other coxswains to all be in the right place at the right time. You will know your steering is improving when you can make it through a practice without your coach saying anything about your steering. You should review the steering chapter and get familiar with your home water. You should also pay attention to how your coach wants things done. This means being familiar with the normal places that you start and end practice every day. Overall, avoid steering like you just drank a gallon of malt liquor. Talk to other coxswains on your team, and pay attention to where you are going. Stop together and maintain your spacing between one another based on the coach's preferences. If you make a mistake, admit it, and do not make it again.

One of the best things you can do to help your coach run a good practice is to work well with the other coxswains on your team. (If you collectively agree to a plan that the coach does not like, at least you are all in the doghouse together.) Talk to each other to maintain appropriate spacing between the crews. Agree with one another on position—middle of the lake, inside, toward the shore—as you go through the practice. Talk to one another as you get pointed between pieces or need to move over during pieces. Agree to points for steering, and communicate how you will approach known obstacles like bridges. Cutting each other off and talking smack will only make the coach angry, resulting in the coach's attitude worsening toward all of the coxswains. If you have an issue with another cox, take it up with him or her off the water, away from the rowers, and agree on how you can work better together. You should absolutely not go to the coach to complain about other coxswains unless you have made a good faith effort to work it out amongst yourselves.

F. Not Wasting Time

A coach comes to practice with a plan for the day in mind. Your wasting time throws that plan off, making the coach frustrated. There are things, like equipment breakage, that waste time but are outside of your control. Then there are things that can be avoided, like rowers being late, having to go to the bathroom, taking a long time on the dock, being careless with equipment resulting in breakage, or just plain fooling around. Those are slightly outside of your control. As a coxswain you have to walk the fine line of being likable and getting people to do what you want—e.g. get off the dock and get going in a timely manner. It's all about setting high expectations for what you expect out of your crew. Social time should be reserved for the pre-practice warmup or after practice. If rowers are consistently late or unprepared, work with your coach to enforce penalties like extra squat jumps or running stadiums. Enforce penalties as a boat, not by individuals. Then there are things that are completely within your control, such as YOUR being late to practice, YOUR not having your equipment ready to go, or YOUR steering your crew into the wrong place. Those are mistakes you want to avoid at all costs.

G. How to Cox a Seat Race

Rowers swapping out for seat racing

Rowers switching seats with one another

Seat races are the best way for a coach to compare the performance of individual rowers on the water. It works like this. Two boats, lets call them A and B, are lined up and raced for a short distance. The coach notes the times and which boat moved the best. Then one rower from each boat is switched, and the race is repeated. The coach continues to switch rowers in various combinations and race the boats. The coxswain has a single job during seat races—steer perfectly straight and keep your mouth shut. The coxswain keeps his or her weight in the boat and sits in a tucked down position as in a sprint race. Between seat races, the coxswain has to work with the coaching launch to switch rowers in and out—this will involve keeping the boat set and directing rowers to assist with holding onto oars and the launch during the switches.

H. How to Run a Land-based Captain's Practice

Many coxswains will have the opportunity to run a captain's practice at one time or another. This might be in the off-season, when the coach is away, or may involve any sort of land-based workout. Here are a few ideas on how to do it without pissing off your peers:

Work with the other coxswains to set expectations. Be consistent, and enlist your coach's directives in setting the workouts.

Do the workouts with your crew if it makes sense. Nothing like a little sweat to earn the respect of your rowers and shed a few extra cookies.

Make it fun. Anything you can think of to make it better. If your team responds to motivational quotes, funny signs, matching shirts, whatever you can think of, do it.

Let people socialize while they are working out. The off-season and off-the-water practices are as much about team bonding as they are about fitness. If you try to stop this, they will turn against you. You want your rowers to consider you one of them, not an enemy spy sent by the coach to watch what they are doing. It is OK to partake in some fun occasionally.

Institute some friendly competition. Consider instituting a friendly intrasquad competition in the off-season, ending with an event including gag prizes, theme squad names/outfits, scavenger hunts, a team breakfast potluck, and the like. Be creative, but keep it within reason. The idea is to start with squads that are as closely matched as possible and really push the team collectively to its limits. Remember, it's about getting fitter as a team, not playing people against each other.

Don't pretend you are the coach. Keep your role in mind, and don't act like you are the coach. You might be in charge, and you might be carrying out the coach's orders, but you are not the coach. Enough said.

I. Practices During the Off Season

Check with the coach first. He or she will help set expectations for the off season and your role in it. Your coach may be counting on you as a team leader during the off-season or expect the rowers to lead. Defer to the coach's wishes and expectations.

Use the off-season to work on your coxing. This includes doing research, watching video, talking with your rowers, working on your notebooks, and evaluating your recordings. Work with other coxswains, and see if you can improve the collective coxing level of the entire team.

Learn to cox on the ergs. Much of the off-season workouts will be spent on the ergs. If your coach has sent benchmarks for erg scores, ask your rowers if they want to be coxed on the erg. Many people hate this. If your rowers do not want to be coxed on the ergs, back off! If you do have rowers who want to be coxed on the ergs, ask each rower what he or she wants to hear. Write this down. Tailor to the individual. Record yourself coxing people on the ergs, and evaluate yourself. Learn to look for technique on the ergs.

Update the coach. Give your coach progress updates, as allowed by your school, athletic department, or NCAA rules. Keep it general and positive. Remember, you are a coxswain, not an enemy informant. If you have suggestions, let the coach know, and come prepared with solutions and ideas.

CHAPTER 7
HOW TO MAKE YOURSELF BETTER

A. The Simple Formula for Getting Better Faster
B. Honestly Assess Your Skill Level—The Coxswain Evaluation Form
C. Write Down Your Goals
D. Research Resources
E. Asking Your Rowers For Feedback
F. Asking Your Coaches for Feedback and Help
G. Working with Experienced Coxswains on Your Team
H. Setting Up Your Recording/Review System
I. Review Your Notes/Recordings—Practice Logistics, Tone, Rhythm, and Technical Calls
J. Self-Analysis—Assessing How Annoying You Are
K. Self-Analysis—Assessing How Boring You Are
L. How to Conquer Self-Analysis
M. Preparation—Writing it Down and Saying it Out Loud
N The Big Notebook
O. The Mini Notebook
P. Practicing Your Calls and Commands Off the Water
Q. Checking In—Evaluating Your Improvement

A. The Simple Formula For Getting Better Faster

It's pretty clear to us that most people want to succeed and become better humans. There is a multi-billion-dollar industry devoted to self-help books. We've never read any of those books, but we are going to guess that the big secret is working hard while making it look effortless. This book will hopefully clue you in on secrets it took us years to learn. But we will be honest—shortcuts are few and far between. There is no substitute for working hard and putting in the hours in the coxswain seat to become a better coxswain. This section was written with the intention of helping you teach yourself to get better on your own time.

Pep talk time. If you are going to get better as a coxswain, it is all in your own hands. Nobody will do it for you. Being a self-starter is the single BEST thing you can do to help your coach out and help your rowers go faster. If you are serious about this, you should invest a minimum of three hours a week beyond what you are already doing in practices. It might seem like a lot, but think about what you waste three hours a week on already.

Here is the formula:

One hour a week of research/feedback. If you want to take it to the next level, you need to talk to everyone you can and read everything about rowing you can get your hands on. Feedback includes getting feedback from your coaches and rowers. Research includes browsing websites on rowing technique, listening to coxing recordings from experienced coxswains, watching national team-level race videos, learning drills, and learning about kinesiology. Research also includes doing ride-alongs, volunteering to cox for other crews, and talking with experienced rowers and coaches. Research does not include searching #rowing problems, watching rowing crash videos, or complaining about your rowers to your friends.

One hour a week of self-analysis. Self-analysis includes reviewing your voice recordings and your written notes of calls and evaluating their effectiveness.

One hour a week of preparation. Preparation includes writing up your notes, transferring notes from your mini-notebook to your big notebook (see below), planning calls, drills, or stories to share with your crew at upcoming practices, planning what you would do differently for the next practice, talking with your coach about his or her vision for practice, and planning your upcoming practice or race content.

Here is how to get started on your path to being a better coxswain:

Acknowledge that it's up to you. Repeat after us—'If I want to get better as a coxswain, I have to teach myself.' Say it over and over again. Nobody is going to do it for you. Trust us on this one.

Figure out what your goals are. Set your short-term goals for each season and your long-term goals for the next two to three. Write those down. You will be putting those in a prominent place in your new rowing notebook (more on that below). Valid goals include smaller things like mastering three new drills or bigger, more difficult things like making the varsity team or being selected to cox for Head of the Charles. Look at your goals often, and figure out what it will take to get there. Keep your goals focused on things that are measurable and achievable. Remember that you cannot control how tall and strong your rowers are or how many experienced coxswains are on the roster ahead of you, but you can control your own progress forward.

Ask for help. We talk about getting feedback in more detail below, but suffice it to say that a successful coxswain is the kind who is not afraid to seek out the opinions of others and make changes based on feedback from rowers and coaches.

Record it. Digital recordings, whether video or audio, are the key to your self-analysis. It's only embarrassing to listen to yourself the first time.

Review and evaluate your progress. Evaluate what you recorded and figure out how you can do things differently next time.

Prepare for success. The big notebook and the mini notebook are the keys to getting better. See more in this chapter.

B. Honestly Assess Your Skill Level—The Coxswain Evaluation Form

We have provided as Appendix E, Coxswain Evaluation Forms for novice/intermediate coxswains and experienced coxswains. It is really important for you to review the list of basic coxing skills and evaluate (honestly) where yours fall on the spectrum. Determine whether you are still in the novice/intermediate category or the advanced category. Then, we recommend scoring yourself on a monthly basis on a 1-10 scale on the items on the relevant Coxswain Evaluation Form. If you are ready for an ego check, ask your coach or a few of your rowers to evaluate you fairly and honestly. (You can cry about it later in private.) This will help identify areas for improvement. Let's face it—nobody is perfect. There are things on the list that we struggle with even after decades of coxing under our belts.

C. Write Down Your Goals

After you have completed your Coxswain Evaluation Form, you should pick a few things you would like to improve upon. It is impossible to work on everything at once, so just plan to work on a few things at a time. If you are not familiar with the concept of SMART goal setting (specific, measurable, achievable, relevant, and time-specific), look it up. We want to stab ourselves in the eye for even suggesting this because this type of thing comes straight from the depressingly gray cubicles of large corporations. However, it has merit. Even if you have never had a real job where you were forced by your department head to write soul-crushingly boring annual goals, you can still make your coxing goals SMART. Here are a few examples:

- "By March 30th [time-specific] I will learn to measure distance accurately, [specific] so I can start my crew's sprint in the right place for sprint races this spring season [relevant]. I will do this by downloading a SpeedCoach type app and testing myself in every practice for the next six weeks [achievable] until I can accurately measure 200 meters [measurable]."

- "I will devote the last four weeks of winter training [time-specific] to learning six specific timing drills [achievable] backward and forward. This will include watching videos of others doing the drills, reading about the drills, and memorizing the calls associated with the drills [specific], so I am prepared to execute those drills when the spring season starts [measurable] to fix basic timing issues in my crew [relevant], including finishes, catching together, rolling up together, and slide speed."

- "My crew complained that I sounded whiney during races last year [relevant], so I will devote the last two weeks in September [time-specific] to lowering the tone of my voice and enunciating [specific] by practicing speaking from the diaphragm and reviewing my tapes after every practice [achievable] to ensure that the squeak and garble is gone from my voice for our first head race [measurable]."

We encourage you to put your goals in a prominent location somewhere you will see them regularly, including on the inside cover of your notebook. We encourage you to talk to your coach about your goals and make sure that he or she agrees that you are focusing on the top priorities for improvement. Chances are your coach will never be thinking about this as much as you are, so he or she may be taken off guard by it. If you suspect that will be the case, just mention it casually, in passing. If your coach disagrees with your improvement priorities, ask for his or her suggestions, and revise your goals accordingly. We do not recommend discussing your goals with your rowers—you just want them to notice the improvement (or not notice and take it for granted).

D. Research Resources

Research can come in many forms—seeking out experienced people, using old school books and magazines, watching video content, or otherwise browsing coxing websites and social media. As a coxswain, you need to be constantly looking for new resources to start learning real rowing technique, what should be done at each point in the stroke, and master all of the drills. Pronto. Then you need to work on racing strategy, watch real rowing at the highest levels, and listen to recordings from really experienced coxswains in race situations.

This section will point you in the right direction of coxing resources, in person, online, and in print. We recommend an hour of research a week or more if you want to get better faster.

Talk to rowing people outside your team. One of the most powerful phrases in the English language is, "Can you help me?" In your local rowing community, there are almost certainly a number of people with significantly more experience than you have. Seek those people out. Ask coaches from other teams if you can ride along during their practices. Ask coaches to sit down with you and go over their practice planning schedules, race planning, or talk about how they evaluate technique. Ask a senior masters sculler out for coffee and pepper him with questions about his glory days back in college in the 1970s. Seek out experienced masters coxes at nearby boathouses, and ask if they might be willing to sit down with you and talk about coxing and share recordings. Sure there are jerks out there, but rowing people by and large genuinely want to help new people, especially those who take an interest in them and are enthusiastic to learn. You can learn a lot from books and the internet, but it is no substitute for building real life relationships with actual humans. The sort of coxswain who isn't afraid to seek out others is exactly the kind of coxswain that people want to have in their boat. You never know when those very same people are going to call you about coxing opportunities like camps, clinics, and races.

Books and magazines. Let us congratulate you for getting your hands on this book. That is a pretty good first step on your journey to coxing self-discovery. In addition to this one, there are a few coxing books out there, but to really take it to the next level, you've got to seek out real rowing books, magazines, and kinesiology journals. We trust you can find them. The books are mostly dry and boring, written by old, mostly British, rowing coaches, but these people know what they are talking about. There are a few magazines that have come and gone in recent years, but you should look for these as well.

Apps. There are a number of ever-changing rowing apps available for your mobile device. We really like the apps that mimic the functions of a SpeedCoach. In other words, apps that give you stroke ratings, splits, and meters rowed, all in real time. These are on the pricey side, but well worth it. Other cheap or free apps worth downloading will give you stroke ratings, workout logs, rowing terminology, and rigging. Your mobile is also the best way to record video and voice, and there are a number of apps that do this. We are not going to recommend any in particular, mostly because new and improved apps come out all the time.

The Internet. You might want to check the Internet for rowing information. Duh. We can tell you that www.row2k.com has been THE rowing site for more than a decade, so we can recommend that one. The www.concept2.com website also has tons of information and rowing workouts. www.youtube.com is a gold mine of rowing videos, both good and bad. We like to search "coxing recording" as a start, but you should use your own imagination. Search terms for specific drills, starts, head race turns, and the like are also worth looking for. There is also an ever-evolving number of rowing and coxing blogs and social media, some much better than others. (You can follow us on all the social media you can think of @shortandsnarkyrowing). We will not mention the surplus of coxing humor, funny videos, and coxswain toss mishaps—you can find that on your own.

E. Asking Your Rowers for Feedback

We will preface this by saying that asking for feedback is difficult and sometimes emotional. It is far easier to bury your head in the sand and think that everything is fine. When approaching rowers for feedback, consider your audience. If you are coxing high school novices, they have no idea what they want while masters will tell you exactly what they want every second of the practice, give you steering pointers, and tell you to take vitamins and wear sunscreen. With newer rowers, keep it general. Ask them things like, "Do you like when I say A or B better?" If you are just joining an experienced crew, ask them before your first practice or at least before you cox for them for too long. If you work with a crew on a regular basis, you should check in with them once a season, relatively early on in the season. Doing it more than that will just give your rowers free reign to vent about every gripe they have about your coxing. This is unproductive, so target doing it twice a year, once in the spring season and once in the fall season. You can talk to individual rowers directly one on one or set up questions in an anonymous online or social media poll. We do not recommend talking to a group of rowers because there is a strong chance that they will influence one another, and potentially you will feel like they are ganging up on you. Do not share the feedback with anyone, particularly if it is hard to hear. Here are a few things to ask a crew you have been working with for a while:

- What do you like about my coxing?
- What do you wish I said more?
- What fires you up?

- What motivates you when you're in pain?
- What do you want me NOT to say?
- Do I talk too much or not enough?

Thank your rowers for providing feedback. You do not have to tell them what the outcome was, and the less you make a big deal about it, the less of a big deal it will be. If the feedback was upsetting or overwhelmingly negative, you are going to have to work hard to get over it. (If you figure out how to do that without eating a gallon of ice cream or crying into your pillow, you are a better person than we are.) But never let them see you upset, or it will only feed into their negative impression of you. Instead use that feedback to get better. Don't dwell on it, but use what they said to drive you harder. If the feedback was that you try too hard, then relax!

F. Asking Your Coach for Feedback and Help

Asking your coach for feedback and help really depends on the coach. Some coaches are very intimidating while others are approachable and easy to talk to. The thing to keep in mind is that the coach has lots of athletes and is probably underpaid. Be mindful of his or her time. You should schedule meetings with the coach off the water and away from other rowers. The beginning or middle of practice is NEVER the right time to go deep on anything with your coach. As a general rule, it is appropriate to approach the coach with technical questions, to trouble-shoot problems, and to discuss new ideas. You should only approach the coach to resolve interpersonal issues as a last resort and in a solution-oriented way. Most coaches would like to be completely insulated from rower drama, so tread very, very lightly if you are going to go down that road. Many coaches prefer email communication, which gives them a chance to think about their responses. You should write down your questions in advance of any in person meeting and consider emailing those to the coach in advance if he or she prefers it. Here are a few things to ask your coach about:

- When you do not understand a workout, drill, or command.
- To ask for input on new things you would like to try with your crew.
- When you have tried all of your options to improve a situation or technical problem and are out of ideas. (Do NOT go to the coach to complain that the boat is unset! It just makes you look like a whiner.)
- To ask for feedback about something specific, such as your race plan.
- To ask for opportunities to get more experience with certain things that the coach might not consider on his or her own. This could include opportunities for ride-alongs with other coaches, asking to cox a varsity boat for a practice, or the opportunity to review your recordings (pick your best and never more than 15 minutes of recordings).
- To ask for general feedback on your progress. Ask your coach to be honest, and thank the coach for any criticism. Ask him or her to use the Coxswain Evaluation Form in the back of this book as a start.

We are going to give you the straight truth—most coaches do not think much about their coxswains. When we coach, we don't like to think about our coxswains at all. That says something because we ARE coxswains. We hate to stereotype, but most coaches put their coxswains into one of two buckets—the problem coxswains and the ones they don't have to think about. When you ask for feedback from your coach, you are probably not going to get much. It is not as though the coach doesn't want you to improve—far from it—but he or she does not really notice what you do unless you regularly cause problems. The problem coxswains are the ones who are never in the place where the coach wants them to be, scream until they are hoarse, give the coach attitude, hit things, or the ones the rowers do not like very much or do not respond to. The rest are considered coxswains the coach doesn't need to think about because they don't cause problems. Your coach is probably relying more on the opinions of your rowers than you can possibly imagine. Keep that in mind. Rower opinion—basically which coxswains can get the rowers to pull hard for them—matters far more than just about anything else. So basically what we are saying here is to follow our advice about how to stay on your coach's good side, and do not expect much in the way of feedback from him or her.

G. Working with Experienced Coxswains on Your Team

We have mentioned a time or two that it really is in your best interest to work well with other coxswains on your team—but in a business-like manner. When you are starting out, your best resources are the experienced coxswains on your team. We especially recommend seeking out the most experienced coxswain on your team—not the ones around your level or slightly ahead of you. One of your authors remembers her first year in college, where the most experienced coxswain was a senior on the men's team. She coxed the top men's boat, and they worshipped her. She carried an almost perfect GPA with a really tough course load and was completely brilliant. She had flawless skin. She had gotten into a top three law school in the first round of admissions and was a dynamo in the boat—totally calm, cool, and fearless. We didn't see her as competition—she was so far beyond us—she was more like a mentor. We watched what she did on the water, listened to what she said off the water, and mirrored her preferred style, tone, and voice. During winter training, we followed her at a respectful distance, watching what she said to her rowers on both technical and motivational aspects. She was more than happy to pass along advice to the younger coxswains, mostly because she didn't see us as competition, but as people who were there to learn. When we were coxing the top boats, we paid it back by mentoring the first-year coxswains. It is good karma, and it will make you feel like you are really helping the team. Experienced coxswains on your team will probably love to be asked about their experiences and generally should be more than willing to offer advice in tricky situations. If there are not any on your team, seek out experienced masters coxswains at your boathouse or nearby clubs.

H. Setting Up Your Recording/Review System

When we talk about the simple formula to improving—research/feedback, self-analysis, and preparation—the self-analysis part is basically listening to recordings from your practices. (Sorry to make it sound so technical—this is all that we are talking about.) To get started with self-analysis, you will need a few things. We recommend a recording device as the most basic. This can be your mobile phone in a waterproof case, or even a plastic bag, or one of those handheld voice recorders. There are a number of mobile apps to download for recording, but most mobiles will have a recorder built into them. A Go-Pro type camera is also highly recommended if you have access to it. You can mount it to face and record you (scary!) or record the rowers. If you are working on steering improvement, mounting the camera facing the bow is really helpful because you can use it to analyze your course. (Watch the video on fast-forward, or you will fall asleep.) Start out by recording a whole practice for the first few run-throughs. It will probably take a little time to figure out exactly how much space your recording device has and what is actually worth recording. As you get better, you can be more selective about recording shorter pieces.

Here are a few recording tips we have learned from experience of doing it wrong:
- State the date and workout at the beginning of the recording in case you don't have time to review immediately.
- Record what the coach says to you and your crew as well as the downtime between pieces.

- When you sit down to review recordings, block off at least an hour with no distractions.

The other thing you should do to prepare for self-analysis is to take a look at the Coxswain Evaluation Form attached at the back of this book. It is not comprehensive, but it will give you a good start of things to look and listen for in your recordings. We highly encourage you to reference the Coxswain Evaluation Form as you begin the self-evaluation process. When you are starting out, each and every recording should be reviewed referencing these questions. Some may apply and some may not given your own situation, what you were doing when you were recording, and what type of practice it was.

I. Review Your Notes/Recordings—Practice Logistics, Tone, Rhythm, and Technical Calls

If you are just starting out with recording your practices, you are going to be overwhelmed, and you will feel like review takes forever. Use the Coxswain Evaluation Form along with the questions below as a guideline. As you get more experience in reviewing recordings, or are working toward more specific goals, you are only going to be listening for specific things, and it will go much faster, we promise.

Here are a few sample questions you could be asking as you review your recordings:

Boat Handling
- Did you get your equipment out of the boathouse and down to the dock without hitting riggers or the boat on anything? Were there any close calls?
- Did you call the right sequences and calls when moving the boats? If not, how would you do it differently next time?
- Was there any confusion or were your rowers talking when they should not have been?

Docking and Launching
- Were you standing by the skeg on the dock?
- Did you bring all of your equipment with you?
- Did you call the right sequences and calls when putting the boat into the water?
- Was there any confusion or were your rowers talking when they should not have been?
- Did you get off the dock in a timely manner?
- Did you land safely?
- Did you misjudge the landing or land perfectly? If you misjudged, what errors did you make? How would you do it differently?
- How did you account for wind/weather/current when docking and launching?

Safety and Steering
- Were you in the right place at the right time the entire practice?
- Did your coach mention your steering? How many times?
- Did you look 360-degrees often?
- Did you take any risks or make misjudgments with steering that you would do differently next time?
- Did you talk to other coxswains or communicate with your coach effectively about position and steering?
- Did you work well to hold good courses for the launch and with other boats on your team?

- Were you prepared for obstacles, other boat traffic, and wind/weather conditions?
- If not, what happened, and what would you do differently next time?

Running an Effective Practice
- Did you understand the practice and communicate the workout to your crew before you did it?
- Did you add pairs in seamlessly?
- Were you in the right place to begin and end all of the pieces? Did your coach comment on your position or have to call you up?
- Did you waste any time? Were there unnecessary lags between pieces that were due to your being in the wrong place, off point, or you failing to keep your rowers from wasting time?
- Were you able to keep the crew focused?
- Was there any talking in the boat or confusion?
- Did you communicate with other coxswains about the workout?
- Did you start and end all of your pieces where the coach intended?
- Were you 'on' for drills and pieces? In other words, did you start and end at the right places and make the right calls for each?

Technical Input
- Did you give data (stroke rating, time, split, etc..) throughout the practice in an effective and timely manner?
- Was the data timed to what the crew was working on?
- Did you keep the crew on track—e.g. monitoring stroke ratings frequently and making sure timed pieces were started and ended at the correct place?
- What were the biggest technical problems with the row? Were you able to identify and correct these issues? What did you say that worked the best? The least?
- Did you understand the technique points that the coach was focused on?
- Did you understand the point of the drills?
- Were you able to apply the drills to the technical emphasis for the practice?
- Were you able to explain the drills correctly?
- Did you call the drills correctly?
- Were you able to translate what the coach was saying in different words? How did the rowers respond?
- Did you bring in components of the drill or remind the rowers what they did in the drills during other parts of the practice?
- Did you work with individual rowers to resolve his/her technical problems without picking on him/her or bullying? Did you let him/her know when he or she was doing it correctly?

Giving Commands
- Was the recording clear?
- Could you clearly hear the sharpness on counts?
- Did your voice sound sharp, crisp, and accurate to the sound of the oars?
- Did you vary your tone of voice?
- Could you hear different levels of intensity?
- Was the intensity level appropriate to the piece?

Intangibles
- How much time did you spend talking to the stroke on the mic?
- Were your calls positive ('control the slide with the legs') versus negative ('don't rush')?
- Did the rowers have a positive experience in practice?
- Did they have fun?
- Did you bring any wit, humor, or good cheer to the practice? Did you keep them entertained?
- Were you blabbering? Whiny? Annoying? Boring?
- Did you sound confident and like you knew what you were doing?
- Were there well-timed (planned) silences or did you talk the whole time? Did you only stop talking in a moment of panic or when you screwed something up?

J. Self-Analysis—Assessing How Annoying You Are

In addition to what you say, there is also the matter of how you say it. When you are listening to your recordings, you should also be looking for common characteristics that collectively add up to an annoying coxswain. Here are few common coxswain sounds, voices, and other odds and ends that rowers absolutely hate. You should be listening for these characteristics in your voice:

The scaredy-cat. Rowers hate a coxswain who takes dangerous risks or talks about how close of a call they had with an obstacle, but they especially hate a coxswain who is afraid of everything that might happen. We are by no means suggesting that you take safety lightly, but even if you are scared, at no time should you let the rowers question your ability to get them safely through the practice and back to the dock. Do not let your crew know you are afraid of anything! When you listen to your recordings, note points where you discuss risks, weather, obstacles, the traffic pattern, or how dangerous other boaters are acting, or you can hear the fear in your voice.

The quiet mouse. Rowers hate a coxswain who is not authoritative on land or on the water. Speak up, be consistent, and do not move boats on land or on the water if your crew is not paying attention to you. When you listen to your recordings, is your voice powerful? Can your rowers even hear you? Do you sound confident and in control?

The bully. Rowers hate a coxswain who bullies the crew. Avoid picking on people or creating a coxswain versus rowers environment. Are you screaming or sounding angry? When you review your recordings, listen especially for repeated picking on the same rower, over and over again, especially in a non-constructive way. Do you ever tell your rowers when they are doing things right? If not, make sure you add it in. We like to compliment each rower on what they are doing right at least once every other practice. If you do it every day it feels forced and fake, (and you don't want to feed their egos too much!) but if you do it several times a week, it sounds genuine. Even the worst rower on your crew is doing something right, so figure out what that is, and make his or her day.

The chatterbox. Rowers hate a coxswain who will not shut up. Think about everything that comes out of your mouth. Use silence to increase the focus in the boat. Remember, just because you can talk the entire row does not mean that you should talk the entire row. When you listen to your recordings, is there ever a break? Is what you are saying at all interesting? Is it so boring and unending that you can barely listen to yourself?

The indecisive. Rowers hate a coxswain who is not decisive or confident. Make decisions quickly and stick to them. Do not explain your hesitation or decision-making process to your crew. Just pick something and go with it. Chances are they will never know there was an issue. Remember, the minute you cede control or show lack of confidence is the minute you become the rowers' doormat. (And if you are not a decisive or confident person by nature, think seriously about whether coxing is the best fit for you.) When you listen to your recordings, listen for moments of hesitation or if you say one thing and then change your mind.

The explainer. Rowers hate a coxswain who explains everything to them. Rowers do not really care about how you are pushing on the steering cords, what the team from another school is doing, or that you are going to slow down as you come through the channel later on in the practice. Experienced rowers really hate it when you explain basic things to them, like reminding them to turn their blades over when they are going to back. When you listen to your recordings, listen for this type of over-explanation.

The distracter. Rowers hate a coxswain who wastes practice time by distractions, unnecessary chatter, or non-focus. When it is time to work, you should be ready to make them work hard. We stress the importance of making practice interesting and fun, but having fun in your crew does not mean that you need to waste time or be distracted during practice. Maybe this is contradictory advice, but we figure you are smart enough to figure it out. When you listen to your recordings, listen for the amount of time you are spending on distractions versus time spent on technical calls and commands. We are huge fans of a well-timed moment of levity, but it should not take up half of the practice.

The negative force. Rowers hate coxswains who are always negative. The ones who are never satisfied with the row, always point out negatives, and never do it in a nice way. When you listen to your recordings, be listening for 'positive versus negative' statements, whether you are telling your rowers when they are doing things right, pointing out a few good strokes in an otherwise lousy practice. Aim for the positive, and if the negative creeps in to your recordings, think about ways to turn the gloom into sunshine for the next row.

The flake. Rowers hate a coxswain who doesn't know the practice, the drills, and cannot correct technique. At the start of every practice, write down the workout and the drills, and take your mini-notebook in the boat with you. We strongly encourage you to read the sections in this book on drills and how to fix basic technique problems. No one expects you to be an expert when you are first starting out, but they do expect you to increase your knowledge quickly. When you are listening to your recordings, listen for your own confusion, your coach reminding you of something, or your asking your rowers what the coach said or meant.

The punisher. Rowers hate a coxswain who calls one power ten after another or pushes the crew beyond their point of reasonable expectations. In other words, a coxswain who does not appreciate the rowers' collective pain. We strongly encourage you to learn to row or at least do some erg pieces to get a better appreciation for what the rowers are going through. Your job is to help motivate them beyond their own limits, not punish them. When you listen to your recordings, listen for what sounds like a military basic training instructor coming through in your voice or an 'I don't care' attitude about the rowers' pain. The alternative, the overly sympathetic cox, is just as bad ("Oh, poor rowers, coach said to do another power ten; I just feel so bad for all of you").

The annoying voice. Rowers hate a coxswain who screams, whispers, baby talks, or whines on the mic. Rowers also hate a coxswain who has repetitive speech behaviors, including saying 'like' and 'um' and 'you guys,' constantly. If you are making yourself hoarse on a regular basis, you should evaluate the causes. When you listen to your recordings, listen for the common problems. Does your voice sound deep and powerful? Are you speaking from your diaphragm? Remember, everyone hates the sound of his or her own voice, so do not be so hard on yourself.

The misjudger. Rowers hate a coxswain who misjudges distance. Get a SpeedCoach or similar app and practice. Learn the distance between landmarks on your lake or river. Practice, practice, practice. Listen for the tell-tale, 'Last ten strokes. OK, five more. Oops, another three.'

The crackly mic. This is not really a coxswain type, but more of something to be listening for. Rowers hate when you crackle on the Cox-Box mic. When you store it wound up in a tight ball, the wires start to break down, resulting in crackling. If you hold it kinked in the boat it may also crackle. Store your mics flat or loosely looped over a hook. If your mic is crackling regularly, it is toast, and it is time to buy a new one.

K. Self-Analysis—Assessing How Boring You Are

If you ask most rowers, they will take a boring coxswain over an annoying one any day. But that doesn't mean you should be aiming for boring. When you are listening to your recordings, you should also be looking for common characteristics that collectively add up to a dull, dull, dull, coxswain—the kind who the rowers tune out because the coxswain isn't saying anything of interest or importance.

We've all been there. Perhaps it's cold, raining, dark, or you are slightly hung over from the night before. Maybe the coach yelled at you for what you feel is an injustice, or your rowers told you that you were annoying for trying to be entertaining. You would rather be back in your warm bed, but instead you have woken up at 5am to sit in a freezing rain and have to be 'on' for the next two hours. Whatever the reason, you do not feel like giving your 100% effort to be sparkling and engaging today. We recommend recording your practices on those types of days when you really do not feel like coxing, the days when you know it will be punishing to listen to your recordings later. This tactic will keep you focused when you feel like phoning it in and will also force you to listen to yourself when you are really not giving your best effort and are at your maximum boringness. To get around the boring factor, when you are going through your recordings, listen for a few key things:

- Does your tone of voice change during the recording? Does your intensity change in relation to the workouts?
- Do you spend lots of time talking to your stroke or the coach over the mic when you should be off mic?
- Do you tend to mumble or just throw words out because you feel like you should be saying something?
- Are you counting accurately? Are the counts sharp and at the right place on the catch?
- Are you filling the entire time with chatter? Are they well timed silences? Are there any deliberate silences? Are there way too many silences?
- Are you screaming, blabbering, or sounding angry?
- Do you sound bored, like you don't care at all, or would rather be anywhere else besides rowing practice?
- Are you saying the same things in every practice? Are they creative at all, or are they the 'stock' phrases that coxswains have been saying for the last 100 years?
- Are you making any effort whatsoever to be funny or interesting?

L. How to Conquer Self-Analysis

We are not going to lie. The first time you listen to recordings it can be a bit disheartening. Getting feedback from rowers and coaches may make you feel like you want to put your head in the oven. You may have a long list of problems identified. Your feelings might be hurt. (If they aren't hurt, you're probably not human.) You feel like you just want to give up and quit rowing altogether. We will tell you from experience, the coxswains who do press on are the ones who will be successful. We will congratulate you for taking the initiative to get better—many coxswains will never do this. The coxswains who do are exactly the determined, problem-solving types who will do well for their rowers and their coaches in the years to come.

Additionally, it is important not to get overwhelmed. You should also remember what we said at the beginning - you should only work on fixing a few problems at a time. Here is what we recommend you do with your first recordings or your first feedback:

Put it on paper. Write down specifically your shortcomings, screw-ups, and deficiencies in your big notebook. (More on big notebooks later in this chapter). Don't be afraid to admit these. It is OK not to be perfect. If it makes you feel any better, just keep in mind that your authors could fill twenty big notebooks with all of our screw-ups and deficiencies over the years.

Make SMART goals. Turn these into a manageable number of SMART goals, and write that in your big notebook.

Figure out next steps. Write down specifically what you would say and do differently next time in certain common situations. Write down how you will work on addressing your problems.

Now that you have all of that written down, you are ready to start with the preparation portion of the formula.

M. Preparation—Writing it Down and Saying it Out Loud

Remember back at the beginning of this chapter when we told you the formula for improvement was research/feedback, self-analysis, and preparation? We are now in the preparation section of the formula. The preparation section relies on writing things down and practicing things out loud.

N. The Big Notebook

The first thing you should buy yourself is a big notebook in which to write things down. This is a permanent record of your coxing journey. Trust us, this is the sort of thing you will be glad you have years from now, and on those bad days to remind yourself just how far you have come. (One of your authors has an amazing coxing notebook that spans more than a decade, and it formed the backbone of this book!) Ideally your big notebook is an extra large binder with looseleaf paper or one of those enormous multi-subject spiral notebooks. Or you can spring for a fancy, hard bound one, or put it all in a giant document on your computer and print it out regularly. Or start a blog. We don't really have a preference, but regardless of how you do it, you should definitely print it out, so you can flip through it, show it to your coach, and review it with others. We like a binder because you can print out on-line research and pop it in as needed.

What goes into this big notebook? It can be your thoughts, musings, reviews of your recordings, race plans, what motivates individual rowers, technical fixes, drills, and the like. When you find good stuff on the Internet, magazine articles, rowing pictures, or make diagrams, pop them in to your big notebook. At a bare minimum, we recommend using it to record daily workouts, drills, what you did right, what you would like to work on, and what you would do differently next time.

Here are examples of big notebook entries:

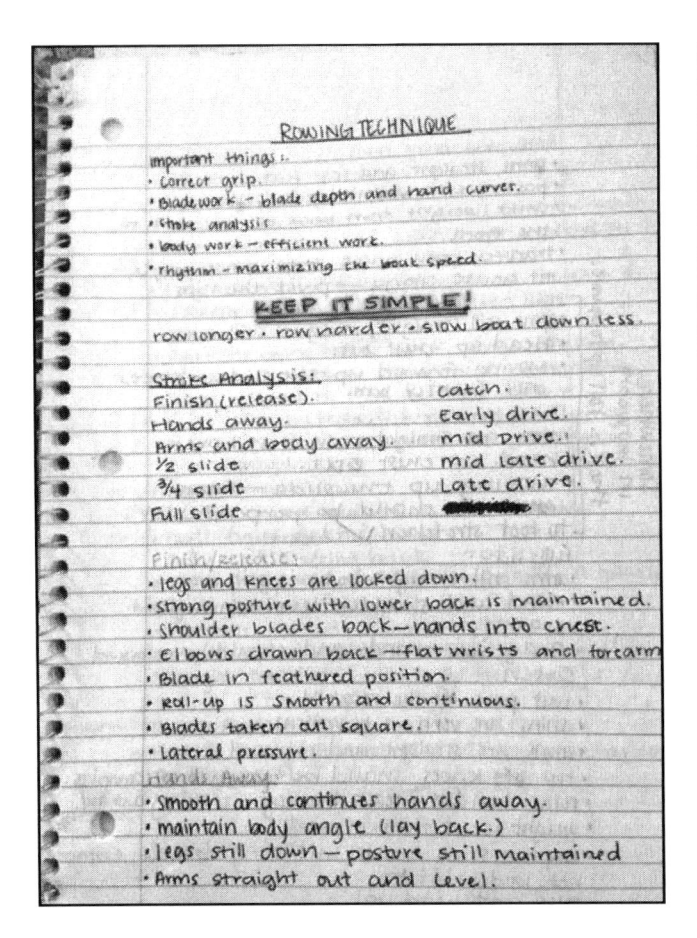

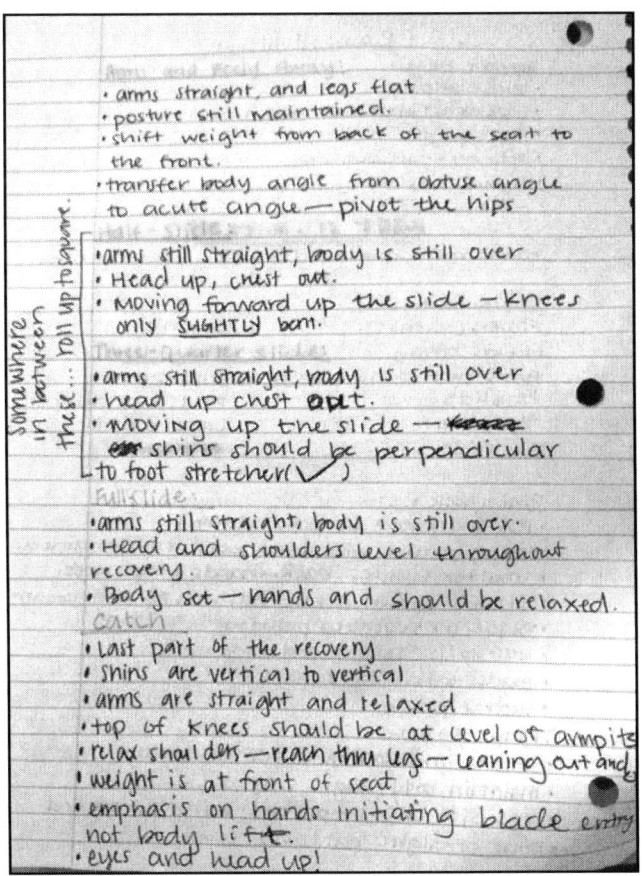

O. The Mini Notebook

The second prong of writing things down is to write down everything you will need for the boat. For this we love mini-notebooks. You might be used to using scraps of paper or printed pages in plastic bags, and you do not really get the fuss of what the mini-notebook is all about. Maybe your coach even gives you the workouts on an index card (bad idea because this won't force you to even look at the workout until you're out on the water!) We might have a hard time convincing you of the mini-notebook's merit—after all it weighs more, is bulkier, and, well, maybe harder to look at than an index card in a plastic bag. We don't have a good response other than to say maybe it is because we are coxswains that are predisposed to like things that are small. All we know is that your authors are huge fans of smaller-sized versions of regular things. Those tiny soda cans, half-size lip gloss tubes, you name it. Perhaps it was out of this love for small things that we discovered mini-notebooks. (Actually it was because we were forced to buy waterproof field notebooks for geology labs and found that they worked remarkably better than index cards or scraps of paper in plastic bags.)

Regardless, you should try it at least. Ideally mini-notebooks should be able to fit into a pocket but be big enough so that you can write everything you need on a single page for each workout. It is inevitable that they will go into the water at some point or another, so consider them to be disposable, and make sure you transfer everything to your big notebook, ideally after each practice, but at least once a week. Then if you lose your mini-notebook or get it wet, you won't have lost all that much. While some coxswains like to take notes on their mobile devices, we the like the mini notebook better because you can see it on paper even when you are using your mobile for other things like recording.

As far as mini-notebooks go, if you are going to bring it in the boat, we think it should be (a) really cute and (b) waterproof. You can find cute mini-notebooks anywhere. We suspect the entire Japanese populous shares our fascination with cute mini-notebooks because they seem to make the coolest versions. Even if you can't go to Japan, we love to buy mini-notebooks in bulk at Asian markets. The best waterproof mini-notebooks are made by a company called Rite-In-The-Rain. Elan Publishing Company also makes great, sturdy waterproof notebooks. Elan's are also designed for field notes and are nice because they have hard covers that can withstand even the worst kind of coxswain abuse. The waterproof mini-notebooks are obviously way more expensive, but they will last considerably longer and are far more difficult to destroy.

A word to the wise—put your mini-notebook in a sturdy quart-size Ziploc freezer bag with a small pen or golf pencil. This will at least double its lifespan, and you will also always have something to write with.

Before each practice, write down a few calls/shares that you want to make sure to say during the practice. This could be key calls that you are working on, something that you want to say in a different way, something that you are trying out for your crew, motivational quote, funny story to share, whatever. It should be just a few key words to jog your memory, not the entire thing. When you get to practice, ask your coach for the day's workout, his or her technical focus, and the drills you will be doing. Write those down. If your lineup differs from day to day, write down your lineup as well. Cram it all on a single page so you don't have to flip around to find it. Open the mini-notebook to today's page, and pop it into your Ziploc bag. Use a binder clip if you have difficulty getting your mini-notebook to stay open to the correct page. Keep your mini-notebook at your feet or next to your body in the coxswain's seat. The important thing is to keep it in a place where you can see it throughout practice, and it will jog your memory.

Here is an example of a mini-notebook entry:

And don't forget to look at it. It's just another piece of junk you have to carry with you into the boat if you never look at it. After each practice you should transfer everything you wrote in your mini-notebook into your big notebook.

P. Practicing Your Calls and Commands Off the Water

As we have been saying throughout this book, if you really want to get better, you have to practice. This includes your commands and your calls. If you really want to get better fast, you need to practice these off the water in non-rowing situations. We are talking about practicing in front of the bathroom mirror, in private, without anyone else around, and making recordings of yourself pretending to cox real boats while not really in a boat. As far as race coxing goes, the best way to practice for races is to practice an entire race, from start to finish, in real time, with your race plan and a stopwatch in front of you. If you do this enough before you race, you will not be nervous, but will feel great, well prepared, and ready to go when the real day arrives. We will get more into detail on this in the racing chapter.

While it may be hard to find the time or interest in getting started, once you start, it's very easy to do. For example, if you are working on sharper counting, practice counting, recording your counting, until you like the way it sounds. As another example, if you are new, and have problems figuring out the commands for moving boats, practice picking up objects around the house and moving them—from waists, to shoulders, up overheads—working on sharp commands as you go through the motions. As another example, if you are nervous about your start sequences for sprint racing, practice your first thirty strokes of the race, practice giving data on rates and other crews, match your voice intensity from the start (whether you want it to be controlled or fired up), help the crew control the slides and feel the power, and add extra focus words in. When you get a version you like, you can always play it for your rowers and see how they respond. This is the type of thing we are talking about.

Be careful with this though—you can get carried away. One of your authors especially likes to fully nerd out on this and has been known to say things like 'weigh enough' to other non-rowers in places like the grocery store, at the gym, at the office, and in social situations.

Q. Checking in—Evaluating Your Improvement

We talked at the beginning of this chapter about SMART goal setting. One of the things that comes after SMART is SMARTER—that 'ER' is 'evaluate' and 'reevaluate.' Basically it means a never-ending cycle of constant improvement, analysis, evaluation, and reevaluation. What could be more frustrating than that? (Well, welcome to real life!) We recommend checking in after about a month of working on your SMART goals or your deadline for completion, whichever comes later. Compare one of your recordings from when you started to now. Determine whether or not you can detect a difference.

Here are a few things to ask <u>yourself</u> during the evaluation and revaluation process:

- Did I achieve my goal? Why or why not? If yes, congratulations! If not, was my goal a good one? What would I change about it if I got a do-over?
- Did the solution that I came up with address the problem? If the solution I came up with did not, who might be able to provide input in coming up with new solutions?
- What step did I take to fix the problem? Did the steps I took fix the problem (or at least make progress toward the problem)? How could those steps be modified?
- Have I mastered the skill I was working on? If not, what would the next goal be?

Then, take steps to <u>indirectly</u> figure out if <u>other people</u> noticed the changes. Here are a few indirect indications:

- Your coach has stopped or at least decreased his or her comments about the problems.
- Your rowers have not noticed the problem or at least complained less about it.
- Your rowers are rowing better, paying more attention to you, etc...

Then there is always the <u>direct</u> route. You can ask. (Shocking, we know!) Keep it low key. You can say to your coach, "Coach, I just wanted to let you know that I've been really working on maintaining good spacing with the other coxswains in practice. I hope you agree that it's getting better." Or you can say to your rowers, "I know you guys hate when I get too frantic in pieces, so I've been working on taking deep breaths, thinking about everything before I say it, and being calmer. I hope you agree that it's gotten a little better." You can always ask your coach or rowers to fill out a Coxswain Evaluation Form and see how the numbers match up to the last one. Remember, if you bring it up, you control the situation, and they can give you their input. Then again, when you mention it directly, they may disagree. We always figure though that it is best to know your status than to guess about it.

Then, when you are comfortable that you've achieved your first few goals, you can draw up a list of new SMART goals and get going on those. It really is a never-ending cycle of improvement.

CHAPTER 8
BASIC TECHNIQUE AND TECHNICAL FIXES

A. What to Look for at Each Point in the Stroke
B. How to Fix an Unset Boat
C. How to Fix Timing Problems
D. Finding and Fixing Miscellaneous Issues

When we asked lots of coxswains what they wanted in coxing training, they overwhelmingly told us that they wanted pictures taken from the coxswain seat. Essentially pictures of what good rowing technique looks like, what bad rowing technique looks like, what to look for when you're crunched down in the tiny black hole that is the coxswain's seat, and how to fix the problems. As you get more experience in coxing, you will gradually be able to feel when certain problems arise beyond just seeing them. While we cannot claim the expertise to pontificate on the finer points of the physics of rowing or advanced kinesiology theories of sports performance, we do know what good and bad rowing technique looks like. Lord knows we've seen enough of the bad to last a lifetime. So coxswains of the world, we staged these photos for you, from the coxswain's seat, showing real rowers, pretending to have technique problems. In reality, all of our model rowers are exemplary and would never make such mistakes.

A. What to Look for at Each Point in the Stroke

Here are some general things you should (maybe) be able to see from the coxswain seat when the rowers are doing everything correctly.

At the Catch. As rowers come into the catch, they should be moving their hands slightly upward from the gunwales and compress to a position where legs are at a 90-degree angle from the bottom of the boat. Bodies should not be flopping forward or 'diving,' but instead rowers have an arch from the lower back with their butts behind their shoulders, are sitting upright, and heads are up. Knees should be separated and upright. Arms should be relaxed and straight, elbows straight, and wrists should be flat and relaxed. The shoulders should be relaxed and upright. Rowers should have their weight on the front of the seat with their chests open and upright. At the catch, rowers will 'hinge' their outside arms from the shoulder, lifting the arm slightly, and allowing the blade to drop into the water. Catches should be sharp, but not violent. Catches should be slightly 'backed in' where the oar is still moving backwards as it enters the water. Doing this successfully will result in 'backsplash.' At the catch, oars should be square in the water enough to cover the blades but not so deep that the shaft of the oar is underwater.

At the Catch

On the Drive

On the Drive. In newer crews, legs should be pressed down first, then bodies should swing into bow, and finally rowers should bring their arms in. As rowers gain more experience, these will be blended into one another more, which actually improves the acceleration of the boat, so long as all of the rowers in the crew are doing it together. As rowers push their legs down, they transfer their weight to the middle of the seats. Regardless of your crew's skill level, bodies and arms should stay in position as the legs are first pressed down to generate the maximum amount of pressure. During the drive, arms should be straight and relaxed with wrists flat, and shoulders should remain relaxed and forward of the hips until the very end. At the end of the drive, weight will be transferred to the back of the seat as backs are swung back into the bow, and arms should be quickly accelerated in toward the body parallel to the water, bending the elbows as the oar is brought in. Elbows should bend in a 'chicken wing' position—not pressed completely against the body and not sticking straight out at a right angle.

At the Finish. As rowers come into the finish, legs and knees are completely down, and rowers should be maintaining a 'sitting up' type posture with shoulder blades back and heads up. As hands come in for the final bit of the drive, rowers should simultaneously push down with their outside arms (the 'tap down') and feather the blades cleanly out of the water (the 'release') with their inside hands. Remember the blade should always come out of the water square and is then feathered.

At the Finish

Hands Away and Bodies Over. Then rowers will quickly push the blades away from the body. At hands away, rowers should have smooth, continuous hands away without any pauses. Rowers should maintain layback position while moving their hands away and then bring their bodies over. On the 'lay forward' (known as 'body preparation') rowers should maintain good 'sitting up' posture with heads up, chins up, and chests up, pivoting from the hips forward.

Hands Away and Bodies Over

On the Recovery

On the Recovery. After rowers have swung their bodies forward, legs should come forward back to full compression. Rowers should be sitting up with heads up and chins up. Slide control is key here, and rowers need to engage their core muscles and hamstrings to put the breaks on the slide.

The Rollup. The rollup or square up should be a quick, singular motion done simultaneously by all rowers following stroke's timing. The roll up is done by squeezing the inside hand and rotating the back of the hand over. Rowers should not use their outside hands to feather or feather by sticking the elbows up, or excessively bending the wrists.

General Bladework. Rower grips on sweep oars should be between two fist distances and shoulder width apart. Hands should be relaxed, and rowers should avoid common problems like gripping and ungripping the oar. Hands should move continuously throughout the entire stroke.

The Rollup

B. How to Fix an Unset Boat

Unset boat (down on Port, up on Starboard)    *6 Seat hands too high*

One of the biggest problems a coxswain faces in the early years of coxing is learning how to fix an unset boat. When the balance is off in your boat, the boat will 'fall off' or 'fall down' on one side. You can feel an unset boat in your back (You will feel like half your body is being pulled downward or that it is a struggle to sit up straight in the coxswain's seat). A boat is considered to be 'off set' when it leans down to one side or the other, typically on the recovery. Being off set can come from a number of factors, including any number of parts of the stroke/timing being off among the rowers, and handle height issues. Here we offer photos (from the coxswain's seat), things to be watching for, and how to fix the problems for some of the most common causes of unset boats.

Handle heights. One major cause of an unset boat is handle heights that are in the wrong place or inconsistent between strokes. This is pretty easy to see from the coxswain's seat, even in the bow. Look at the heights of the handles, how far off the water the blades are, and how the shafts compare to one another. You should be able to identify the oars (and the rowers attached to them) that are at the wrong height.

Port handles too high, Starboards too low

2, 4 hands inconsistent heights with 6, stroke

Generally, inconsistency is the biggest issue. The most basic fix for set is having rowers find their marks. Finding their marks means sitting at the finish with hands by the body with the blades square and buried until the boat comes to 'level' set point. Then have them sit at the catch with blades square and buried until the boat comes to 'level' set point. Have them then pull through a few strokes, one at a time, stopping in between each, between the catch set point and the finish set point. Focus on keeping handle heights level and consistent between the catch and the finish set points. After you have them move between their 'marks' a few times, watch the blades, and look for rowers who are pulling in higher or lower than the rest of the crew. Watch for other stuff going on (people leaning away from their riggers or otherwise throwing off the balance with their body weights in a weird place, timing issues, etc…) because handle heights are rarely the sole problem in any newer crew. Try to isolate which rowers are causing the problem. It probably will not be just one person. An individual rower's handle height being off causes a ripple effect through the rest of the crew as they try to compensate for the person who is off. If you find handle heights consistently problematic in your crew, it is important to single out individual rowers by name who are off from the group and offer specific corrections. Don't leave that person alone until you are satisfied that he or she is in the right place. Many rowers do not know when they are right; they only know when they are being corrected, so give positive feedback when people hit the right spots. Keep in mind that even if you fix handle heights, other factors related to timing will likely be contributing to the bad set.

Dropping the hands at the catch or lurching into the catch.

Dropping the hands at the catch, also known as 'skying the blade' because it causes the blade to pop up in the air, is a big problem in newer crews. (Some experienced rowers never quite get it either.) This may be caused by rushing the later half of the recovery in a fear of being 'late' to the catch or by rowers who fail to get their bodies over before they start compressing the legs on the recovery. In the coxswain's seat you will notice the blades that pop up toward the sky.

4 seat dropping hands at the catch, skying blade

It's pretty easy to see anywhere in the crew, even in the bow. Try to identify the cause of the dropped hands. Is the rower failing to get his or her body over before compressing on the recovery and lurching forward into the catch? If so, remind the crew to swing the bodies forward after the hands come away. A drill that emphasizes bodies over, such as Cut the Cake, or a two-part pause drill, pausing at hands away and then bodies over, is a good fix for this. Is the rower rushing the slide and lurching into the catch? This can also be addressed with a two-part pause drill with moderate pressure at a really low rate, pausing at hands away and then bodies over, reminding the rowers to slow the slide down after the second pause. Or is the rower just doing something like dropping his or her hands thinking he or she is going to get a better catch if the blade crashes into the water from 18 inches up instead of 6? This one is best fixed by reminding the crew that they need to be coming up with hands level and then lifting the hands slightly up (or letting go/dropping, whichever image your coach prefers) and letting the blade resoundingly plop into the water.

Over-compression/head dropping. In newer crews, you can also have balance/set issues as a result of poor posture and over-compression especially at the catch. Novice rowers especially will drop their heads and take a 'dive' toward the stern as they come into the catch, often called 'diving at the catch.'

From the coxswain seat you should be able to see it in the bodies of your stern four rowers, but it is harder to diagnose in those toward the bow. (Hopefully your coach will notice because it is easy to see from the launch!). You may also feel 'check' in the boat. If you suspect that this is happening, do some stationary catch placement drills, and remind your rowers to sit up, arching from the lower back and engaging their

Stroke overcompressing and dropping the head

core muscles with heads up, chins up, looking over the head of the person in front of them. Use the ergs as a teaching tool to demonstrate proper compression (with shins essentially straight up and down, arms outstretched, chest and head up), so rowers know where to sit, and remind them of sitting up when you're in the boat. If you get tired of telling them to sit up, phrases like 'chins up' or 'look high' seem to resonate with some crews.

4 Seat Rushing the Slide, Hands too High

Rush. Rowers moving too quickly up the slide on the recovery, known as 'rush,' cause lots of problems in crews. One of the main issues is that it results in the rowers' body weight being thrown at different speeds toward the stern of the boat. A typical problem is that rowers rush the last half of the recovery, which makes them lurch into the stern, and often drop their hands at the catch, which impacts the set of the boat. See the paragraph above for more information on this. From the coxswain's seat, you can see people rushing if the blades and the shafts of the oars are moving faster than the other blades around them, or more likely, you feel 'check' in the boat and see the boat crashing down to one side right before the catch. If rush is a consistent problem in your crew, slide control drills like How Low Can You Go? and pause drills that include pauses at body over or at half slide can be effective. Remind rowers to engage their hamstrings and decelerate as they come into the catch and hold themselves up with their core muscle groups. The older, more out of shape, or lazier your rowers are, the more rush is a problem because it is just plain less effort to control the slide. If your crew falls into one of these categories, you are going to need to think of creative ways to talk about slide control.

Leaning out. While some people just like to lean out of the boat for no apparent reason, most of the time you will find individual rowers leaning out the wrong way trying to fix the set, which then makes other rowers sloppier or more inconsistent on their attention to balance. This overall situation contributes to a really, really, really bad row. From the coxswain seat, it is pretty easy to see if someone is leaning out the wrong way. Depending on how your coach likes the rowers to compress, you should at least see some 'leaning out' or 'curving around' toward each rower's own rigger at full compression as they come into the catch.

5 Seat leaning out to the wrong side

Stroke overcompressed, learning too far out, but correct side

If you do not see one person's head at this point, this should be a red flag that that rower is either not getting full compression, is late coming into the catch, or, more likely in newer crews, is leaning the wrong way. Talk to your rowers about curving around their own riggers, keeping the outside shoulder slightly higher than the inside shoulder, getting their outside hands all the way around, and 'dropping' the blade at the catch using a 'hinge' of the outside arm coming off the rotator cuff of the outside shoulder. You can add some catch placement drills and stationary catch drills if the problem occurs at the catch. If rowers are just leaning out generally on the recovery and during the drive, single people out individually. If rowers are leaning because they are trying to fix bad set, remind them that this only contributes to the problem of bad set. Then you as the coxswain need to find the cause of the bad set and fix that.

Starboards pulling in lower than ports

Side dominance. We do not have a good term for this, but sometimes, especially in crews where experienced rowers have to row with newer ones, you will find a situation where two or more rowers on one side (port or starboard) deliberately or coincidentally are pulling in high, which ensures that the boat will fall down to the other side. From the coxswain's seat, you will be able to easily see this—handle heights on one side will be much higher than on the other, and the boat will be down on the low side. You can remind rowers on the 'down' side to lift their handles, but focus on singling people out on the 'high' side and call them out by name. Half the time you will suspect that they are doing this deliberately. Most of the time you will be right. You can stop rowing and check marks as an effective fix, but punishing the 'high' side by making them row with square blades is also effective (or it might make the situation worse!).

Dumping into the lap. Another cause of bad set is the terrible technique of rowers 'dumping' the blades into their laps. In other words, they are pulling in straight to their belly button or in a big curving arch that ends at the belly button, (not pulling in correctly at mid-chest level and moving the hands down and away as they feather out of the water). This tends to result in the blade 'washing out' or popping out of the water early and throwing off the timing of the finishes in the boat generally. This is a hard one to see from the coxswain seat, especially if it happens with rowers closer to the bow. What you may notice is the blades washing out and the boat falling off set or wobbling at the finish. In newer crews, some rowers like to lift the oar handles up toward the sky about mid-drive (digging too deeply with the oars, which you can easily see) and then bring the handle down

Stroke dumping hands into the lap

straight to their laps (popping the blade out early, which you can also see). You can generally remind rowers to pull in straight and level to mid-chest, but this is a good opportunity to correct individual rowers who are doing weird things with their handle heights on the second half of the drive. Remember to let your rowers know when they are doing it correctly, too. Drills that help include finding your marks, rowing on the square with outside arms only, and even focusing on the correct heights during a standard pic drill can all be helpful.

Uneven pressure off the feet. This is a common problem in novice crews often because rowers do not fully realize how important it is for them to push off the foot stretchers with an even amount of pressure from both feet. It is really difficult to tell that rowers are doing this, but if the handle heights look consistent and even, uneven foot pressure might be a likely culprit that is contributing to an unset boat. Reminding rowers on a regular basis to push evenly is a good idea.

Stroke, uneven pressure on feet

Failing to put lateral pressure on the oar against the oarlock. Rowers in both sweep and sculling boats need to push laterally with their oars to exert outward pressure between the collar band of the oar and the oarlocks to keep the oar in place. Often in novice crews, rowers will forget to exert the lateral pressure against the oarlock, causing the oar to 'separate' from the oarlock, which can significantly impact the set of the boat and can cause serious loss of control of the oar, crabs, and other problems. Remind rowers to use their outside pinkie fingers to push the oar toward the oarlock, and talk about the importance of connection between the oar collar and the oarlock.

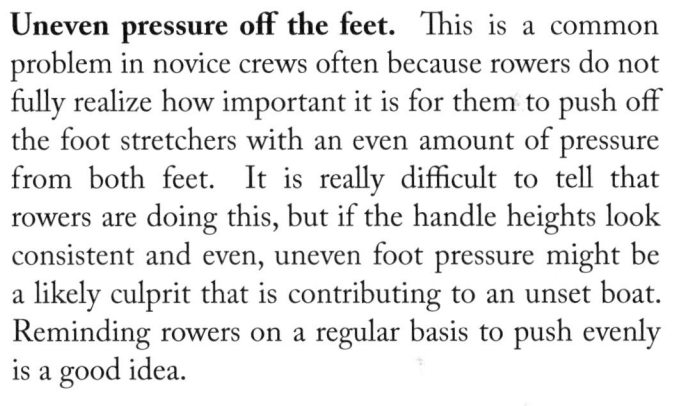

4 Seat No Lateral Pressure on Oar Against Oarlock

Timing Problems. Timing problems are big, often hard to pinpoint, and a major contributing factor in offset boats. This means that the timing sequence is generally off among one or more rowers somewhere in the stroke. That narrows it down, right? In a typical situation, hands are slow out of bow or coming out of bow at different times, which impacts the timing of the bodies swinging forward, which in turn tends to result in rush up the slide (fear of being late) on the later half of the recovery, which results in hanging at the catch or squaring up at the wrong spot or time and often missing water. It might also result from people getting stuck at the finish, which in turn makes them late up the slide, square late, and wash in to the catch after the rest of the blades have connected, slowing down the run of the boat. As a coxswain, you can feel timing problems in what is known as 'check'—essentially body weights of different rowers are doing different things and going in different directions, slamming your back into the back of the coxswain's seat or making you feel like you are lurching forward and backward. We address common timing problems in more detail below, but just know that typically timing problems are the result of a combination of factors, so there is not one easy fix from the coxswain's seat. This is also why you have a coach!

C. How to Fix Timing Problems

If you have been coxing for more than a month or two, it should now be obvious to you that while the rowing stroke is simple, technically a lot can go wrong. After years of observing bad rowing, here are some of the more common problems and how to fix them.

Out of sequence drive or recovery. The proper rowing drive sequence involves pushing the legs down, then opening the back, and then bringing the arms in toward the body. The proper recovery should first push the hands away, then bring the body over, and then compress the legs. One of the biggest problems we see in newer crews is rowers with out-of-sequence drives or recoveries that do not follow the appropriate progression. You will see rowers who open the back up early, forget to pull in, fail to get their hands away, or bodies over before the legs come up, and the list goes on. This tends to happen when you ask the rowers to pull harder or increase the rating beyond a certain rower's comfort zone. They panic and suddenly forget everything they have learned. With a newer group of rowers, it will generally be only a few people who creates 99% of the problems, so as a coxswain, your goal is to get those people back on track without picking on him or her too much. From the coxswain's seat, you should be able to see that one or a few oars are consistently in the wrong places. You will also note your coach, hopefully, calling the culprits out. If one rower is struggling, we like to take the opportunity between pieces to go through the stroke sequence in a stationary position with just that rower or pair going through the proper sequence with blades flat on the water. You can also generally remind the boat to follow the backs of the person in front of them. If you are coxing a newer crew, whatever you do, do not let your crew start giving pointers to the out-of-sequence rower. Take control and keep working on it, but do it in a positive and productive way. Work with the rower off the water on the erg, stressing proper technique, including at higher pressure or ratings. The good news is this problem will improve in time.

4 Seat, slow hands away, not tapping down and feathering out with the rest of the crew

Throwing open the back early/tensing the shoulders. When rowers have out-of-sequence drives, one of the common mistakes is opening their backs up early. This can be from overly tense shoulders or just plain thinking that they can generate more power from their backs. With your stern rowers, you should be able to see it pretty easily. You will note that the back opens before the legs are all of the way down, often accompanied by an upward arc on the oar handle. Basically they will try to pull with their backs and their legs simultaneously or push weakly with their legs. Often these rowers will not lay back because they have exhausted themselves pulling the whole weight of the stroke with their backs. This is hard to see from the coxswain seat if it occurs in the bow of the boat, but be watching for oars that go deep in the early part of the drive and come out of the water early (often resulting in a pause at the finish). You may also be able to see the upward arcs on the oar handles. If you have rowers with this problem, remind them to push with their legs, thinking about the idea that 60+% of your power in the rowing stroke should come from the legs. Remind them to keep the shoulders up but relaxed. If specific rowers have a tendency to yank with their backs, remind them of the proper drive sequence, and do not be afraid to call them out individually.

Stroke throwing open back too early

Lack of body preparation. When rowers have out-of-sequence recoveries, they typically fail to get their hands away quick and then get their bodies over. Instead, you will see them lurching forward right before the catch. This should be very evident with your rowers in the stern although hard to see in the bow.

Watch for handles that are slow to come toward the stern and especially any oar handle that is dropped at the catch. To fix this common problem, remind your crews to get the hands away quick, and swing the bodies over after the hands come away. We like to add a two-part pause drill with a pause at hands away and then a pause at bodies over. Drills like Cut the Cake and accelerating the hands away at double their normal speed also can be helpful. Remind rowers to swing from the hips into the lay back, and the 'lay forward,' and follow the backs of the person in front of them.

Stroke, no body preparation coming into catch

Rushing the slide. Sure we talked about this in the previous section, but it bears repeating because slide rushing is one of the most common issues in crews of all levels. When crews are rowing well, the drive should be quicker than the recovery. Rushing the slide means that rowers are zipping back up the tracks toward the stern on the recovery. They might be pulling up on the backs of their feet inside the shoes; they might be just lazy and are doing it because it is easier than recovering in a controlled manner, or they might be getting thrown up to the stern by others

4 Seat rushing the slide

who are rushing. You will notice rush from the coxswain's seat when you see everyone flying fast forward toward you, possibly even faster than during the drive, and can feel it in your back as you get thrown back into the back of the coxswain seat. Generally the stroke is going to be trying to hold back the thundering herd behind them, and you will see everyone 'beating' the stroke up the slide. You will feel it in your back as the body weights of the rowers fly up. So what do you do about it? As we mentioned in the previous section, slide control drills like exaggerated ratio drills, How Low Can You Go?, and pause drills that include pauses at body over or at half slide can be effective. Remind rowers to engage their hamstrings and decelerate as they come into the catch and hold themselves up with their core muscle groups. If you are dealing with a newer, older, lazier, or more out-of-shape crew, rush will always be a problem. As a proactive coxswain you are going to need to think about things you can say to slow them down, using your tone and rhythm to match the desired ratio.

Slow or late roll up. Another very common timing problem in crews of all levels is squaring up (also called rolling up) at the wrong time. Ideally, rowers should square their blades all at the same time, following stroke seat, in a quick motion as the oar handles pass over about mid-calf/ankles, a bit beyond 3/4 slide, on the recovery. What tends to happen instead are the following problems:

- Rowers delay squaring until the very last minute (called 'flip catching'). As far as flip catches go, very experienced crews can pull off the flip catch, but for the most part, your coach will probably want your team to roll up early.

- Rowers fail to fully square their blade when they put it into the water (called 'washing in'). In addition to contributing to bad timing problems, washing in is also a big problem because it causes crabs when the oar gets sucked into the water when it is not fully square. As a coxswain, you can easily see blades that are not going in totally square. Call those people out! Do not wait until they catch a crab.

6 late to roll up, 4, 2 ahead of stroke   *Stroke 'late' to roll up, others ahead*

So what causes the slow or late roll up? If the set is bad, the rowers toward the bow (especially on the 'down side') are most likely to have a hard time squaring up on time and tend to flip catch or wash in because they feel as though they can't get their hands low enough or get their blades out of the water enough without dragging. As a coxswain you should be looking for all eight blades squaring up together. Another common problem is that when set is off and the boat is down on one side, rowers on that side cannot get their oars up off the water enough to square without dragging. If a certain seat is late or a side is down, call them out. It should be as simple as working to correct the set first or calling out the individual rower. You can say something as simple as, "Four seat, you're late rolling up. Square up earlier." Keep reminding them a few times, and let them know when they get it right. Make sure you also remind your rowers not to focus their attention on looking at their blades but instead following stroke's blade.

Not catching together. Catching together, where all eight blades enter the water at the same time, is critical to the speed of any boat. The first few inches of the drive have the greatest potential to make the boat move forward, but when rowers are late or early, the 'off' blades act as an anchor, slowing the boat down. The catch is also by far the easiest place for a coxswain to observe timing problems. Catch problems typically fall into one of a few categories including pausing at the catch and waiting for the stroke to arrive (this is also a sign that the early rower is rushing the slide), catching early, or catching late. The single best thing you can do as a coxswain is to call people out individually. Let rowers know that they are late or early or "hanging" (waiting around for the stroke). Keep reminding them a few times, and let them know when they get it right. Make sure you also remind your rowers not to focus their attention on looking at their blades, but instead following stroke's blade. Drills to improve catch timing include the chop drill, the slap drill, and the whistle catch drill.

6 seat catching too early

Uneven pressure from one side. This is a common problem in crews at all levels. Essentially it means that your ports are pulling harder than your starboards or vice versa. If it happens at full pressure, it means that one side of the boat has stronger people on it or at least people with more effective application of power through the water. You will easily be able to tell if you have uneven pressure if you put your rudder at dead center, and the boat consistently pulls to one side. If you think it is as a result of lack of effort by certain rowers, call out that side, by name if you have to. You can get your point and tell your crew that you will be keeping your hands off the rudder, and warn them that if they crash, it will be the weaker side's fault. You can keep your rudder at dead center and tell them it is going to be a 'ports versus starboards' race to see who is stronger and warn them that you are not going to steer at all. If you genuinely have a situation where certain people (or just one person) is far stronger than the rest, you can either have them back off or resign yourself to being on the rudder the entire time.

Ports out-pulling Starboards, making boat swerve

Pauses. Rowers tend to add in unwanted and undesirable pauses in two places—right before the catch and right after the release. Some rowers rush up to the catch and then pause there for a second to wait for the stroke and everyone else to catch up to them because they are trying to avoid being 'early' in catching. This bad habit is sometimes called 'hanging at the catch.' You can see it from the coxswain's seat in your stern rowers, but it is hard to detect elsewhere. Listen to your coach correcting individual rowers for this practice, and keep an eye on the known usual offenders. Remind them to slow the slide, and point out when they get up too early ahead of the stroke. Two part pause drills, making a pair with the offending rower row alone for a few strokes, and stationary catch placement drills are good fixes for this, but generally it is just a bad habit among certain rowers, and a simple reminder should do the trick. The other place where rowers stop unnecessarily is after the release. This even worse habit is called 'getting stuck at the finish,' and it is very common in new rowers who think that by finishing their stroke, they are entitled to a 0.5 second breather to stop and look around. You may see this from the coxswain seat if you notice one oar that is not moving toward you after the finish, but it is usually pretty subtle. Generally reminding rowers of quick hands coming out of bow, tapping the oar down and away, and accelerating their hands away and bodies over should do the trick. We also like to teach our novices that the stroke should end at hands away, not at the release. Get your rowers in the habit of ending at arms away after every piece and trying to balance the boat, which should reinforce this idea that the stroke ends at hands away. You can also make them row at arms and backs only, focusing on the tap down and hands away.

D. Finding and Fixing Miscellaneous Issues

Just when we think we have seen about all the weird technique problems and mistakes, a new group of novices will come along with a different set of problems. Here are a few other things that you should be looking for from the coxswain seat.

4 seat oversquare at the catch

2 late, 6, 4 washing in, missing water, generally sloppy

Sloppy bladework. One of the other things that many crews experience during normal practice is times of overall sloppiness with bladework. This means that the blades lack sharp precise appearance when entering and exiting the water, or you are not hearing consistent sound from the riggers. As a coxswain you should be able to feel when the crew is catching together (you can feel the boat being 'picked up' as the oars lock onto the water), and, conversely, when you do not feel that 'grab,' it means that the oars are not going in together—the result of timing being off and probably also sloppy bladework. You may also be able to feel blades dragging on the water or kicking up water, which can also be the result of sloppy bladework. As a coxswain, you should be watching for this sort of non-descript issue. Remind your crew to sharpen it up periodically. Good drills for combatting general sloppiness include square blade rowing, eyes closed, chop drills, whistle catches, and reverse pic drills. You can also do some silent focus tens to 'listen to the boat' or 'feel the boat.' Remind them to listen to the sound of the blades against the riggers and the sound of the catches going in. Toward the end of the practice, especially on the cool down, is the best time to watch for and work on clean bladework.

6, 4, 2 undersquare, washing in, and missing water at catch; stroke also pulling in too deep

1, 5 coming out too early, missing water at finish; 3 washing out and missing water at finish

Missing water. A very common problem for newer crews, and even some experienced ones, is missing water. Missing water is when a rower fails to pull a stroke that is the same length as the rest of the crew or pulls a very short stroke that makes an incomplete 'sweep' through the water. It is possible for rowers to miss water at the front end of the stroke (failing to compress fully or failing to drop their blade into the water when they are at full compression) or the back end of the stroke (failing to bring the oar all the way to the body or otherwise bring the blade out early). From the coxswain seat you can see missed water easily. You'll notice blades that don't go back 'as far' as the other blades, blades that come up with all the other blades but are not dropped into the water when the others drop—taking part of the leg drive with the blade in the air instead of in the water—or blades that come out earlier than the rest of the rowers and don't get as close to the boat as the other blades do. If all rowers are missing water, the arcs of the oars will be very short in the water. Remind rowers to lengthen out, remind them to drop the blades in right when they are at maximum compression, and remind them to stay long and bring the oar all the way to the body. Stationary catch placement drills and chop drills are good for missing water on the front end of the stroke, and exaggerated layback drills are good for 'holding the finish' and preventing blades from coming out early.

6 seat washing out and missing water at the finish   *5 seat washing out and missing water at the finish*

Washing Out. Washing out is when rowers fail to bring their blades out of the water square following a complete stroke. This is caused by several things but is mostly attributable to feathering the blade underwater. Washing out diminishes boat speed, makes the row sloppy, and all-around impacts the timing of the other rowers in the boat. As a coxswain you can easily see blades that are not coming out square or that certain blades are coming out early. Do not hesitate to call rowers out, and remind them to bring their oars all the way to their bodies, lengthen their layback, come out square, and get the finish turns together.

Washing In. Washing in is when rowers fail to fully square their blade when they put it into the water. In addition to contributing to bad timing problems, washing in is also a big problem because it causes crabs when the oar gets sucked into the water when it is not fully square. As a coxswain you can easily see blades that are not going in totally square. Call those people out! Do not wait until they catch a crab. Washing in is generally caused by squaring up late and then rushing to put the blade in the water while it is still under-squared. The best way to solve washing in problems is to accelerate the hands faster out of bow at the finish, and make sure that the rower has enough time to come up the slide and square up with the stroke.

6 seat washing in

Gripping too tightly. Another issue we see frequently, especially in newer crews, is the problem of gripping the oar incorrectly. The oar should be gripped tightly enough to control but lightly enough that the hands are relaxed. We have heard that the general rule of thumb is that rowers should grip the oar enough so that a single sheet of paper could fit between the hand and the oar. We are not really sure if we buy that standard, but suffice to say if you can see white knuckles or veins bulging on your rowers' hands or they have constant problems with blisters that never go away, they are probably gripping too tightly. Remind them periodically to relax their grips, particularly those individuals who have this problem consistently.

Stroke gripping too tightly; outside hand too far away from the end of the handle; hands too close together

Sroke feathering with both hands, over feathering with inside hand

Feathering with both hands. Another issue with newer rowers is feathering with both hands or with their outside hand. You will notice the outside wrist bending when it should be flat in the stern, but otherwise this is hard to see from the coxswain seat. Remind rowers periodically that they should only be feathering with their inside hands. Drills like inside arm only and outside arm only rowing are good for this problem.

Bent wrists. We also see the problem in newer crews of weak wrists or wrists bent at weird angles. Generally this means that the rower is holding the elbow at the wrong angle, failing to pull in evenly, is not getting a clean release, or has some other issue. Wrists should be held flat throughout the stroke. You can see this fairly easily with your stern rowers. It is hard to detect in the bow, although if you see an elbow sticking out or not coming past the body at the finish, this should be a red flag. This is something that your coach will likely see easily, so be listening for this correction, and make a mental note to remind the offending rowers frequently. Generally speaking, remind your rowers to pull in evenly and keep their wrists flat. One old-fashioned solution is to tape straws or popsicle sticks on the top of your rowers' wrists.

Over-bent wrists

Under-bent wrists

Digging too deep. A common problem in newer crews is digging too deep with their oars. Novice crews often feel like they are pulling harder when they dig deep with the oars. This is not true! Ideally, only the blade should be covered, not the shaft of the oar. Putting the blade in too deeply creates drag and slows the boat down. Putting the oar in too deeply also means that the rower is pulling in too high, which can impact the set and is inefficient—often resulting in pulling in an upward motion on the oar and throwing the back open early. You can easily see oars that are too deep from the coxswain seat. Look for oar shafts that are underwater. Single out rowers reminding them to pull in lower with the handle and drive with the legs.

4 seat too deep; 2 seat slightly too deep

Stroke pulling in too deep (but this is the least of this crew's problems)

Loss of focus. One of the biggest problems we see in crews of all levels is loss of focus. It usually happens when the practice is not going well or the coach came over and yelled at the crew. Sometimes it's when you're having too much fun! Here is how you bring it back.

7 seat, looking out of the boat

Stroke and 7 laughing (NO fun, rowing is serious!)

- **Acknowledge the situation.** If things have gone south, let the crew know that you need them to get back on track. If you're taking a break from a moment of joking around, let the crew know that it's time to get back to business.

- **Focus on rhythm elements of the stroke.** Exaggerating the sounds of the oars against the riggers, the down and away of the hands at the release, the blades going into the water together, the swinging forward and swinging back of the hips, or deep breathing.

- **Close eyes.** Throw in ten strokes with eyes closed to force the crew to listen to the boat. Have them open their eyes for ten, and then surprise them with ten more strokes with eyes closed.

- **Silent tens.** Throw in a silent ten (eyes closed optional) to force them to listen to the boat.

- **Quotes.** Add a motivational quote that you have in your back pocket for situations like this.

Caution that this might have the opposite effect and turn all of them against you.
- **Threaten punishment.** For situations when the crew is deliberately not listening to you, this is the equivalent of your dad telling you that he is going to turn the car around. You can always ask them if they want to go back to the boathouse and do a 10k on the erg.

CHAPTER 9
WHAT TO SAY, HOW TO SAY IT, WHAT NOT TO SAY, WHEN TO SHUT UP

A. Categories of Things Coxswains Say
B. What to Actually Say
C. Positive versus Negative and Follow Ups
D. Long List of Boring Phrases Your Coach Probably Thinks You Should Say
E. How to Speak into a Cox-Box
F. How to Count
G. Enunciating
H. Rhythm
I. Intensity
J. Fixing the Sound of Your Voice—Learning to Speak from the Diaphragm
K. What to Avoid Saying
L. Signs That You Might Be Boring and Annoying
M. The Lost Art of Silence—Strategically Timed Silences

A. Categories of Things Coxswains Say

What you say in the boat can be put into a number of categories:

Specific technical. This includes pointing out specific technique corrections for individual rowers (e.g. "Three seat, keep your hands up as you come into the catch").

General technical. This includes words and phrases designed to improve rower technique in the boat generally, but not directed to anyone in particular (e.g. "Let's get heads up and chins up as we come into the catch").

Data. This includes giving specific information on rating, split, time, position relative to other crews (e.g. "We're at a 28, two minutes to go in this piece").

Equipment and human logistics. This includes information to do with equipment, breakage, or fixing things, rower readiness, and the like (e.g. "Weigh enough; four seat jumped her track; we're going to wait for her to put her seat back on and adjust her foot stretchers, so it won't happen again. Count down from bow when ready.").

Course logistics. This includes information to do with your course, including steering, feeling rudder, the boat's course, obstacles up ahead, or upcoming stopping, turning, and the like (e.g. "We've got a stopped novice eight up ahead in the wrong place. To get around them let's add pressure on port for five strokes, ports let's go, 1-2-3-4-5, OK, back to even pressure").

Workout information. This is typically given at the start of practice, letting the crew know what the workout will be and where you are going (e.g. "We're doing a steady-state aerobic row down to the old power plant, 45 minutes at a 22-24 rating, at 90% pressure").

Motivational. This includes words and phrases that fire your crew up, and you know your crew will hear and will make them pull harder or break the tension. They can be quotes from famous people or as silly as you want to make them (e.g. "Let's take a ten for Jen's white tube socks!").

Compliments. This includes what you like about what your rowers are doing. (It must be genuine, so don't say it if it is not true!) If someone is having a great practice, let them know. If they are terrible, but they have great enthusiasm, also let them know. Make sure you spread the love around too—praise should not go just to the all-stars, but to the unsung mediocre or downright bad rowers, too. Work it in naturally so it doesn't seem fake or forced.

Extras. This includes funny stories, anecdotes, or observations about what is happening around the boat currently (e.g. "Whoa, coach just went for a swim; let's go back and see if she makes it back to the launch OK").

Obvious/non-specific complaints. This includes things that come out of your mouth that shouldn't, including observations on your own personal situation or problems with the boat (e.g. "We're down on starboard again").

Unmotivational. These are the mood killers that a coxswain should never utter (e.g. "You guys look really tired today").

B. What to Actually Say

This is the section you have been waiting for. Here is a list of categories of what to actually say in the boat:

Things that give the rowers specific instructions in a non-confusing way.
"Last two strokes. 1-2-weigh enough!"
"We need to get our point a bit more toward starboard. Two seat touch it one light stroke."

Statements that fix problems in a positive and specific way.
"Five seat get your hands out of bow a split second faster following stroke."
"I'll count ten catches to get our timing back. Nice and sharp on my count, 1-2-3…"

Do statements.
"Let's control the rush by engaging the hamstrings and slowing the last half of the recovery with stroke."
"Ten for clean finishes together."
"We're at a 26; let's take it up 2 to a 28, over 2, following stroke, ready, 1-2."
"Let's get our set back by having three seat and five seat lower their hands on the recovery on this next one."

Statements that express confidence and that everyone is in this together, including the cox.
"We've got this!"
"We just took two seats on them, let's hold it across the line!"

Information on your coxing or conditions that will impact the rowers.
"We've got a wake coming over port side in about three strokes. Be ready for it."
"You're going to feel a little rudder for the next few strokes."
"Let's remember to square up early with this tail wind."
"A sailboat is headed right toward us. I will give you advance warning if we need to stop."

Statements that feed their egos in an honest way (do not overdo it, and only say it when it is true!)
"You guys look really strong!"
"We've really flown the first half of practice; keep up the good work!"
"Three seat, your hands look great at the finish."
"We're getting great run; let's keep sending those puddles away."
"Stroke is dominating the rating changes; let's follow right with her."

C. Positive Versus Negative and Follow Ups

Both Specific Technical and General Technical information should be given in a positive light. Rowers get down on themselves when their coxswain takes on the persona of nagging or pointing out all of their flaws. Sometimes it's hard to remember, but here are a few examples:

Make it positive and ask for something specific. Instead of saying, "Three seat, stop skying your blade," say, "Three seat, push your hands away slightly higher on the recovery, making sure you are holding consistent height as you come into the catch."

Make it positive and get the boat working on something together. Instead of saying, "We're down on port," say, "Let's get our set back. Tom and Brian, lift your hands slightly on the recovery. Good, that made a difference. Now, let's get our finishes together. I'm going to count ten at the finish for quick hands out of bow, 1-2-3, etc…"

Stay on it until it's right, or you've passed the point of futility. After you have corrected a rower's technique specifically, stay on it until he or she does it correctly. As soon as the rower does it correctly, compliment him or her on it, and make a note of the change and how it improved the boat overall. If he or she doesn't get it after two or three reminders, he or she probably won't, so just let it go. You can talk to the rower individually after practice or to your coach if you think it is a big enough issue that it is impacting the entire boat. Check back later in the practice and remind the rower or compliment him or her again depending on how it is going.

D. Long List of Boring Phrases Your Coach Probably Thinks You Should Say

Most coxswains we talked to have asked what they should actually say in the boat. That is a tough one without any good answer. We talked about the general categories above, but that is not what most coxswains want. They want the words and phrases that will make their rowers pull hard for them and pay attention and correct bad technique all at the same time. They want the words that will get bad practices back on track and make good practices even better. We hate to break it to everyone, but there are no such things. Sure, we have seen plenty of coxing advice that talks about things like 'magic words' or 'what your rowers want to hear.' (We even came across a coxing manual from a club that we will not name that actually suggested saying 'razzmatazz' as a 'magic word' to get crews going. We know that if we were rowing and heard something like 'razzmatazz,' we would laugh out loud because that is about the dumbest thing ever.)

While there are no such things as 'magic words,' there are plenty of conventional things that coxswains and coaches have been saying for decades. We came up with a list of as many of those as we could think of. Some of these are useful, but we are going to be honest with you and say that not all crews want to hear this stuff. For many crews, the best thing a coxswain can say is nothing at all. Here are the boring catch phrases, in no particular order. These mostly fall into the general category of General Technical corrections and Motivation. Be warned they are all things you've probably heard before, but we use them all of the time (OK, we use some of these all of the time):

Catches

"One splash, all eight blades"
"Single splash at the catch"
"Quick/crisp/clean/aggressive/powerful/sharp catches"
"'ATCH…'ATCH…'ATCH"
"CHAAA….'CHAAA…'CHAAA…'CHAAA"
"Drop the blades in"
"Let's see some backsplash"
"Bury that blade"
"Back the blade in"
"Back it in"
"Backsplash"
"Strike"
"Build it"
"Lock on together"
"Lock the first few inches"
"Nice and sharp"
"'ATCH together"
"No hesitation"
"Pop it at the catch"
"Drop it at the catch"
"Crush it at the catch"
"Take out the hang, drop it in quick"
"Lift the outside arm and let the blade fall in"
"Catch connection together"
"Feel the first two inches of the catch together"
"Let's get that lock on together"

Drive

"Quick in the water"
"Power in the water on the drive"
"Jump with the legs"
"Stand on those stretchers"
"Stomp on the footstrechers"
"Crush the footstretchers"
"Explosive off the footstretchers"
"Big jumps off the footstretchers"
"Quick legs down on the drive"
"Press those legs down"
"Power on the legs"
"Legs down smooth"
"Squeeze"
"Pop off the stretchers"
"Make those quads sing"
"Big legs"
"Quick legs"
"Quick kick with the legs"
"Send this boat with the legs"
"Move those puddles past the coxswain seat"
"Kick those legs down"
"Just a blade full of water"
"Move the water with your blade"
"Send it away"
"Pick up the bow with your blade"
"Accelerate through the water"

Finishes

"Out together"
"Finishing together"
"Clean/quick/sharp/crisp finishes"
"Tap it down and away"
"Quick hands in, quick hands out"
"Fast hands out of bow"
"Body angle before the recovery"
"Down and around"
"Accelerate the hands quick out of bow"
"Clean releases"
"Clean finishes"
"Into your marks"
"Right to your mark"
"Finish"
"Swing forward with the back in front of you"
"Clean and out"
"Finishes out together"
"Sharp blades out of the water"
"Send it"
"Send it away"
"All the way through"
"Take 'em out square, and send 'em away"
"Hold the finishes into the body"
"Bring it to the body"
"Bring the oar handle to the body"
"Push off the tiptoes into the finish"
"Clean tap downs"
"Tap it down and away together"
"Tap it down, light hands out"
"Lengthen it out"

Recovery/Ratio

"Controlled with the legs"
"Creep up the tracks"
"Connection through the water"
"Long and controlled"
"Take it down with the legs, on this one!"
"Make the ratio change on this one, ready slow!"
"Nice and long"
"Decelerate through the recovery"
"Put the breaks on through the slide"
"Get that ratio back"

Recovery/Ratio (cont'd)

"Let the boat run out from under us on the recovery"
"Let it come from the drive, slow recovery"
"Hold yourself off"
"Fast hands, slow slides"
"Be patient up the tracks"
"S-L-O-W on the slide"
"Smooth push together as you come into stern"
"The catch can wait"
"Let's help the stroke out by slowing down for him/her"
"Control up the slides"
"Engage the hamstrings and hold yourself off"
"Quick drives, slow slides"

Set/Timing

"With the stroke"
"Watch strokes blade"
"Following the stroke"
"Even handle heights"
"Tap it down and away together"
"Everybody with stroke"
"Matching together"
"Control your handles, don't let them control you"
"Don't let the boat dictate you"
"Strike out for the gunwales"
"Low hands away across the lap"
"Consistent hands out of bow"
"Hands up for the catch"
"Consistent handle heights"
"Bodies over the keel"
"Quick hands out of bow to set this boat up"
"Starboards/ports lift your hands"
"Level hands"
"Deliberate hands away"
"Push that oar away level"
"Pull into your marks"
"Lets get back to our marks"
"Squaring up together"
"Square it up with stroke"
"Square it up over your ankles"

Consistency/Body Position/Balance

"Find those handle heights"
"Pivot around your own rigger"
"Swinging the hips together"
"Hands level on the recovery"
"Consistent handle heights away"
"Keep the hands level up the slide"
"Find your spot and focus"
"With your stroke's blade"
"Find the middle ground"
"Sit tall and breathe"
"Square up together"
"Swing with the backs"
"Swinging into bow together"
"Let's get it back together"
"All eight swinging together"
"One catch, one finish"
"Catch together, finish together"
"Hands up into the catch"

Rhythm/Swing

"Swing"
"Swinging together"
"Layback into bow together"
"Swing into bow together"
"Let's see those nice laybacks"
"Let's move our body weight together, stern to bow, bow to stern"
"Find that swing"
"In together, out together"
"Long laybacks"
"Send it long"
"Lengthen out at the finish"
"Sit up and breathe"
"Lean back into the finish"
"Swing the backs together"
"Feel the boat run"
"Feel the boat run under you"
"One crew"
"All together"
"Put some lipstick on it"

Generic Motivation/Power Phrases

"Make this count"
"Strong legs"
"Sit tall"
"Be strong"
"Strike with the oar"
"We've got it"
"Send it away"
"You've got it"
"You deserve it"
"Send this boat"
"Power through the water"
"Send this bow up out of the water"
"No limits"
"Own it"
"Bring it"
"Kick it"

Generic Motivation/Power Phrases (cont'd)

"We've got only got one chance to do it right today"
"Hang on that oar"
"Take that seat…its yours"
"Big, ugly catches"
"Send the boat"
"Fire it up"
"Strike while the iron is hot"
"Let's move those puddles away"
"Send the boat"
"Push those legs"
"Jump off your footstretchers"
"Grip it and rip it"
"Make this the best ten strokes of the race"
"Make it count"
"Walk away"
"Walk it out"
"I want their coxswain/stroke seat/5 seat, etc…"
"We're taking it together"
"Get those heels down"
"Explode off the stretchers"
"Do it now, its now or never"
"Power up those drives"
"Let's see that intensity"
"Strong legs"
"Attack at the catch"
"Big, powerful catches"
"Powerful and controlled"
"Walk with the legs"
"Take no prisoners"
"Drive it down"
"Let's bend those riggers"
"Keep it strong"
"We've got 'em now"
"Long and strong"
"Make your hands fly"
"Swing it and bring it"
"Let's walk through them"
"We can handle them"
"We're walking like crazy"
"Empty the tank"
"Power through"
"We own this lake"
"We're dominating this course"
"We've got the best line"
"We're taking names"
"Give 'em open water"
"No one in this crew is letting you down; don't let them down"
"Show me how much you want it"
"Show this entire boat how much you want it"
"You know you want it"
"Time to prove it"
"No one is going to stop us"
"Make this next ten strokes count"
"Let's fly"
"Let's break free"
"No passengers on this boat, only crew"
"We're not stopping for anyone in this race"
"We're walking straight through them"
"Now or never"
"Swing for the finish line"
"If you're not pushing the boundaries, you're not doing it right"
"Walk it across the line"
"We won't give an inch"
"Put that bow ball across the line first"

E. How to Speak into a Cox Box

First of all, wear your mic on your head. We see lots of coxswains who like to hold their mics in their hands. This is a junior varsity move if we ever saw it. Wear a hat if you think it messes up your hair or is uncomfortable. You need both hands for your steering and holding your body in place, and by putting the mic in your hand, you are subtly impacting the set, whether you realize it or not. Plus, holding it in your hand makes you look dumb. Maybe even dumber than wearing that mic on your head. Wait, you say, you like to bring the mic closer to your mouth when you get intense. Fine, we say, that is what the volume knob on the Cox-Box is for. It is fine to turn the volume up or down when you feel like it. You should also turn the volume knob to 'off' when you are talking 'off the record' to your stroke or communicating with your coach, other coxswains, or other boats on your waterway. Once you get into the habit of adjusting the volume, you will completely forget about the need to hold the mic in your hand.

Optimally, the Cox-Box mic should be about two inches or less from your face. You do not want it interfering with your peripheral vision, nor do you want to even be aware of it. If you hear an echo in the boat, it is too loud. If your rowers cannot hear you in the bow, the volume is too low. Ask the rowers, and learn the appropriate volume for each boat/Cox-Box combination.

F. How to Count

We know what you are thinking—do we really need a section on how to count? Yes! You would be shocked by how many coxswains don't know how to do it correctly.

Keep it by ten. First of all, you should never count above ten, and if you start a ten, you should finish it. It is fine to add other words into your counting, and even skip a few numbers or reverse order, so long as your counts of ten are accurate. For example, "Let's take a ten for pushing the heels down to the footstretchers." "1-2-get those legs down-4-5-6-7-three more strokes, nice and solid with the legs, 9, last one, push the heels down, 10." It is fine to call things like, "Last thirty strokes," but instead of counting from one to thirty, you would count in three sets of ten. Be aware that counting to ten three times in a row without saying anything else will drive your crew crazy. Instead, keep track of where you are, remind the crew as you go, and break it up with other words. For example, if you were going to take the last thirty strokes of the piece, instead of straight counting, you could say: "Last thirty strokes, here we go. 1-2-3-let's focus on big leg drive here. Bow pair, big pushes from you, make sure your blades are connecting with the water with everybody else. That's it, bring it all the way through, solid connection off those stretchers-9-10. Next ten, keep giving us those big legs, 3-4-5-6, pound these out now. Less than fifteen strokes to go; let's see that jump back off the stretchers together. Keep standing on those legs. Come on, last five strokes of the piece, big pushes off the stretchers, 2-3-last two strokes-1-2. Paddle it out."

Counts should be sharp. You do not need to pronounce the entire number. For example, "'un-two-'ree-'or-'ive-si-sv'n-e't-nine-ten" is fine. You do not have to overdo it, but particularly at high rates, you are not going to have time to add every syllable.

Perfect your timing. Make sure your counts are timed EXACTLY on the point of emphasis, typically as the stroke's blade enters the water. If you are working on other technique issues, for example, quick hands away, your count would be exactly at the point where the stroke begins to push his or her hands away.

G. Enunciating

When you are 'on' in coxing, your words should be sharp at all times. Enunciating can only help this. Pronounce words clearly and sharply. For example, instead of saying 'tweny,' as in conventional speaking, you should be saying 'twen-TY.' But wait, isn't this the opposite of what we just told you with counting? Yep. It will be up to you to find the balance.

H. Rhythm

The rhythm (or the timing and speed of your words) should match what you are asking your crew to do. If you are talking about quick, sharp catches, you should count or speak (e.g. 'ACH together') with the emphasis on the exact moment that the stroke's blade hits the water. If you are emphasizing a slow recovery, your words should be purposeful and s-l-o-w to match the time it takes to come up the tracks in a controlled manner. In other words, if you tell them 'slow up the tracks' in a really frantic, hurried voice, it kind of defeats the purpose. Matching the rhythm is as important as tone to setting the overall look and feel of your coxing style. Start out by saying a few things to match the rhythm of the rowers, and then gradually expand your repertoire.

I. Intensity

In real life, you may never think about the sound of your voice consciously, but chances are you are varying the intensity of your voice without even realizing it depending on the audience. The trick to maintaining any sort of rower attention in races is to vary the tone, rhythm, and pacing of your voice. Particularly for races, you want to convey calmness AND intensity, often at the same time. This is no easy task. Your primary modes should be:

In charge coxing. In charge coxing should resemble your professional, at work phone voice, down a few octaves. You are the authority; you are in charge; you are the voice of reason keeping your crew focused. Your voice should sound crisp, confident, and calm. Think about the announcers reading the news on nationally broadcast public radio programs. They sound believable, intelligent, knowledgeable, and in charge. This is what you are going for.

Fired up. Fired up coxing is big, bold, and a little bit arrogant. It should convey competitive fire, encouragement, bordering on urgency, and intensity. This should make your rowers take notice and should match the rhythm of the strokes. Think about sports commentators during big moments in games. They sound excited, but not frantic, in the moment and incredibly enthusiastic about what is happening. This is your target.

Silence. In practices and head races you should plan on some short, strategically-placed silence—you do not have to talk the entire time. Talking for hours or even 15 minutes straight is a lot for your rowers to hear and process. Chances are the less you talk, the more likely they are to listen to what you are saying when you do say something! Tailor the silences to the situation, and give them something to think about while they do it. For example, it is appropriate to say, 'We're going to take a silent 20 strokes to listen to the boat,' or 'Let's do a focus 20 for swing into bow.' Then you shut up and don't say anything until those 20 strokes are over. Again, silences should be short, strategic, and are best left to the middle of the row when not much else is going on. It would be poorly-timed to add silences when you are in the midst of transitions between pieces, short pieces, doing drills, docking or launching or in the middle of the action during a head race. If you are going to shut up at any of those times, make sure your crew knows the reason and feels confident that you have it under control. For example, you can say, "We have a collision between two crews up ahead. I'm going to focus on my steering for a few strokes. Let's keep it strong, eyes in the boat, and follow stroke. I will let you know if you are going to feel any rudder." Silence during sprint races is never a good idea!

Intensity in Practices. Your intensity in practices should vary and increase at the appropriate moments (the end of pieces, and whenever you are at full pressure and especially on power tens). You should be relaxed during paddle pressure or lower pressure pieces, and your voice should particularly become less intense on the cool downs. Maintaining an intense voice is no easy task because it is just a hair away from screaming, blithering, or going crazy. The trick is to maintain your voice from your diaphragm (more on that to follow in this chapter), keeping your voice low, but purposeful. You can get excited (that is the whole point, after all), but at no time should you lose your cool. The best way to channel intensity is again to think about sports broadcasters—the game may crawl along at points where they convey business-like information to the audience—then when something interesting happens, and their voices become more intense until the ball goes over the fence, into the net, or toward the goal. That is exactly the way you want to run a rowing practice. If you are super intense all of the time, even when paddling between pieces, your crew would no doubt tune you out completely. (It would be impossible to keep that kind of enthusiasm up for any length of time).

Intensity in Races. We have talked throughout this book about developing your own coxing style. Particularly in races, you can either take a laid-back, business-like approach, perhaps punctuated by motivational intensity (which we have grown to prefer) or going full intensity throughout (which we relied heavily on during our junior and college racing careers). There is no question that the right motivational calls will fire your crew up, but the question is, can they stay engulfed in flames the entire race, or do you want a slow burn? Or do they need intensity at all? Again, it really depends on your crew.

- **All business.** This style relies on 'in charge' coxing throughout the race. You are the bus driver, and you are executing the race plan. It can work especially well for serious masters crews who are 20 or 30 years past their glory days and are fired up enough just to be alive, in the race, and not experiencing chest pains. This type of crew is most likely to become easily annoyed with 'fired up' coxing. If you are coxing a crew like this, they will let you know how they like it. Trust us on that one.

- **Slow burn coxing.** The slow burn is a mix of 'in charge' and 'fired up' coxing styles. We like the slow burn approach these days, particularly for head races, for several reasons. First, with newer crews, or for bigger races, crews are amped up and nervous enough on their own. Amped up, nervous crews tend to rush the slide, go out too fast, and fail to pace themselves appropriately. If the coxswain is calm, cool, and under control, he or she can help the rowers relax and build at the appropriate speed. Second, an outright aggressive approach is tough to sustain for even an entire six or seven minute sprint race, let alone a 15-20 minute head race, without resorting to being a screaming, blithering idiot, unless you have lots of coxing experience. Third, there is the question of impact when you constantly hit your crew over the head with motivational phrases and try to sustain such a high level of intensity. Will your crew keep listening to you, or will they tune you out? How many minutes does it take for you reach the point where you become just background noise? Lastly, can you keep up with technical changes and give your crew the appropriate data when you're coxing at such an intensity level? Some crews, and some coxswains, can handle it, but many cannot. This goes back to knowing your crew and knowing their style.

- **100% fired up coxing.** Some coxswains attempt to maintain the 'fired up' mode the entire time. It can work, but this is hard to achieve because if you are completely fired up the entire time, your rowers may quickly tune you out. This style also lends itself to rowers going out too hard and too fast, rushing slides, and hitting the lactic acid wall half way through the race. You also will not be able to 'go up from here' with your voice during big moments in the race and may have trouble getting your rowers to bring their best at crunch time when you need them to because you have been so intense the entire time. On the other hand, we have had lots of success with an intense, aggressive coxing style from the start of the race to the finish line, and these have been the most exciting racing seasons of our careers. The coxswain is ON, and the crew knows it. Many crews, fast high school and college-aged crews in particular, prefer the in-your-face, aggressive type of race coxing. Six minutes is not that long really to keep fired up. This take no prisoners approach can work especially well if your crew identity for the season is 'fast crew with an attitude,' or you are trying to cultivate such a reputation.

J. Fixing the Sound of Your Voice—Learning to Speak from the Diaphragm

Another major complaint that rowers have with coxswains is that their voices are annoying. Here are what we think are the worst offending types of coxswain voices. (Picture what each of these sound like, and when you are listening to your tapes, listen for shades of these.)

Boot Camp Instructor
Fire and Brimstone Preacher
Baby Voice
Whining
Half Asleep/Under the Influence of Sedatives
Hyperactive Cheerleader

But what does a good coxswain sound like? Well, we think James Earl Jones would make one heck of a coxswain, if you could squeeze him into the coxswain seat. He sounds trustworthy, likeable, and confident, with that deep, deep voice that we could listen to all day – which is probably why insurance companies hire him.

If you have been coxing for any length of time, you have probably heard that you should be speaking from your diaphragm. What does this really mean? Well, we are not speech therapists, singers, or experts of any sort in this arena, but we know what sounds good. It is a coxswain who speaks with a deep voice, from the middle of the chest, with clear, understandable tones. (Arguably, in the paragraph above, both the boot camp instructor and the preacher are speaking from the diaphragm, too, but not what you are shooting for.)

So how do you talk with a deeper voice? We took some cues from our favorite place—the Internet. Here are a few things we learned:

Record, record, record. We are telling you that anyway, but listen to what your voice sounds like on tape, and try to make it a few octaves deeper.

Practice speaking deeply. The Internet also recommends practice, practice, practice.

Find a voice role model. The Internet suggests watching old movies from the 1940s and 1950s or emulating old-time movie actors like Clint Eastwood and Lauren Bacall. People don't really talk like that any more, but it will help you get the idea. Listening to sports announcers is also suggested.

Stay hydrated. Relax your vocal cords by drinking hot beverages like warm water with lemon or herbal tea with honey, or swallowing sips of water repeatedly before you practice speaking deeply.

Project loudly. Project as though you were in front of a room trying to get the people in the back row to hear you clearly.

Use your lungs. Breathe deeply and push the words out from the lungs.

Stand up straight. Good posture is supposedly helpful for generating enough air out of the lungs and the diaphragm. Difficult from the coxswain seat, but you can definitely sit up straight at some points.

Avoid nasal, growling, rasping, or whispering tones. You should avoid these anyway in the rest of your life!

Hum. Practice humming in your throat with your mouth open and your chin pointed downward. Do that in private because we know nothing more annoying than people who hum in front of others.

The best thing we recommend is keeping the sound of your voice in mind as you review your recordings, and see if you can identify what triggers you to be shrill, high-pitched, or whiny.

K. What to Avoid Saying

We wish we could write a book on what coxswains should never say. (Oh wait, we are…) Here are some general categories that hit the coxswain low points. If you say these things on a regular basis, it's pretty much guaranteed that you will not be coxing for long. Here are some of the worst offenders:

Statements that cause confusion.
"Weigh enough in two."
"Er…ports…no wait…er…starboards…wait I meant ports."
"Three and four add in on two, 1-2. Five and six add in."

Statements that express doubt, confusion, lack of confidence, or incompetence.
"I have no idea what I'm doing!"
"Oh my god!" (followed by silence)
"Oops, that was close." (followed by silence)
"Whew, we almost hit that bridge. My bad!"
"Sorry, what was I doing again?"
"Wait, didn't coach say we were supposed to be doing this piece at a 24?"
"Did coach say two three-minute pieces or three two-minute pieces?

Statements that make it worse or illustrate that you have no idea what the rowers are going through.
"Wow, you guys look really tired today."
"I bet this hurts."
"I'm sure you can't wait to have a double cheeseburger when this workout is over."
"Ugh, you can really smell the sewage treatment plant today."
"It's taking us forever to get through this piece."
"Only 49 minutes to go!"

Statements that belabor the obvious in a non-specific way.
"We're really off set."
"We're down on port."
"Everybody is off."
"We're not rowing well at all today."
"Anybody else agree that this is a terrible row?"

Non-constructive criticism of the coach, other boats, or specific rowers.
"Can't believe that coach is making us practice starts again. I'm so sick of it!"
"I hate the cut the cake drill. It doesn't do anything."
"Three seat in the 2V boat isn't even getting her blade in the water."
"Tyler, you are totally off today. Get it together!"
"Meghan is the worst cox on the lake. Look how she just cut us off again!"

Complaints.
"This coxswain seat is so hard, my butt is falling asleep."
"I'm so cold I can't feel my toes."
"I wish I was on spring break already."
"Rowing in the rain sucks."

Don't statements.
"Don't rush."
"Don't be late at the catch."
"Don't sky."

Repetition.
"Let's do a power ten…let's do another power ten…ok guys, one more power ten…great, now one more power ten…"

"stroke-stroke-stroke-stroke-stroke-stroke-stroke…"

Gossip.
"I heard coach is going to cut Mike after that seat race last week."

"Of course those varsity heavyweight men want a cute girl to cox them; maybe she'll hook up with stern pair like the last one did."

Constant counting. Really, you want to avoid sounding like a crazy person, and this is a sure fire way to sound crazy.

Chatter, Blabber, Screaming. Take it down a notch or two.

L. Signs That You Might Be Boring and Annoying

When researching this book, the rowers we talked to had no shortage of complaints about their coxswains, but chief among them were coxswains who were boring or annoying. Both types successfully got their crews to tune out during practice. So how do you tell if you are boring or annoying?

If you lose your voice often, especially in races, you are probably screaming. That is annoying.

If you talk constantly, that is annoying.

If you complain, whine, or bring your own baggage with you into the boat, that is annoying.

If you say the same things over and over again, that is boring.

If you repeat, verbatim, what the coach says, over and over, that is boring.

If you talk in a monotone, that is boring.

If your tone does not match the intensity of the practice, that is annoying (and possibly also boring).

If you put absolutely no outside effort into your coxing off the water, that, in and of itself, is annoying.

If you are talking to your coach, your stroke, or other coxswains over the mic, that is annoying.

If the mic is too loud or too soft, that is annoying.

If you forget the workouts, screw up the drills, or lose your counts or where you are in the piece, that is annoying.

We could go on and on, and the rowers we talked to did. So how can you avoid these things? Mix it up! Record yourself and listen to what you sound like!

M. The Lost Art of Silence—Strategically Timed Silences

One of the common problems with most coxswains is that they feel like they have to talk all of the time. They feel like they are not doing their job unless they are talking. Plus, by nature most coxswains are chatterboxes. We are here to tell you many crews will tune you out no matter what you do. With those crews especially, if you are going to say something, it had better be relevant, or it had better be interesting.

We are huge fans of deliberate silence as a way to get your crew to listen to you again in practice. (We do not recommend silences during a race situation!) You can either tell your crew that you are going to shut up, or you can just do it.

Here are the few situations where you can use silence to your advantage:

When you need to steer. There are plenty of situations where you are steering through tight spots on the rowing venue, heavy boat traffic, potential hazards, or you otherwise just need to focus on your steering. If you are an experienced cox and your rowers trust you, you do not even need to tell them why you are being quiet. With newer crews, or crews who don't know or trust your coxing abilities, make sure you distract them, and lead into the silence by making them feel secure that you can handle what is going on around you. Give your rowers something else to focus on. For example, it's ok to say, 'Everything is good, but we've got a lot of other traffic on the lake right now, and I'm going to focus on steering for a bit here. Let's keep heads in the boat, and I want you guys to focus on sending the puddles out for the next couple of minutes,' and then do it. Your rowers will appreciate it.

Long rows. During long pieces you often want the rowers to focus on listening to the boat and feeling the boat. For example, you can say, 'Let's take the next few minutes to focus on swinging into bow together,' and you can just shut up for a few minutes.

When the rowers tune out. When no one is paying attention to the coxswain, one way to fix it is just to stop talking. Let it last a few minutes. We think it takes at least that long for some tuned out rowers to realize that the coxswain has stopped talking and will start to pay attention. After the silence you had better come up with something really good and motivating to say to get the practice back on track.

Really great rows. Sometimes the row is so great that you don't want to break the swing. Just let them go and enjoy the ride.

During eyes closed. It's a nice break for the rowers and reminds them to focus on feeling the boat and listening to the boat.

During periods of intense coaching. When your boat is one-on-one with the coaching launch or you are doing camps or clinics with lots of instruction, it's easy for the rowers to get overloaded. During these times, your function is as the driver. You should keep your mouth shut except to give instructions to keep the boat on course. Pay attention to what the coach is saying—maybe you can even learn something.

On days when it truly sucks. We've all had truly terrible practices. If the practice is truly miserable and anything you say is only making it worse, we are fine with just shutting up. At that point, it does not matter what you say, and saying anything is only going to be perceived as annoying or fueling the fire.

CHAPTER 10
PRE-RACE DAY—LOGISTICS, RACE PLANS AND RACING STRATEGIES

A. All About Sprint Races
B. All About Head Races
C. Developing a Race Plan
D. Racing Strategies
E. Derigging and Loading the Trailer
F. Coxswain's Role During Travel
G. Weigh Ins
H. Sportsmanship and the Rules of Rowing
I. The Night Before the Regatta

Races are usually won and lost long before race day. Certainly your crew should be putting in a good effort in practices, during off-season training, eating well, and getting into the right mental state. As a coxswain, it is even more important that you are putting in the effort before race day. This means being prepared for your race, including developing and practicing a race plan that you have committed to memory.

A. All About Sprint Races

In North America, the UK, and elsewhere, sprint races are generally run in the spring and summer. Races are typically 2,000m for juniors/high school, college, and open rowers. Masters sprint races are generally 1,000m. In sprint races, two to eight crews are lined up at the starting line and start simultaneously down a straight course. Generally, each crew has its own 'lane' divided by a line of buoys, although some sprint race courses are not buoyed, and, instead, crews steer toward numbers or other geographic landmarks. Larger sprint races may have enough entries to have heats, followed by the top finishers in each heat advancing to the Grand Final and lower-finishing crews going to Petite Finals and in larger races to Third-Level Finals. Some larger events also have Repachages, which allow crews finishing in the middle of the pack in heats to compete for a second chance to qualify for the Grand Final.

B. All About Head Races

In North America, head races are generally run in the fall, while in the UK and elsewhere these races have more of a fall and winter schedule. Head races are typically 5,000-6,000m long along rivers. Many courses are known for their bridges and tight corners, and because of this, head racing presents more of a challenge for coxswains. Head races have staggered starts; crews leave the starting line at different times, spaced out over uniform intervals of anywhere between 10 and 30 seconds between crews. Generally the fastest ranked crews are started first, and the slowest crews are toward the back, although seeding is usually based on the prior year's results and is not an exact science. Given the distance of the these courses and the staggered starts, head races are exciting to watch around bridges and corners where crews attempt to overtake one another. Larger regattas can have 50 or more entries in each event. Head races are considered to be a 'gentleman's race' because no one is ever sure of the outcome until hours later after the results are tabulated.

A variation of a head race is sometimes called a 'turn the stake' race, typically used where the rowing venue is not long enough to accommodate an entire 5,000m head race course. Instead, crews turn around a series of buoys half way through the race and head back toward where they started or row several circuits around a loop course. Like traditional head races, these races are typically 5,000-6,000m long and involve a series of crews starting at staggered intervals. Generally these races are also challenging to cox because of the turns and because timing when to pass other crews is critical.

C. Developing a Race Plan

Unless you are working at a very high level as a coxswain with a very inexperienced crew, you are going to need buy in on race plans from your coach and your rowers. We have news—despite how they are oftentimes made out to be, race plans are not rocket science. Nor are they an exact science—things happen during races that are outside of your control, and while you are going to follow your race plan, you may have to figure out how to respond without much time to think about it. Regardless, the single best thing you can do as a newer coxswain is to commit your race plan to memory. Practice coxing it in real time before the race until you know it by heart. Failing that, write it on an index card, put it in a Ziploc bag, and tape it somewhere inside the boat. Refer to it often. We have sample race plans at Appendix D.

D. Racing Strategies

In sprint races, as a coxswain your calls can focus on your own crew, on the other crews, or on both. Here we outline a number of strategies, both internally focused (rowing your own race) and externally focused (focusing a lot about other crews). Internally focused races are great for crews who are not going to be very competitive, crews of egomaniacs who care more about themselves than their opponents, nervous/easily distracted crews, or crews who are motivated by their own things. Internally focused races are also great for crews who are heavily favored to win, where the competition is somewhat irrelevant to their race. Externally focused races are great for crews who are heavily favored, who want to mess with the minds of their opponents, crews in races where all the boats will be closely matched, crews who are possibly not the lead crew but are in the mix to finish in the top positions, crews who respond well to what other people are doing, and crews who contain highly competitive individuals who will rise to the occasion by being compared to others. Most coxswains will use a mix of internally and externally focused calls. The other thing to keep in mind about racing strategies is that a good coxswain will be able to change the plan on the fly depending on what is happening in the race. You should always have a plan B, plan C, and plan D depending on what other crews do.

INTERNALLY FOCUSED RACING STRATEGIES

Start Fast, Stay Fast, Finish Fast. This type of racing strategy (also known as the 'even pace') is most common with top level crews. The crew goes out as hard as it can sustain and holds a steady pace at top speed with rowers' energy 100% completely depleted at the finish of the race. Splits among all of the 500 meter blocks of the race are comparable. There is little focus on other crews; it is an internally focused racing strategy. Coxswains stress internal motivation and worry less about position relative to other crews, except at the very end of the race. This is the preferred racing strategy, especially for experienced crews who know the upper limits of their potential, and using this strategy tends to produce the fastest times.

Go out fast, then settle in. This type of racing strategy is common among inexperienced through intermediate racers, including masters crews, particularly recreational ones, and novice juniors and college crews (often employed unintentionally). Crews try to get as big a lead as they can off the starting line and then settle in. The first 500m will be the fastest of the race. Again, this is an internally focused racing strategy, where the crew focuses on getting out as fast as possible, and then pushes at a sustainable pace.

Crews tend to underestimate how much energy they have left and are unlikely to produce their best times. There is also the danger of going out too fast and then having a major dropoff in power in the middle and end of the race, known as 'fly and die.' Overall, this is not an optimal racing strategy.

Go out fast, row moderately in the middle, bring it up at the end. This is probably the most common racing strategy for crews of all levels. In this strategy, your crew will have a good clean start and then settle in to a sustainable level, focusing the middle of the race on body swing and picking the boat up. Then, in the last 500m, the crew focuses on the final sprint. Coxswains should focus on explosive power off the legs in the first 500m, lengthening out and swinging together to generate good boat speed and run in the middle of the race, and again explosive power at the end. At the end of the race the coxswain can focus a bit on other crews, but the race is primarily internally focused.

Start slow, pick it up as you go. In this strategy, you start off slow, and as you go, the power comes up. The first 500m is the slowest, the middle of the race is slightly faster, and the final 500m is fastest. This type of strategy is good for very new novice crews who might be running on pure adrenaline and nerves at the start. The idea is that the coxswain keeps the nerves down by keeping the pace slow and easy and letting other opponents catch crabs because they started too high. Crews gain confidence when they see that they can move the boat well, even if they are in last place off the start, and will gain even more confidence by catching other crews as they falter. Coxswains should focus on swing, length, and controlled recoveries for the first 500m at least. If the crew can sustain, the coxswain should then gradually bring the rate and power up. Calls should be very internally focused on technique, catching and finishing together, and application of pressure at the correct place in the stroke.

EXTERNALLY FOCUSED RACING STRATEGIES

Start Fast, Stay in Front. With this racing strategy, the crew focuses on getting out as fast as possible as a psychological advantage over other crews and then maintaining their lead, just enough to keep the other crews from passing at the end. The coxswain of the lead boat will slow the leading crew down to stay just far enough ahead of the other crews through the finish. This is a risky strategy because you never know when another crew will make a move, and such move can surprise your crew, crushing the psychological advantage. There is also the danger of going out too fast, building up a large amount of lactic acid, and then having a major dropoff in power in the middle and end of the race, known as 'fly and die.' Needless to say, this is not an optimal racing strategy.

Come from behind. This is a very risky strategy employed by experienced racers who want to gain psychological advantage over their opponents and generally mess with the minds of others. We see this frequently especially with experienced masters crews. In this strategy, you get off to a slower start in the first 500m, and then, after other crews have forgotten about you and possibly backed off on the pressure, in the second 500m block, you take the pressure up in an attempt to close the gap and blow past the crews in front of you. An even riskier strategy is to wait until the third 500m block to attack, making the second half of your race much faster than the first half. This is a very risky strategy because your crew may not have enough room to catch the lead crews and also because you will have wasted the first half of the race rowing sub-optimally. That said, some experienced masters rowers thrive on this type of excitement because they have been in so many races and have gotten bored with the standard race plans.

Leapfrogs. This strategy is often employed by very experienced racers, particularly scullers, but also in sweep boats, when their crew is heavily favored to win the race. The idea is that the lead crew gets out in front to a comfortable lead and then goes easy until they are challenged by another crew. When another crew makes its move, the lead crew explodes to get away from them. While this type of racing is exciting and makes for a great race as a coxswain, the crew will be unlikely to have a great time with all of the backing off and charging ahead.

Sneak Attack Moves. This is a smart strategy for crews who are rowing against closely matched rivals, particularly other teams that your team sees frequently. With this strategy, the crew starts out with the pack rowing at a fast/moderate pace. While the crew employs a 'normal' race plan, it adds in a few power 20s or ratings increases at odd times in the race—such as 600m and then again at 1150m—to confuse and surprise the other crews. The coxswain should focus on using the legs to pass other crews during those moves and be very externally focused for that time period. Likewise, the coxswain should be prepared for response or sneak attack moves by other crews, being ready to throw in an additional move as needed. Be warned, however, that this strategy can backfire if enough moves are added, rowers can experience serious lactic acid buildup and not have enough 'left in the tank' for the last 250m of the race. Additionally, your crew cannot use the moves at the same point in the race week after week, or your rivals will figure it out and potentially respond in kind.

The copycat. This strategy is good for crews who might not be at the top of the pack but know that they can compete with the leaders for at least part of the race. With this strategy, your crew specifically plans to go out as fast as the lead crew off the start and stay with them for as long as possible. As a coxswain, you should be very externally focused on what the lead crew is doing. When they make a move, you make the same move. You can even repeat their coxswain's calls. Chances are your crew will turn in a faster time, and the lead crew may be rattled to see that you are able to hang with them and are copying what they do. This strategy can also seriously backfire if the lead crew pulls away—your crew will become frustrated, and you will have to refocus back to an internally-focused race or find another crew to copy.

E. Derigging and Loading the Trailer

If you are traveling to a regatta, in most cases your equipment will travel with you. Boats, oars, and other equipment are loaded onto a boat trailer and towed by a truck. The trailer is typically driven by a coach, the rigger (a person who rigs the boats), or other athletic department staff member. With masters programs, the trailer may be driven by a rower or even a coxswain. We will not get into trailer safety here, except to say that all boats should be safely loaded, strapped down, and flagged. A few lucky programs have "people" to take care of loading and unloading boats for travel to regattas, but the vast majority of teams load their own boats.

Before you leave for an away regatta, you will spend a few hours de-rigging all the boats (unscrewing the riggers from the boats) and loading the trailer. Coxswains should come prepared for boat de-rigging with plenty of wrenches, bungee cords, and a head lamp or flashlight. Mark your wrenches with your name or color scheme, or you'll never get them back! You should also bring an eagle eye to retrieve dropped nuts and bolts in dense grass or parking lots.

You will likely be supervising de-rigging your boat or boats and getting your equipment onto the trailer. You are going to be in charge of supervising your crew taking riggers off the boat, getting riggers, seats, oars, slings, and other equipment organized and loaded on the trailer, and getting the boat loaded safely onto the trailer and strapped down. De-rigging is a huge pain but try to see it as a fun team-bonding time. Keep in mind this is where it is incredibly important to command authority over the rowers. Once you get your boat's stuff loaded, organize your crew to help others on the team get their boats de-rigged and loaded. Don't forget your Cox-Box and charger. You may have at least one in your personal custody during the race travel period.

Here are a few thoughts on de-rigging and loading boat trailers:

- Your job is to cox the rowers loading and unloading boats. A commanding presence is required.

- Your first few times loading a trailer, you should observe experienced coxswains and do what they do. Follow their lead, and, if in doubt, ask the coach or experienced rowers how you can be helpful.

- You will, at a minimum, be in charge of overseeing your crew de-rigging your boat. This includes:

- Taking off the riggers and making sure all of the nuts, washers, and bolts make it back onto the boat before it is loaded.
- Organizing and securing all riggers for your boat in an organized fashion (in rigger bags or strapped/bungeed together) and getting the riggers onto the trailer.
- Organizing and securing all seats for your boat in an organized fashion (typically in crates or boxes) and getting the seats onto the trailer.
- Organizing and securing all of your oars for your boat (often in oar bags, oar boxes, or just placed in the bottom of the trailer) and getting these onto the trailer.
- Getting your Cox-Box AND CHARGER onto the trailer or bringing it with you in transit.
- Assisting the coach in loading slings, tool boxes, bow numbers, spare parts, first aid kits, tents, chairs, and other equipment onto the trailer.
- Flagging your boat. (In other words, putting a brightly colored flag on the end of your boat.)
- Loading your boat onto the trailer. This is like a giant game of Jenga and should be left to the coach's design. Follow directions, and load your boat in the assigned order.

F. Coxswain's Role During Travel

The best coxswains trend either toward completely hyper-organized control-freaks or the opposite end of the spectrum bordering on ADHD. If you're in the latter category, read this section. If you're in the former category, you're way ahead of us and probably don't need this book at all.

If you're new to racing, you will be shocked at how much stuff goes into regatta travel. Some lucky clubs and universities have paid staff to rig, drive trailers, and manage logistics, but for the rest of us, it's all hands on deck for a race travel. As a new coxswain, it's important to clarify your regatta-travel role beforehand with your coach. Generally this will involve:

- You will likely be in charge of 'head counts' for the rowers in your boat in transit and at all times during the race. It is pretty tough to have a good race when you left your six seat at a rest stop in Delaware. You're going to be the one to make sure everyone is present and accounted for every step of the way from the time you leave to the time you race. Masters rowers will need almost no coordination, while juniors will need a lot. (Consider your audience before you tell a 60-year-old district court judge to check in with you before he goes to the bathroom.)
- For juniors ONLY, remind your rowers about bringing all of their own personal gear and equipment. Many a uni or socks have been forgotten. If your team doesn't have a regatta-packing checklist for rowers, you could always create your own. If you are flying to the regatta, remember to pack your uniform and essentials in your carryon luggage. If you're coxing masters, trust that they are old enough to have figured it out by this point. Reminding them to bring their socks or get to bed on time will only make them want to punch you.

G. Weigh Ins

Many larger regattas have coxswain weight minimums. If you are racing at one of these races, you will be required to weigh in at the racing venue either the day before the race or the day of the race. Most coxswains like to weigh in as early as possible. Make sure you are aware of the times for the coxswain weigh in and are prepared with your gear. At most regattas, you will go inside a designated tent or weigh-in building and step on some sort of industrial scale, and the race officials will certify that you meet the minimum or not. You will probably get some sort of wrist band as well. If you do not meet the minimum, you will be required to carry sand with you in the boat on race day. Plastic bags and sand will generally be available in the weigh-in tent, but some races require coxswains to bring their own extra weight. Generally speaking, a coxswain is required to weigh in wearing only the racing uniform of a unisuit and socks. Some races weigh you in with shoes on; most weigh you in without shoes. Some races allow you to weigh in wearing racing splash jackets. Jewelry, watches, additional clothing, and the like must be taken off before weighing in, even if in reality you will probably be wearing all kinds of extra clothes when you race.

We have seen people try to cheat and weigh in with multiple wrenches crammed into their sports bras, five pairs of underwear, wet hair, you name it, just to be a pound or two heavier. We even knew a cox from a rival university who was a double amputee and very conspicuously always weighed in with his prosthetic legs on and then took them off and left them on land for races. True story. Race officials never said a word about the crate of nine pairs of shoes and a pair of legs leaving the dock. We would never condone cheating, and neither should you. Taking a few pounds of sand in the boat is not the end of the world. Plus we don't feel sorry for you if you are one of those lucky people who can just eat whatever you want and never gain a thing.

If you are close to the minimum weight, but slightly under (and by slightly we mean within 1-4 lbs/.5-1.8 kg), you can always go for the old standby trick and try to drink as much water as you can to 'make weight.' A liter of water weighs 2.2 lbs/1 kg. Drinking more than that is ridiculous, terrible for your body, and will make you feel miserable for the entire day, and you'll probably end up peeing in the boat on the warm up which will not exactly endear you to your rowers. Don't be stupid and drink too much water. People have died from less. A liter, on the other hand, seems pretty reasonable. We don't encourage these kinds of stupid coxswain tricks, but being well-hydrated probably will not hurt you too much, and everybody else will be doing it as well. We personally are big fans of eating sushi with lots of soy sauce the night before the weigh in, which makes you retain water like crazy (making you heavier), but is not too high in calories.

H. Sportsmanship and the Rules of Rowing

Rowing is one of those old school sports that prides itself on a tradition of refined behavior. While the Brits seem to favor rowdy drinking as part and parcel of the rowing culture, regardless of which side of the pond you are on, on race day, it goes without saying that there is no place for cheating, bad behavior, or harassment of other teams. We may have mentioned this a time or two in this book, but only because we think it's extremely important—be nice and polite to opposing teams, coaches, race officials, and anyone else you meet on race day, especially when you are wearing your team uniform. Congratulate the winners, and offer 'nice race' to the losers. Rowing is civilized in that regard. Even though some races may involve gamesmanship or even crashing or clashing of oars, this is not hockey where fights break out or even baseball where bench clearing brawls happen from time to time. Rowers are expected to be on good behavior at all times and to behave like ladies and gentlemen on race day.

Rowing also has very clear rules of racing that govern everything from rower conduct to racing protocols on race day. All of the major national rowing governing bodies have these rules posted online. In the U.S. they can be found at www.usrowing.org, in Canada at www.rowingcanada.org, in the U.K. at www.britishrowing.org, in Australia at www.rowingaustralia.com, and so on. The rowing governing bodies in other countries also publish and update rules of rowing for their respective countries. These rules are updated from time to time, and all coxswains should get their hands on a copy of the rules before coxing any race. There is no excuse not to read them. These rules cover everything from policies on cell phones in the boat during races, coxswain weight limits, start procedures, and protests. Not all races that you will compete in will be subject to governing body rules, but even non-sanctioned local races generally strive to follow these as best practices. Local races may have additional, specific rules governing racing and rower conduct, such as the infamous public urination ban for rowers on Lake Quinsigamond in Massachusetts, to name just one. Reading the national and local rules for each regatta will make you a better student of the sport of rowing and give you an advantage when it comes to racing. We must say these rules are not like tax codes or biochemistry books—they are intended to be read by participants of all ages. Do not be scared of them just because they have roman numerals and lots of sub-headings. We also strongly recommend that you read the sections on sportsmanship in Chapter 11.

I. The Night Before the Regatta

A coxswain has a few roles the night before the regatta. The biggest of which is to be a positive force of action for your rowers and your coaches. Put a smile on your face no matter how tired you are, and keep your crew moving and entertained. Here are a few specific duties:

Rig. If you had to load your boats at your boathouse at some point before your arrival at the venue and your race, you're probably going to be supervising re-rigging of those very same boats. At larger races, crews will be assigned parking spots, and at smaller races, it will be first come, first served. You never know quite what your parking situation will be, but you will be responsible for getting boats off the trailer, rigging them, and strapping them back down, either in slings or back on the trailer. A coxswain should be prepared for a rigging session with many wrenches (Mark them with your name, or you'll never get them back!), and an eagle eye (and a flashlight) to retrieve dropped nuts and bolts in dense grass or parking lots. This is basically the reverse of de-rigging, which you did a few hours ago at your boathouse. You will be groggy from travel and not really feel like it. Fake a positive attitude, and try to make it as much fun as possible. The faster you rig, the faster you can go to your team dinner or get to sleep.

Set the mood. For juniors ONLY, try to bring the energy level down the evening before the race. It is always a great idea to have a boat meeting, where you talk about the logistics of the next day, talk about your opponents, the lane assignments, go over your race plan, visualize the race, and cox and imaginary race with them. If your team is prone to giggling, nerves, and generally high level of energy, ask the team parents to help keep people focused. But the boat meeting should be just for your boat, not for parents or coaches, and should last no longer than half an hour, less if at all possible.

Visualize. Consider a pre-race visualization with your team. Find a quiet hotel room. Turn the lights down and get into the right mood. Light some scented candles. Get a little weird. Go through your race plan. Do it in real time for sprint races, and hit the highlights for head races. See Chapter 13 for more information on this.

Get to bed early. Do we really need to remind you of this?

Charge your Cox-Box. Enough said. Especially if you are sharing Cox-Boxes, make sure they are fully charged, and do not forget to bring the charger with you to the racing venue.

Miscellaneous. No texting, no social media, no temptation of the hotel hot tub, alone or in a group.

CHAPTER 11
RACE DAY—ALL THINGS RACING, FROM THE DOCK TO THE FINISH LINE

A. Your Race Day Gear
B. Writing it Down
C. The Coaches and Coxswains Meeting
D. Your Role on Race Day
E. Pre-Race Checklist
F. Launching
G. Race Warm Ups
H. Navigating the Marshalling Area
I. Sprint Race Starts
J. Step by Step Tips for Coxing a Sprint Race
K. Step by Step Tips for Coxing a Head Race
L. After the Finish
M. Protests
N. Accuracy and Misinformation During Races

A. Your Race Day Gear

In the heat of everything that is going on leading up to race day, it is important to take care of yourself as the coxswain, even if you won't actually be rowing. This means getting some sleep the night before the race and being prepared with the right gear, drinking plenty of water, and eating healthy snacks on race day. You also need a pair of great sunglasses, sunscreen, cough drops, lip balm, a hat, and the team uniform. Also bring your index card in a Ziploc bag (see next section), athletic tape, a wrench, and some really basic first aid stuff. We try to wear as little as possible for warm weather races—just a uni and flip-flops. For cold weather races, take care of yourself—bring a pair of warm socks, long trou, a long-sleeve shirt, and a splash jacket. A really small backpack with zippers—more than just those cheap drawstring bags—is also really nice to have in the boat to hold all of your gear. (We didn't specifically say fanny pack, but we aren't afraid to admit we could rock one if the mood were right.) Bring socks. Bring two pairs of socks for water launches. You are more effective if you are not freezing, and being focused and comfortable will do far more for your crew than the extra weight of a pair of wool socks! One more time, let us remind you, do not forget the Cox-Box and charger.

B. Writing it Down

In addition to your other gear, the single best thing you can bring with you in the boat is your race plan and for head races only, the course map.

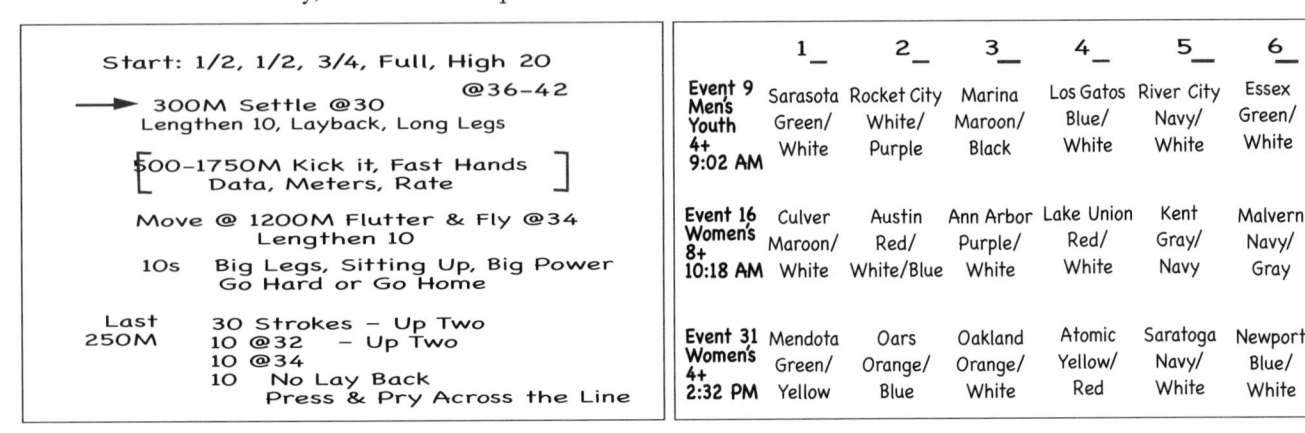

```
Start: 1/2, 1/2, 3/4, Full, High 20
                              @36-42
   → 300M Settle @30
     Lengthen 10, Layback, Long Legs

   ┌ 500-1750M Kick it, Fast Hands  ┐
   └         Data, Meters, Rate      ┘

     Move @ 1200M Flutter & Fly @34
          Lengthen 10

   10s    Big Legs, Sitting Up, Big Power
          Go Hard or Go Home

   Last   30 Strokes – Up Two
   250M   10 @32    – Up Two
          10 @34
          10  No Lay Back
              Press & Pry Across the Line
```

Sample Index Card-Front

	1	2	3	4	5	6
Event 9 Men's Youth 4+ 9:02 AM	Sarasota Green/ White	Rocket City White/ Purple	Marina Maroon/ Black	Los Gatos Blue/ White	River City Navy/ White	Essex Green/ White
Event 16 Women's 8+ 10:18 AM	Culver Maroon/ White	Austin Red/ White/Blue	Ann Arbor Purple/ White	Lake Union Red/ White	Kent Gray/ Navy	Malvern Navy/ Gray
Event 31 Women's 4+ 2:32 PM	Mendota Green/ Yellow	Oars Orange/ Blue	Oakland Orange/ White	Atomic Yellow/ Red	Saratoga Navy/ White	Newport Blue/ White

Sample Index Card-Back

Get a large index card, put it in a Ziploc bag, and affix it somehow to the boat. Some coxswains tape it inside the boat. We've seen others rubberband it to their leg, attach it to a coxing kit, or something else. Some coxswains write on their legs with permanent markers (we do not recommend this, although some coxswains swear by it). Just get it in a place where you can see it at a glance and don't have to fool around with it or run the risk of dropping it or losing it. This is not the kind of card you use for final exams, where you try to cram 50 calculus formulas on a single index card because the instructor said you could bring only one card in. We like to think about the card as a quick reference. If you make the type too small, you won't use it. You also don't want the inside of the boat to look like the control center for launching a space shuttle. Keep it on a single card and keep it simple.

So what goes on this card? We recommend the following:

Race Plan. This should diagram/outline all of the moves, plans, major land marks, and the like. Make it a picture, so it's easy to use. This should be an easy reference for you.

Race course map. This is the big one used for head races only. You want the major landmarks for the one mile, two mile, three mile, and where to start the sprint. You want it to show the traffic patterns for the race, warm up, and marshaling area. You want it to show all major obstacles and bridges. This can be combined with the race plan on a single card if that makes it easier.

Key calls. Make a list of motivating things you want to make sure you bring up during the race. Keep it short. Keep it simple.

Times and lane assignments. Other organizational details such as your race times and your competitors' should go on the back of the index card. For sprint races, write down your opponents' lanes and opponents' blade colors if you are not familiar with them. For head races, write down the starting order and opponents blade colors if you are not familiar with them.

C. The Coaches and Coxswains Meeting

Most of the smaller local races, and even a few of the larger, better run races, have a race day meeting known as the 'coaches and coxswains meeting' or some variation on it. As a coxswain, you may be responsible for representing your boat at the meeting, which is almost guaranteed to take place at the crack of dawn (often in the dark) on the morning of race day. During this meeting, race officials will let you know what the starts will be like, any obstacles to be aware of on the course, and any special rules that will govern the race.

They will also point out major landmarks on a map and explain the launching, warm up, and race protocols and traffic patterns. We will warn you that at this meeting there is always one dumb giant sculler who will be standing directly in front of the course map. If you're short, duh, don't be afraid to politely elbow your way to the front. Ask questions if you have them, and don't leave the meeting until 100% of your questions are answered. You need to understand the starting commands, traffic patterns, how the lanes are numbered, and any relevant landmarks, so you can convey this information to your crew where needed and avoid penalties. Although these meetings are a staple of local races, the bigger races tend not to place much emphasis on them, and, even with the smaller races, you can often find relevant race information online. Some smart coaches even let their coxswains sleep in and fill them in later.

D. Your Role on Race Day

As a coxswain you will likely have a lot of responsibility on race day, including the following:

You may be responsible for race day logistics. For juniors ONLY, remind them that eating fried food from the vendors or shopping at the booths is reserved for AFTER the race. For juniors ONLY, keep them out of the sun, remind them to drink water, eat healthy energy foods, and put on sunscreen. Make sure everyone knows the appointed time and meeting place before each of your races. Masters should have it covered.

You will be responsible for being well organized on race day. You should memorize your race times, your lane assignments, and the names and blade colors of every other crew in your race. You should know the location of all of your equipment, have your bow numbers and pinnies, and if you are hotseating, you should know who you are hotseating with and when their race ends or starts.

Do your job. The bottom line is that your responsibilities on race day are to (a) get the crew to the starting line on time with the right equipment, (b) steer a good course, and (c) execute the race plan. Simple.

E. Pre-Race Checklist

You want to have a game plan in place for race day. Rowers should meet at an appointed time at least an hour before your race is scheduled to start for sprint races and 90 minutes ahead for head races where you need to row up to the starting line.

35 Minutes before launching. Thirty-five minutes before launching, identify the location of all of your equipment. This includes Cox-Box, tool kit, bow number, bow pinnie for cox and bow seat plus safety pins (if the race has them), oars, boat, seats, etc… Give the boat a once over, checking that the boat is pitched, all riggers are tight, and that the equipment is ready to go. Specifically designate a few gear helper people—parents, spouses, rowers who are not racing, or coaches—to help you get your oars down and take your shoes back up. Let those people know exactly where to meet you and exactly what time you will be launching.

Thirty minutes before launching. Thirty minutes before launching round up your entire crew, get them to the bathroom, get a snack and some water down their gullets, and lathered up with sunscreen.

Twenty minutes before launching. Twenty minutes before launching, sit down with all of your rowers for a quick pre-race boat meeting to recap what was said the previous evening and the race plan. Be enthusiastic and upbeat, and reiterate a few key tens that you will call to motivate the crew. Keep it to no more than ten minutes.

Ten minutes before launching. Ten minutes before you launch, have your crew go on a quick jog (all together) and/or stretching warm up (all together). Allow for a few last minute nerves to send people running to the bathroom. Use this time to make sure you know where your equipment is and track down your designated gear helper people.

Five minutes before launching. Five minutes before launching, get all hands on the boat, and walk it down to the dock or beach launching area.

At the dock. At the dock or launching site, make sure gear helper people have a crate for shoes and other items and know to meet you after the race.

F. Launching

It is hard to give you a general rule on how far in advance you should launch. Each race is different. You need enough time to get up to the starting line with the other boats in your race and warmed up, but you do not want to be sitting out on the water taking up valuable space in the marshalling area and getting cold or doing so much warm up that your crew is tired when it actually comes time to race. Consult with your coach at the beginning of the day. If you are the nervous type, build in an extra five minutes over what the coach suggests to make yourself feel better. Also keep in mind that at bigger races your crew may be standing for considerable time with the boat trying to get off the dock or off the beach for a water launch. Get your place in line, and make sure you let your crew take the boat down to waists as you wait. Keep a mental note of where other crews in your race are as you are in line to dock. You will probably be grouped together, and if you don't see them around you are either late, or you are launching way too early. You will keep tabs on these crews during the warm up and in the marshalling area as well. On the dock you are in charge of wrangling your gear helper people to take your crew's shoes (We like to leave ours on, but some coxswains don't want to carry the extra weight of even a pair of running shoes!). Listen to the dockmaster, and get your oars in and off the dock as fast as possible. Your crew needs to get safely off the dock and out of the launching area before they tie in. Water launches tend to be far more chaotic than dock launches, and can be extremely intimidating for coxswains. You will have boats coming in after their races, along with crews going out for upcoming races. As a coxswain you have to balance being respectful of other boats, protecting your equipment, especially keeping your skeg from getting ripped off on the bottom of the river, and fighting to get your crew launched or back in. The best advice we can give you is to keep calm, and politely tell other coxswains what you're doing if they are in your way, and ask them (also politely) to move for you. Coxswains who are not assertive will find their crew blocked in or languishing on the beach, so it is very important to speak up, and fight for your spot (in a nice way).

We should also mention hot seating. Hot seating is the situation where your team has entered more races than it has trailer space and equipment for, and you have to share boats and/or oars with other crews, either on your own team or borrowed from another team. When you are hot seating, you are often in a huge time crunch, waiting on another boat to come in, and have to very quickly swap out sets of rowers and hustle to the starting line. If you are the coxswain in the first race, you should fight your way into the dock or beach launch as a courtesy to the crew you're hot seating with (some times jumping the line) by letting the dock master and other crews know that you have to hot seat. If you are the coxswain in the later race, and are hot seating, it is crucial that you assert yourself to get your crew out of the launching area as fast as possible, and work hard to convey a veneer of calmness on the row up to the start. Rowers who are frantically rowing at full pressure on the warmup to get up to the line rarely have a great race. While you can't do much about hot seating or time pressure, you can do your best to keep them calm.

G. Race Warm Ups

Race warm ups will be done against the race traffic pattern, generally in tight spaces. Your job as cox is to avoid other boats and obstacles and get your crew warm, calm, and ready to race. With sprint races, the traditional warm up includes doing some start sequences (start+10 high, start+20 high, start+20 high, settle, 10 at race pace), and throwing in a few high 10s at race pace to get the crew moving and warm. Remember that some races will ask that you stop rowing on the warmup if a race is coming down the course. If the race is running behind, find a shady spot and stop for a few minutes while you give them a pep talk, but keep the crew moving for the most part. For head races, you will likely have considerable distance to cover, typically the entire length of the race course, so your warm up will be steady state rowing with a few (not too many) tens at race pace. With sprint races the warm up is just one giant head game where every crew is trying not to look at every other crew and pretending like they don't care what other people are doing around them, but really giving everyone else the once over. As a cox, you should be completely focused on your boat and reminding them to keep their eyes and heads in your boat. Talk about how strong your crew looks, some basic motivational speech, and how excited you are to race. Do not talk about what other coxswains or crews are doing, how big the other crews look, or any attribute of anyone else's warm up. It's a head game, though, because you are going to be doing nothing but sizing up these other crews. Be respectful of others. Do not do starts straight toward other boats, and keep a distance—but keep an eye on them because the marshal will call all of the crews in your event up together.

H. Navigating the Marshalling Area

Whether the race is large or small, sprint race or head race, you will probably find yourself in a marshalling area with a set traffic pattern upstream from the starting line. In the marshalling area crews go in a big circle or sit on the edges until their race is called up. Your job in the marshalling area is just as it is on the warm up—keep your crew calm, be upbeat, pump their egos up, and keep them warmed up. Avoid crashing into anyone else or going too fast or near to other crews. Do not let your rowers look at any other crew—you can look all you want, but do NOT talk about what you are seeing, and don't let your rowers or other crews catch you staring. Make sure you know where the other boats in your race are, and be within earshot of the marshals. When your race is called, you will proceed to the line, in order. Do not cut anyone off, and if other coxswains who are ahead of you are not paying attention, it is fine to say things like, 'bow number 357, River Rowing Club, the officials are calling you. We will follow behind you guys.' In fact, it is pretty darn intimidating to the other crews. Let's just say it, we are bossy and proud of it. You need to have a little ego, and in the marshaling area, well, use your own imagination. Be nice and be polite, but it is OK to talk to the other coxswains if they are in the wrong place or you need to move around them, particularly crews in other later events who are in your way. We can't stress this enough—you are on the record—so be polite, nice, and never, ever use words that could be held against you later. If anyone wishes you luck, you can respond for your crew. We are not huge fans of exchanging pleasantries before the race, but we always say, "Thank you, you too." Make sure your rowers stay focused with their heads in the boat if you are talking to other coxswains.

Trust us when we say that even the best run races have their snags and inefficiencies in the marshalling areas and around the starting line. Officials are only human, and those humans may be currently dealing with wind, waves, weather, timing equipment issues, rowing equipment breakage, missing/late crews, medical emergencies, and a whole host of other things. The nicer and more polite you can be to the officials and race volunteers, the better. Raise your hand when they talk to you, and say please and thank you. Remember that without them donating their own time and expertise, you would not be racing.

I. Sprint Race Starts

Sprint Race Starts—Stake Boats

Many sprint races have stake boat starts. Stake boats are floating platforms that rowing shells back into, where the shells are held in place until the race starts. We have seen stake boats take many forms, including rafts, docks, small sailboats, coaching launches, and pontoon boats. The stake boat is anchored at a fixed location, and a volunteer 'holder' is lying down on his or her stomach on the platform and holding the boats into place until the official starts the race. (If you really want to get some practice with rowing starts, volunteering as a stake boat holder is a fantastic learning experience! You will see every start strategy in the book and see how starts can go wrong. It will underscore the importance of a good, balanced start. It is also far more physically demanding than you might expect. At least one rowing club we know of in a university town gets its stake boat 'volunteers' from the local police department's community service program. The positions are filled by undergraduates who were unlucky enough to get caught drinking and are now sweating off the previous night on a pitching dinghy out in the sun.) Fancier 'stake boat' systems at major rowing venues include specially designed dock systems that automatically hold boats into position.

As a coxswain, your biggest challenge with stake boats will be backing into them. Generally the officials will call the crews up in order, and the crews with the higher lane numbers will cross over into their lanes first. As soon as you reach your designated lane, have your crew stop and do a river turn with short, choppy strokes at arms and backs only. Make small adjustments, and try to make sure you don't cut anyone else off or cross into anyone else's lane. Back it in slowly. Even if you are off angle, as soon as the stake boat holder volunteer grabs you, you can have your individual rowers scull blades to get everything lined up. Sculling blades, also known as 'pinching,' is when a rower grabs the blade of the rower sitting behind him or her and makes a few short, choppy strokes with arms and backs to move the boat's point. Typically you will ask two seat to scull bow's blade or three seat to scull two seat's blade. While you are pointing, your hand should be up—this is the signal to the officials that you are NOT yet ready to start.

Backing into stake boats *Sculling blades*

Don't be the last crew to get lined up—nor do you want to be the first. If you are first to get aligned, chances are the wind or current will blow you off point. If you are the last, you may be yelled at and could be penalized by the officials. Try to be in the middle of the pack. If you are asking individual rowers to scull blades, have them over-point, knowing that the current will probably take you to the correct point by the time the other crews are lined up. If it is taking an incredibly long time for the other crews to get lined up, have your rowers stay in position to scull blades until other crews are at least 'attached' to the stake boats. When all crews are 'attached' to the stake boats, let your crew know. Make sure you are monitoring what is going on and communicating with your crew in a calm, confident, under control voice. Do not talk over the officials or give your crew extraneous information on what other crews are doing or talk about what a disaster it is getting all of these crews lined up. (Rest assured, it is always a disaster getting crews lined up, especially if there is any kind of wind or weather.) You need to keep them calm, so any communications to them should be calm and confident. Keep your hand up at all times until you are ready to go. Try to be the second to last coxswain with his or her hand to come down (You don't want to be last, or you will look like you are the problem). When your hand comes down, say to your crew 'my hand is down.' When all of the hands of the other coxswains have their hands down say, 'All hands are down." If that changes you can say, "One hand is up. Now all hands are down." Try not to overdo it or overload your crew with information. Saying, "All hands are down" just lets your crew know that the officials are about to start the race.

Sprint Race Starts—Floating Starts
Floating starts (also called 'rolling starts') are starts where there is no platform. Boats line up at the starting line, and officials ask crews to move up or back down until all of the crews (at least in theory) are aligned. These are the hardest for any coxswain. Make small adjustments, rowing or backing only by your stern pair, and, by all means, listen to the officials. We're also going to admit a little secret to you—it is almost impossible to get alignment of six, or seven, or even three crews if you have any kind of wind or current. Obviously it goes without saying that you want to race with utmost integrity, but the reality is that some crews will be slightly ahead, and some crews will be slightly behind. Do we really need to tell you that if you have a choice, you want to be one of the crews slightly ahead? As with stake boats, when your hand comes down, let your crew know. When all hands are down, let your crew know. Again, you ideally want to be the second to last coxswain with his or her hand down, but do not keep your hand up if you truly are pointed and ready to go unless you want to annoy the officials.

Starting Commands
If you went to the coxswains meeting, asked your coach, or browsed the regatta's website, you should know the starting commands. If not, ask the officials in the marshalling area. Be polite. They might be annoyed with you, but it's better to be 100% clear. Starting commands vary from race to race. The trend in recent years is toward a countdown start, where hands are not recognized. In other words, once the officials start their 5-4-3-2-1 countdown, they don't care if you are not perfectly pointed or have your hand in the air. Some officials use a two-part command such as "attention…GO!" or a three-part command such as "ready…set…ROW!" Other races are started by some sort of megaphone alarm or marine air horn. It really depends on the race.

Tricks for the Start—Sprint Races

Get yourself in the right head space. We get nervous just thinking about the starting line of a sprint race—but in a good way. Those butterflies in your stomach mean that you are alive and challenging yourself to do something that scares you a tiny little bit. Even if you are nervous, now is the time to get yourself together. Slap your own face if you have to. You should be personally focused on beating the other coxswains by being the best cox you can be. Take some deep breaths, and imagine just you and the other coxswains fighting for world domination. Whatever it takes to pump you up. Keep it calm. Keep in mind that when you remind your rowers to take a few deep breaths and clear their heads, do it yourself, too.

Get your Cox-Box timer and recording set up. Zero out your Cox-Box timer because it is game on! Make sure to zero it out just before you start because if your stroke moves that magnet, it will start going even before the race has started. If you are recording your race (which we always recommend), get that set up, too.

When in doubt, get balanced. If there is any kind of wind or weather, you will probably not be perfectly, perfectly straight at the start. That is just life. However, your crew needs to be balanced at the start and get the blades in together. This is something your crew can control. Focus on this.

Make small use of the rudder. If you are off point at the start (and believe us, it happens, either due to wind or weather, uneven pressure from rowers, or some member of your crew missed water), you are going to be going fast enough that a little tiny bit of rudder is all you need to correct the course and keep out of the lane next to you. It is natural to want to oversteer, but try not to let it happen. If you cross lanes at the start, officials WILL notice, and the likelihood of colliding with another crew is high—you could be penalized, and regardless, it will slow you down considerably.

Start over if you have a crab or miss water. We told you at the beginning of this book that the rowers we cox are not going to the Olympics, and that we designed this book for others in a similar situation. All we can say about crabs and missing water is that they will inevitably happen in novice crews, and even occasionally in experienced ones, and the best coxswains are the ones who can respond to the situation without missing a beat. If you have a massive crab in the first ten or twenty strokes of the race, stop the crew, get the oar back, get them pointed, and start them (from the top) again. Tell them it is a do-over, and they have a second chance to have a good start. Then get on it immediately. It may not be too late for your crew because if it is a novice race, chances are some other crew will also have a massive crab, and you still may be able to catch them.

Consider the brilliance of the 'just row' start. In newer crews a start sequence with all of its half and 3/4 slides might be too complicated and more likely to slow the boat down than speed it up. Consider just starting to row at full slide for your start. One of your authors had a hugely successful sprint racing season one spring using no start at all. After about twenty strokes there was no difference in the crews anyway, and often our crew was ahead.

Focus completely on your steering at the start. As a coxswain you should only be looking ahead at the start, for at least the first thirty or so strokes. Focus on keeping your keel in the mid-center of your lane and away from the buoy lines. Do not worry about what other crews are doing or how your rowers are rowing. Steer straight, go through your starting commands, and let the rest sort itself out.

J. Step by Step Tips for Coxing a Sprint Race

Start + First 25 strokes

As the starter says 'go,' or otherwise indicates the start, check your Cox-Box timer, your steering, and your point. If you are the slightest bit off, immediately give a tiny bit of rudder and then push the steering back to even. Make sure you are making small, small, small adjustments. It is almost certainly your rowers' fault, not yours, but you've got to fix it immediately. Telling one side of rowers to pull harder is impractical during the start sequence, so use the rudder. Beware that your rudder can get out of control if you make more than a tiny adjustment because you may not be used to the power of the start, or the boat lurched to one side or the other due to inconsistent application of pressure from the rowers or a crab. If you oversteered to one side, steer small in the other direction to get it back—don't overcompensate on the other side, too! You want to be looking ahead and focus on getting your bow perfectly in the middle between the buoy lines. While you are getting your course, your calls should be the starting strokes mixed in with specific technique. This should be rote and easy for you to say without thinking because all of your emphasis should be on getting your bow in exactly the right place centered between the lanes. Your voice should serve to keep your crew calm, and your voice should reflect confidence and control. Practice your calls in advance until you can do them in your sleep. For example:

> "1/2, 1/2, 3/4, full. High for twenty. That's 1-big legs here-3-4-pound these out-6-7-let's see that power-9-10. We're at a 39. Ten more, just like that-2-3-you guys are crushing it off those stretchers-5-6-we're still at a 39-quick hands, let's see it-7-8-settle to a 31 in two-1-2. SETTLE! Let's lengthen out here for the next ten. We're at a 32. Let's bring it down one over two strokes with stroke seat. 1-2. That's the way. Nice long legs, you're at a 31. Nice work. Now let's hold it here at race pace at a 31."

While you say all of that, regardless of what is happening around you, get your steering straight, and focus internally. Your bow should be perfectly centered, and your crew should now be at race pace. It always goes by in a blur and is over before you know it. Just thinking about the first strokes of a sprint race gets us all excited inside. This is the reason you cox!

After That

As soon as your crew has settled at race pace, look around. You should be around the first 250-300m in at this point. Assess where every other crew is. Let your crew know, being honest and realistic, but keeping it positive. Here are a few examples:

"We are currently in second place. Prep is in the lead by half a boat length, and we're sitting three seats up on Central and two seats up on St. John's. Collegiate and Jefferson collided with one another after Jefferson caught a crab and crossed the lane line, so we're not going to worry about them."

If the boats are still clumped together (which they typically will be at this point), just simply say, "It's a really tight race coming out of the start. Prep is out ahead by two seats, and all the other crews are about even. We are all hanging together in second place."

If you are way behind, tell your crew that but spin it positively. For example, "We're at the back of the pack, but we are just going to row our own race and not worry about the rest."

Then, go right into a technique call for 10. Start working on keeping legs long, sitting up and breathing, swinging into bow together, and the like (emphasizing moving on other crews if you are taking a more externally focused approach.)

Rest of the First 500m

In addition to steering straight, your top priority in this section of the race is to make sure your crew is at their ideal race pace and is maintaining their ratio. This part of the race sets the tone. Continue to give them ratings, and continue to work on slide control if things are crazy or rushed. Make sure you express the immediacy of the situation and give them clear instructions. For example, "We're at a 31, and now is the time to slow those slides down! We're going to bring the rating down two, on the recovery, following Jessica's lead as stroke. Let's go down two, over two, with leg control. Here we go, 1-2 you're at a 30. We need more control on those recoveries. We still need to bring it down one over the next two strokes. Hold off with the legs as you come up, keeping the drive quick. Make it happen NOW! 1-2. Great work; we're at a 29; let's hold it here." Follow up by adding some technical calls into the mix, especially those focused on slow recoveries, quick hands away, swinging into bow together, following stroke, and the like.

500-1500 meters

During the body of the race, assuming your crew has a handle on its ratio and is at decent race pace (which is a pretty massive assumption), here are your priorities as a coxswain:

Keep your steering and watch the major landmarks on the course. As you move into the body of the race, as a coxswain you will continue to focus on keeping your bow pointed perfectly in the middle of the buoy line, but you are also looking for landmarks—you need to look for the 500m marker, the 1000m marker, the 1500m marker.

Don't watch the rowers. Here is a little secret no one will ever tell you. It is incredibly tempting to watch your rowers (and the rowers in other crews), especially if they are flopping around and totally exhausted, making extremely unattractive faces and sweating profusely. That sheer, unadulterated power and range of the human experience during extreme exertion can be mesmerizing. Do not give in to temptation. The only reason you should be watching your rowers is to look for major things—namely rush, major problems that are creating big set or timing issues, crabs, medical issues, or someone about to fall out of the boat. Now is not the time to point out (or even notice) that five seat is tapping down a smidge lower than stroke or seven seat could stand to move his foot stretcher settings up a notch or two. Especially do not look at the rowers in other crews—you are only watching the other crews as units. (Although we are not above eyeing up coxswains in other crews as an intimidation tactic!)

Watch where other crews are. You will also need to be watching where other crews are and if they are moving on your crew. How often you share these positions with your crew will depend on whether you are rowing an internally or externally focused race. If you are rowing an internally focused race, only give positions of other crews every 300-500m or so. If your crew is very far ahead, the rowers will be able to see the other crews, and you should remind them of that. If your crew is DFL, continue to tell them that, "We are rowing our own race," and refrain from mentioning that everyone else has at least three boat lengths of open water on them. If you are in the middle and you are rowing a more externally focused race, you should give them frequent updates, especially as you move on crews or have crews move on you. It should not be a play by play. You are not doing color commentary of the race from the sidelines; you are giving your crew relevant information. You want to give them enough information so that they feel informed about how far behind the leaders they are and crews that might be gaining on them. Only worry about crews that are relevant to your crew. If the leader is three boat lengths ahead, don't worry about them. Same with the crews at the back of the pack (your rowers can see them anyway!).

Make your moves according to race plan. Give your crew advance warning before your pre-planned moves. If you are going to add a spontaneous move on another crew for tactical purposes, let your crew know that, too.

Other things to communicate to your crew:

Meters left in the race. You can let your rowers know when you cross the 500m mark, the half way point, and the 1500m mark. Sprint races go by so fast that there really isn't a whole lot of time between the major markers. Don't dwell on distance until about the 1250m, especially if your crew is inexperienced. Experienced crews can handle the information earlier in the race and more frequently, but in general, meters left is an end of the race bit of information. Think about how you communicate that information. Some crews would rather hear "We've got less than 50 strokes to go" (be really sure you are correct!) while other crews would prefer "Only ninety seconds left" or "600 meters to go" or "We've got less than two minutes left in the race." Ask your rowers what they would prefer to hear.

Ratings. Give your crew ratings every 20 or so strokes if they are having problems maintaining a consistent rating. If they are locked in at a good race pace, you can do it more infrequently, typically with something like, "Ernesto is doing a great job maintaining that 32."

General motivation. Whether it is a quote from a famous Civil War general or taking a ten for your bow seat getting her braces off yesterday, have at it. Only say it if you know it will make your crew go faster!

General technique 10s. Keep it general—focusing on things like finishing together, getting the lock on at the same time, feeling the swing of the boat—not directed toward any one person.

Last 500 meters

Generally speaking, around the 1500m mark, you want to give your crew a good assessment of where all of the other crews are, and in your own mind determine who you can beat. If you are close to one or more other crews, this is the now or never point in the race. Your race plan should dictate the strategy for the most part, but often the coxswain will have to make the call on the fly. Adding in some focused tens to catch certain crews is fine in some circumstances, but beware that overdoing it could cause your crew to run out of steam and get passed in the final few strokes of the race. Again, consider where you are and whether you are rowing an internally or externally focused race. Most crews are going to be heavily externally focused in the last bit of the race. As you cross into the last 250-300m left in the race, you should refer to your race plan for the components of your final 'sprint.' Generally you will have about 25-35 strokes left at this point. Now is the time to pull out all of the stops. Many crews like to add 'sit up' tens, 'dig in' tens, or the like, where the layback is mostly taken out, and the rating gets taken up. (Consult your coach and your race plan before you do it.) Focus on keeping your point straight (It is easy to get off point if you are looking sideways at other crews), accurately estimating how many strokes the rowers have left, and where you are in relation to all of the other crews. Telling your crew to empty the tank, especially if it is the last race of the day, may do the trick. If you really genuinely don't know how many strokes are left, keep it generic by saying things like "This is the last bit of the race" or "Let's explode off those stretchers for the last strokes of the race." Your rowers will hate you for not knowing, but it is better than telling them they have ten left, and then calling another ten. (And after the race, read up on Chapter 5 on how to teach yourself to estimate distance accurately.) When you can visually see that you are within ten strokes of the line, you should call a 'final ten.' Again, try to time it exactly. Rowers hate to hear 'last ten' and then 'two more.' You are finished when your bow ball crosses the finish line. Switch your timer off immediately and burn that time into your brain. Bring them down to a paddle as soon as you cross the line unless you are on a very short course and are told to stop immediately after the finish.

K. Step by Step Tips for Coxing a Head Race

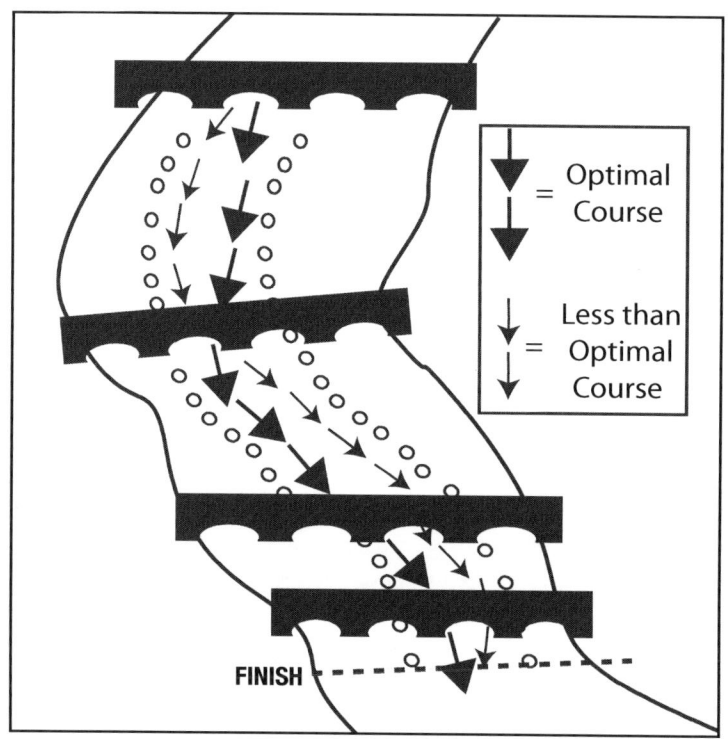

Coxing a head race is a whole different animal from coxing a sprint race, but it still comes down to the same coxing qualities. You need to be organized and have it together on land enough to get your crew to the start in a timely manner; you need to find the shortest possible course; you need to motivate your crew; you need to keep them relaxed, particularly during times when they are passing or being passed, and you need to encourage them to push through their own limits. Head races are long, and you may need to help the crew pace itself, bounce back from being passed, and see the light at the end of the tunnel when they are at the 4,500m mark and don't think they can go another meter.

Steering in Head Races. For head races, the coxswain's course has a much greater impact on the race's outcome. In other words, you have far more to screw up. The fastest course is always the shortest line between the points. You have got to be aggressive in holding your line, especially in big races where there are many other crews to contend with. Look ahead, find the line you want, and follow that. If you are unfamiliar with the race course, consulting aerial maps of the course is the best thing you can do. It is critical that you know the shortest course from maps, so you can follow it on the water. Look at the race course maps from prior years, and see if you can figure out the shortest points around each turn and bridge. Memorize these. We cannot stress this enough.

Head racing is also exciting in that you cannot plan for everything. There are many variables that are just not present in sprint races—namely other crews, bridges, obstacles, and turns. Other crews will collide, crash, get in your way, or pass you from behind. We've seen everything from major debris in the river to unruly spectators create trouble for crews. While the perfect course is out there, sometimes the smartest and fastest course is not the perfect one given conditions on the course. For example, it is generally faster to move out of the way and avoid the trouble—this will likely slow you down far less than tangling/interlocking oars with another crew or crashing through debris just for a negligible patch of water. The most successful coxswains are also the ones who take the long view—that means sometimes taking the outside of one turn might put you in perfect position for the next turn. Ask yourself if you can realistically pass the crews around you before you run into obstacles. Once you pass that crew, what is coming up ahead—is it a major turn, more slow crews, tight spots on the course, an S-curve in the river? Thinking about what comes next is the most important thing you can do. Sometimes it makes sense to drop rowers out or back off on the pressure if it means avoiding trouble. No matter what, safety should be your first priority, and if you need convincing on this, search the Internet for photos or videos of heinous crashes at major head races. We will be as aggressive as the next cox if our crew can back it up, but if not, the smart way to go is to hang back and take the safe route. Maybe your crew can save its strength by going easy for a little while and then breaking free from the other crews as soon as you hit a wider spot in the river. Perhaps you need to hold the line on a turn to set up for the next one, even if it means delaying passing the crew in front of you. Again, it goes back to doing your homework before you get on the water and knowing what is coming up ahead.

Tricks for the Start—Head Races. Head races have staggered starts where crews are sent off the line in intervals of anywhere between 10-60 seconds depending on the race. Your crew crosses the line when the starter calls you up, right? That seems simple enough. Think again. We will preface what we are about to tell you by saying that we cannot emphasize enough that you want to race ethically and show good sportsmanship at all times when coxing races. It reflects poorly on you, your team, and your school/club when you don't. That said, there are a few tricks when it comes to gaming the spacing between crews in head racing starts. Most head races, particularly the bigger ones, stagger starts by 10-20 second intervals.

The jump start. If you are a top seeded crew going off the line first, it may be to your advantage to go off the line as fast as possible to get away from the other crews—if the buffer is more than 10 or 20 seconds, all the better. You can blast off as soon as the marshal starts calling you up—get your crew up to full pressure as quickly as possible. This might catch the crews behind you off guard, building in more than a 10 or 20 second buffer behind you, and giving you time to 'get away' from the trailing crews. It will motivate your crew immensely to see how much open water distance they are getting from the trailing crews. (However, this can also backfire because then you will not know what is going on in the pack, and serious racing could be going on behind you—don't lull yourself into complacency if you cannot see the rest of the pack!) If you are in the middle or back of the pack, particularly if you are a faster crew, again you may want to start as close as you can behind the crew ahead of you. Passing a boat immediately will fire up your crew and set a great tone for the rest of the row. Unless, of course, there is a major obstacle near the start which will make passing difficult, in which case you need to hang back as long as possible. (We can recall one year at Head of the Charles, coxing a slower crew and going off the line one boat ahead of a US National Team training camp crew. Our only goal was to hold them off long enough to not crash at the BU Bridge, about 150 meters from the start. They caught us almost immediately after we had gone under it. Had they jumped the start even more than they did, it would not have been pretty.) Jumping the start also works for slower crews who are worried about being passed immediately by trailing crews in situations like the one above.

The hang back start. If you are a really fast crew and are at the middle or back of the pack (either as a late add, due to poor seeding, or just because no one realizes how fast your crew really is), it can also be a good idea to hang back a bit from the crew in front of you, giving them 20-30 seconds or more of a lead. The more the better in many cases. Then when you cross the line at full speed, you can put off catching up to the crew just ahead of you for a while (Your rowers will be amped up at the start anyway), and then after they settle in, you will be up near the pack and can start passing crews left and right. It is also advisable in situations like the one described above where there is a major obstacle right near the start—if you start with more of a buffer, it will give the slower crews in front of you the opportunity to clear the obstacle, so that you do not get into trouble at that point.

Again, keep in mind that you need to pay attention to the officials and not make them mad or get a penalty. You also want to discuss your plan to get ahead or hang back with your crew and make sure they know what is about to happen. Regardless of how you start, you want to be rowing at full pressure at the point your bow crosses the starting line. Also make sure you zero out your Cox-Box timer as your bow crosses the start line.

Head Race Calls, Situations, and Strategies. Basic head racing strategies are similar to sprint races, just a lot longer. The 'go out fast, stay fast, finish fast' is the one employed by most crews, some more successfully than others. General idea is that you hit your sustainable race pace from the start and pull harder when you are passing other crews or trying to hold off crews from overtaking you. Other crews hit their sustainable race pace early and then sprint at the end. Generally most coxswains focus on getting a good groove going for their crew by emphasizing technique, good ratio and swing at race pace at the beginning of the race, and then moving into a more motivational role as the race goes on. If you think about the head race in pieces, it kind of goes like this:

Start + First 1,000m

The crew is most likely to be rushing, excited, and nervous. The crew will have a lot of energy at this point, so you ideally want to make up some ground on the course. Focus on keeping them calm, getting the race pace locked in, and getting the ratio under control. Your calls should be focused on ratio, power on the drive, and swinging together. You want to make sure they are at race pace and not going out too high, or the rest of the race will be bad news.

1,000m to 4,000m

After the first 1,000m, the technique of the crew will start to fall apart, and rowers will start to tune out. Focus on technique calls, use rower's names (not just seat number), very short, strategic silences, and make sure your calls are emphasizing common technique problems. Good calls focus on reminding the rowers to keep sitting up, keep their heads and chins up, sit tall, keep the strokes long, and make sure catches are together. Motivation calls should increase in frequency the further on in the race you get. Major landmarks on the race course are excellent places to take certain 'moves' or make certain calls, so make sure those are clearly outlined on your race plan. Specific calls to pass things like buildings, bridges, and boathouses are great things to get your rowers amped up during the most tiresome part of the race. The good news with the middle of the race is that this is where most of the racing and passing action happens. If you are lucky, you will get to use other crews to motivate your crew. If you are unlucky, it could be a long, slow slog through the middle of the race, so you need to use geographic markers to make it more interesting. We also like to employ a 1-2-3 minute alternating call sequence during the middle of a long head race. For one minute focus on a technical aspect such as quick hands away, sitting up at the catch, or getting fast hands out of bow. For the second minute do some unique calls or talk about certain members of your crew, like your engine room, your bow pair, or your stern four (This will be repeated, so that by the end of the race, everyone in the crew got their moment in the spotlight!). Then in the third minute work in a 'move' or big push for power, focusing on leg drive, sending puddles away, and the like. Ideally you are using key landmarks for the 'power' minutes, although this might require a bit more advance planning. Repeat this as needed during the slow parts of the race. Ideally you want to put all of this on your race plan index card, so you can easily refer to it during the race. No need to tell your crew about it because chances are they will not even notice.

4,000m to Finish

Rowers will be completely exhausted at this point, and the big focus should be on simple rhythm, teamwork, and the fact that it will all be over soon. Reminding them that they are pulling for each other as much as themselves, their team, or their school is usually effective. This is the point where you want to dig deep into your knowledge of your crew and use your secret weapon calls. If you have rival crews in the same race, even if they are nowhere nearby, thinking externally and making those calls can also be effective. Basic technical calls related to sitting up, breathing, and reaching out are also good at this point in the race. Make sure you are accurate in estimating distance to the finish and timing your calls and execution of the race plan accordingly.

Head racing strategy is much more nuanced than sprint racing and very situation dependent. Here are some basic things to communicate to your crew throughout the race:

Meters left in the race. Head races are long. There is no getting around it. You can let your rowers know when you cross the first mile marker, the half way point, the last mile mark, and the like. Don't dwell on distance until about the last 1,000m, especially if your crew is inexperienced. Experienced crews can handle the information earlier in the race and more frequently, but in general, as in sprint races, meters left is an end-of-the-race bit of information. Again, as in sprint races, think about how you communicate that information. Some crews would rather hear, "We've got less than 100 strokes to go" while other crews would prefer "600 meters to go" or "We've got less than two minutes left in the race." Ask your rowers what they would prefer to hear and how early on in the race they want to hear meters. The absolute worst things a coxswain can say in a head race are things that emphasize how much the crew has in front of them, such as, "We're four minutes in, only about 17 more to go" or "We've only got 4,500m left!" Those phrases are soul-crushers, and you can watch your race chances go down the drain. When you do communicate distance early on in the race, make sure you hide it in something better, like fun tens for inside boat jokes, or when you are about to catch up and pass another crew. Then they will forget all about the meters.

Ratings. Give your crew ratings every 200m or so if they are having problems maintaining a consistent rating or rush becomes a problem. If they are locked in at a good race pace, you can do it more infrequently, typically with something like, "Frederica is doing a great job maintaining that 28; let's make sure we are helping her out with slow legs on the recovery."

General motivation. Again, head races are long, and it is one of the coxswain's jobs to make them more bearable. Interesting motivational tens are surefire, and you want to save your best stuff for the big head races. But remember, only say it if you know it will make your crew go faster!

General technique 10s. Technical tens are a big part of head racing. We highly recommend you keep a long list of them on an index card or mini-notebook and bring it with you for the race. You want to mix it up enough so you are not repeating yourself over and over again. As in sprint racing, keep it general—focusing on things like finishing together, getting the lock on at the same time, feeling the swing of the boat—not directed toward any one person.

With head racing you have far less information about where other crews are in the race. In some cases, particularly where race organizers did an excellent job of seeding the crews or in races with long intervals between starts, you will be on your own for the vast majority of the race and will be forced to row your own race.

You will likely be in several different situations at different times during the race including the following:

Catching and passing another crew. Passing boats in head races is the kind of thing coxswains live for. The memory of it makes winter training almost bearable. Here is the situation—you are coming up on a crew that started in front of you. They are slightly slower (or a lot slower) than your crew. You need to pass them while holding the best possible steering course. As a cox you will have a lot going on when you are passing another crew. In order of priority, you will be focusing on:

- **Thinking ahead.** Regardless of how exciting it is to pass other crews, steering the best possible course with an eye to what is coming up ahead is a higher priority. This means the shortest distance from point A to point B, making sure you have the right angle on the upcoming turns, and are setting up not to crash into other boats up ahead. You must always be thinking about what is coming next, not just the crew you are passing. If the crew you are overtaking does a good job of holding you off, you will need to think about your spacing while rowing broadside to this other crew around the next crew, the next turn, or the next bridge in the race. If that is not incentive enough to get your rowers to pull harder to pass the crew, we don't know what is.

- **Don't crash.** Avoid clashes with oars from the other crew. A little tap or two is no big deal, but full interlocking oars will slow you down like you would not believe. (Although it is exciting, and this is the main reason large crowds of people come out to watch head races!) Avoiding crashes may mean telling the other crew to yield to one direction or the other. Sometimes other crews will not yield, either due to coxswain inexperience or just plain unsportsmanlike conduct. Then you are faced with the choice of running into them or going around them, varying your ideal course. (Believe us when we say we will let that other coxswain know, in no uncertain terms, where they need to go. By that we mean toward port or starboard, not some other places we'd like to tell them to go! Remember, keep it clean, or you could be penalized for unsportsmanlike conduct.) As aggressive as we tend to be, sometimes the best approach is to just go around them. Make sure the officials are watching and hopefully giving them a penalty for failure to yield. If you have to deviate course, play it off for your rowers, and by all means keep them calm and internally focused (see below). Sometimes you just plain have to back it off a little if you are in a tight spot between a bridge or several crews. It is not an ideal situation, so that is why our first point about steering and looking far ahead is so important.

- **Keep your rowers calm.** Keeping your rowers focused internally, not looking out of the boat at the other crew, especially if there are oars clashing or you are yelling at another coxswain, is a tough balance. Those things tend to stress the rowers out, so you need to give them a warning about what is about to happen, remind them to keep their heads in the boat, and keep your voice calm and collected, even if you want to jump out and strangle the coxswain of the other crew. Remind your rowers that their job is pulling hard while your job is steering—if they are looking out of the boat, they are making the boat go slower.

- **Walk on through.** Motivating your rowers to 'walk through' the other crew is next on the list of priorities. You should be practicing walking on other crews in practices, but generally speaking it will go like this, "We've got deck to deck connection with Prep; now let's walk through them. Push with the legs here for ten; I want their coxswain. 1-2-3. Got it, our bow seat is on their coxswain. Big legs here 4-5. You just took two more seats. Push with the legs; I want bow on their 4 seat. 6-7. We're on their 4 seat. More big legs, 8-9, we're pulling up even now, only one seat back. That's it; walk with the legs; we are dead even now; I'm on their coxswain. Let's walk through them now. Push here. I'm on their stroke seat…" Again, remember how important it is to move through crews to maintain your optimal course. You can always remind them that if they don't pull hard now, they will be rowing more meters during the race.

Being overtaken by another crew. There is nothing more demoralizing than being passed in a head race, especially if you end up rowing mostly by yourself for the rest of the race. We say motivate your crew to hold off the other crew as long as possible, make sure you know the protocol for yielding, and then go back to maintaining your ideal line. It is often more strategic to let an opposing crew walk through you to maintain your course than to battle it out with them for five minutes on a less than ideal course.

Sitting on another crew. Sometimes you will find yourself in a situation where you are just sitting on another crew. This doesn't do anyone any good because eventually you will have two crews rowing side-by-side trying to navigate tight turns and obstacles on the course. The two crews are evenly matched and are just sitting there, and both crews are pulling at full pressure. This is the time to pull out a rating change. Make a call to go 'up two over two,' and then demand that the crew follows stroke. Talk about what a great job stroke is doing and that everyone else in the crew needs to pull these twenty strokes at a higher rating for stroke seat. Do the high twenty. If you are still sitting on the other crew, down shift it, and take twenty strokes at a lower rating, and then take it up again. Repeat as necessary. You can also trying feeding your crew's ego and communicating a sense of urgency. You can tell your crew that they are stronger. You can tell your crew that for tactical purposes they need to put you into position to get the best angle on the turn. You can also try playing to your crew's logical side. We have had success telling our crew that they had two choices for the race—to continue to sit with this other crew and row an extra 400 meters over the length of the racecourse or to pass this other crew and shave off that extra minute of rowing. You would be surprised at how good pulling hard at the present moment suddenly sounded.

Rowing by yourself with no other crews around. Often you spend the majority of a head race rowing alone. Often you can see other crews far off in the distance up ahead or behind, but no one is moving on you or challenging you. This might seem dull, and it kind of is, but the good news is you can steer the ideal course. Your big challenge during these periods of rowing by yourself is to keep your crew appropriately motivated. You can take the internally focused approach and talk about things like technique, take tens for fun things that you know will motivate your rowers, give lots of information on rating and the like, OR you can be externally focused, talking a lot about what is probably happening up ahead or behind with other crews passing. You can also externally focus on your known rival crews who are at other points on the race course and take some tens for pulling harder than they are. Then there is always the old coxswain standby of pretending to pass other imaginary crews, particularly rival crews who started well before or after you did. Be warned though that some rowers get into racing imaginary boats, and others may shout expletives from the bow and threaten to throw you out of the boat for doing it. Make sure you ask in advance.

Navigating a turn. Some head races have a few big turns. Then there are others that require you to navigate a serpentine course of multiple S-curves. If you are rowing by your lonesome, you should have no problem taking the perfect course around a turn in the race course. As you come into the turn, remember that the fastest course is typically closest to the buoy line and as far away from the shoreline as possible. If you maintain your line off the riverbank, you will be rowing extra meters! Make sure you know the regatta's rules—most races allow your oars, but not your hull, to extend over the buoy line, while others impose penalties if your oars cross the buoy line. If you have an S-curve situation, following the straightest possible line between the two curves is generally the best course. If you get into trouble with other crews around pushing you into the curves, you can add a bit of rudder, or in tighter curves you will have to have the rowers on the inside of the turn shorten up their strokes and apply less pressure while the rowers on the outside of the curve will be lengthening out and powering up.

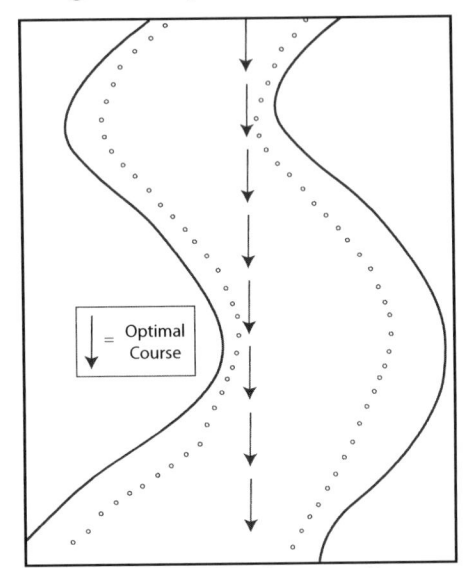

Best course is the shortest distance

It is inopportune to try to pass crews on the turns in a race course, but this is the stuff that makes coxing interesting. You have to find the balance between fighting for your best course and thinking realistically about whether or not you can get through the other crew before pinch points on the course, especially turns. Consider whether crashing or clashing oars will be a possibility and whether it makes sense to hang back and take a break and instead pass the crew later on. If you are being overtaken on a turn, it is always better to just drop off the pressure in your crew to stay on the racecourse, even if it means rowing extra meters close to the shore, than to be forced off the racecourse and get a penalty.

Clashing Oars. Even the most cautious coxswains can find themselves in situations where blade clashing is inevitable. We try to avoid it at all costs (see the section above) because it really does slow you down considerably, but if you are in the situation, do not panic. Staying calm is the best thing you can do for your crew. Let them know it is coming, which side the clash will happen on, which seats will have their oars clashed, and back off a bit. Just go ahead and drop the power off until you are untangled. If you are the overtaking crew, say directly to the other coxswain that you are overtaking them and have priority, and tell them which direction they need to yield. Then as soon as you are untangled, do some tens for swinging into bow together, sitting up tall, and deep breathing to get them back into a good rhythm. Basic counting at the catch and finish, using the classic calls 'CHA' or 'catch…send…'hatch…send…'hatch…send' counted exactly at the catch and finish is also a proven winner. This is also the time to remind your crew that it is anyone's race and that other crews have probably also had clashes on the course. Then, reaching deep into your bag of coxswain tricks, pull out one those motivational calls that show you truly understand your crew and what makes them tick to kick some fire back into them.

Head Race Finishes. One of the most challenging parts of head racing is figuring out where to start your sprint (assuming your race plan anticipates a sprint). Generally you want to start thinking about your finish about 2 to 3 minutes before the end of the race, depending on your crew's experience level, pain threshold, and race plan. You will need to have a good idea of where you are in the race, how long your crew will take to finish, and how exhausted your crew is, but the general rule is with three minutes to go, or roughly around the 750m mark, you are focusing on taking the power up a bit, moving the rate and power up with two minutes to go, or roughly around the 500m mark, and for the final minute, or roughly around the 250m mark, full on sprinting out across the line. Adjust accordingly, depending on how fast or experienced your crew is. Again, it is critically important that you can recognize major landmarks on the course and use those as benchmarks for the distance left in the race. When you can actually see the finish line and think you have about 20-25 strokes to go, call "last thirty strokes!" Rowers tend to shorten up, especially inexperienced ones, and race plans tend to call for that shorting up, which will result in more strokes than you think. Plus, you may not be 100% accurate, but it is better to err on the side of overestimating than underestimating. The worst thing you can do is call the sprint or the last 20 strokes, row them out, and then find yourself still not at the finish line. (If you have never rowed on the course, use the aerial maps and whatever information the race organizers have provided so you know where certain things are—bridges, spectator areas, major buildings, etc… Write those down on your race plan notecards, and use those as cues on race day.) You are finished when your bowball crosses the finish line. Switch off your Cox-Box timer immediately, and burn that time into your brain! As your crew crosses the finish line, bring them down to a paddle, but do not stop rowing!

L. After the Finish

Let your rowers drink copious amounts of water, and check to make sure there are no major medical problems. If there are, alert an official immediately. Wish your competitors a 'nice race.' Then get in line to get back onto the dock pronto because docking will be just as hectic as launching was. Unless you are having some sort of medical issue with your crew or need to hot-seat, you should come in in the order you finished the race. Make sure you are flagging down your gear helper people who hopefully have your crew's shoes. Then get your equipment washed, derigged, and back onto the trailer before you let your crew wander off.

M. Protests

A protest is essentially a complaint to the officials by the coxswain immediately after your race in regard to the conduct of another crew or what you believe to be an unfair situation. In our collective 20+ years of coxing experience and hundreds of races, we feel lucky to say that we have never had to protest a race, nor have our actions ever been subject of another crew's protest. They are not all that common and are generally associated with the larger head races. Then again, some coaches are aggressive, hot-headed, or just like to create controversy, so if you're on a team like that, you might see a lot of protests.

The common protest situations are as follows:

- **Somebody else's malfeasance cost us the race.** Team A protests that Team B failed to yield or deliberately stopped or blocked Team A and cost Team A the race. In a head race situation, unless the action was so egregious, this one is rarely a winner and is rarely worth protesting. In a sprint race situation, where another team crossed into your lane and slowed you down, you should definitely not hesitate to protest, especially if they finished ahead of you.

- **Somebody else's malfeasance caused us to be penalized.** Team A protests that Team B forced it off the course due to a rule violation by Team B, and the officials unfairly gave Team A an undeserved penalty. This one has the best chance of success, particularly if you have witnesses. If another crew forced you off the course due to their own deliberate actions and the officials saw it, and you are 100% likely to be penalized, it is worth lodging the protest before you come off the water.

- **Officials were wrong protest.** Team A protests that Team A was given a penalty for missing a buoy or some other infraction that never actually occurred. Team A protests that Team A was given a penalty when the crew that actually missed the buoy or failed to yield was Team B. In most head races, you will not know whether or not you were assessed a penalty until hours later. You can always complain later, and something may happen, but it may be tough to prove, and it will probably be too late to do anything about it.

- **They cheated, and the officials didn't see it.** Team A protests that Team B missed a major buoy or otherwise violated the rules, and the officials didn't see it happen. Team A noticed that Team B was rowing with experienced rowers in a novice race. Team A wants the officials to give Team B a penalty or disqualify them, which would put Team A into a higher finishing position. This might stand a chance, even if it will look like sour grapes. It is still worth lodging this protest if you have good solid evidence and feel like you have a chance at the medals.

Here is what we will say about protests—don't count on them. If you are going to go down that road, you need to be familiar with the race's protocols for lodging them and the national governing body's rules for protests in general. Most protests must be done on the water immediately after the race, and if you come to shore, you lose your ability to protest. In larger races, your coach will have to submit an often substantial fee just to lodge the protest, so you had better be sure you have good grounds to support your claims. The real truth about protests is that there are no do-overs in rowing. If the officials reject your protest, you are out the money you spent on the protest fee. Generally if your protest is successful, the crew that violated the rules will be penalized. Sure, that means that you beat them, but unless you finished second behind the offending crew, it is generally small consolation. Depending on the race, the officials may have seen the violation anyway and were going to penalize that other crew regardless.

N. Accuracy and Misinformation During Races

The last thing we will say about racing is about accuracy and misinformation during a race. Be honest and accurate during races. If you lie on a regular basis, your rowers will stop trusting you, and that is the kiss of death for any coxswain. However, it is OK to lie (a little bit) if it makes the race go better and they will never find out that you lied. Sometimes you need to tell a crew that they took a seat from a boat they are just sitting on, or that they are looking strong even when they really are not. It is OK to pump up their egos, and that does not make you a liar. Instead of lies, if anything, we prefer omissions—instead of telling a crew that they still have 4,500 meters left to row, just plain don't mention it! If your rowers ask and you genuinely do not know the answer, it is OK to tell your crew that you don't know something. Be honest, and admit you don't know, and then change the subject. An old standby is always, "Keep your head in the boat, and let me worry about it." This does not, however, mean that you should voluntarily offer up your own incompetence or ignorance on a silver platter. Saying things like, "I have no idea how long we have left in this race," without any provocation or inquiry from your rowers does not instill confidence. Instead, you wait until you can see a landmark and then tell them where you are. Be honest, but be strategic about it.

CHAPTER 12
GETTING TO KNOW YOUR CREW AND WHAT MAKES THEM TICK

A. How to Get Inside the Heads of Your Crew
B. Close But Not Too Close
C. Get to Know Other People's Motivations
D. Sappy or Effective?
E. What Really Motivates People?

At the start of this book we mentioned that we don't cox crews that win national championships or train for the Olympics. One of the major things that separates the top crews from the rest of the rowers on the planet is that the very top crews are incredibly internally motivated to pull hard. Top coxswains who steer these crews have the luxury of not having to worry about motivating people who might not feel like pulling very hard some times. However, when you're coxing for regular rowers—whether they are juniors or senior masters—they often need a bit of motivation from their coxswains. Occasionally they need a vast ocean of motivation. That's where you come in.

A. How to Get Inside the Heads of Your Crew

Hard to believe but rowing, especially steady state rowing for long periods, can be soul-crushingly boring, painful, and exhausting. Getting your rowers to stay focused and push beyond their own limits is your goal in every practice and in every race. Achieving that is not easy. What works in practices will not necessarily work in races. Moreover, what works one day may not work the next. We wish we could give you a magic formula on how to break through to your rowers. The closest thing to a secret is to really get to know people on an individual level and as a crew, and set that mood. You are spending 20+ hours a week together, after all. Here are a few things to think about when it comes to motivating your crew:

Take a page from the advertising world. You're in charge of harnessing that 'boat culture' and 'branding' your crew. Some crews are all business. Some crews position themselves as the alpha crew, and your job is to keep those egos inflated. Some crews position themselves as underdogs, so you need to fan those flames of being underrated. Some crews are full of pranksters and want a cox to crack jokes and keep them entertained. Some crews want to be constantly reminded in practices about how hard their opponents are training to make them pull that much harder. You've got to figure out what makes your individual crew tick. At the beginning of the season, or as soon as boats are set, you want to observe the crew and the rowers in it. If you're a new cox, watch to see who the natural leaders are on the team. What is their style? Where they go the rest will probably follow. Especially with novice crews, the cox can play a huge role in influencing the culture of the boat. If you're an experienced cox, you can pretty much dictate what the boat culture will be based on what you think will work for the rowers. Structure your practice calls and conversations accordingly.

Experiment and ask for feedback from your rowers. Think about potential calls and structure for each practice, and test it out. Maybe one day you're focused on what your big rival team is doing today. Maybe the next day you're focused on pumping up your crew telling them how strong and fast they are. Maybe the next you're focused on retribution for what happened in a race last season. See what calls actually make the boat go faster. Those calls that really work should be used sparingly.

Diversify your calls. If your crew responds to a call, think about 50 other ways to say it. See how other words that mean substantially the same thing can work.

Tap into the ethos of your boat. Really, when you spend countless hours a week with the same people, it is inevitable that a certain unique relationship and personality develop for the group. If you can tap into this, far and away this is the most motivating of all. The inside jokes, experiences, and time spent together that lead to shared experiences that no other group of humans on earth has ever experienced collectively together—this is the stuff that is pure coxing gold. We can't tell you what it will be for your group of rowers, but this is what you need to be tapping into.

B. Close But Not Too Close

In order to really figure out what motivates your rowers, you have to put yourself into a bit of a cultural anthropologist role. This means keeping yourself at arms length from your rowers on some level. This is fairly easy when you're coxing masters, but extremely difficult at the high school and college level because most of your rowers will be your best friends, too. Watch what people say and do, identify the leaders on the team, and focus on them.

C. Get to Know Other People's Motivations

Here is a radical idea for coxswains everywhere. Ask your rowers what motivates them. Every crew is different. Masters women will talk at you for an hour in great detail, while high school boys will look at you like you have three heads and shrug. If they can't tell you what motivates them, why they row, or what it is going to take to pull them through a tough piece or race, give them some examples. Ask them to rank motivating phrases or cross out what wouldn't work for them at all. Your authors have had crews be motivated by vengeance, rivalries, patriotism, school pride, retribution from past races, animal imagery, divine providence, zen feelings of peace and harmony, and completely made up words which meant different things to each member of the boat. Some men's crews go straight toward the war analogies, and do not stop when things get gross. Every crew is different. You will probably be surprised what you find out.

D. Sappy or Effective?

Over the years we've come across a lot of coaches and coxswains who have based motivating a crew on sappy inspirational quotes and platitudes. They like to scatter them on bulletin boards and send out a 'quote of the day.' There are literally hundreds of websites, bloggers, and social media users that are offering up inspirational rowing quotes, memes with inspirational rowing quotes, general sports training inspiration, and the like. Some are rowing clichés, some are from famous coaches, and others are just platitudes on the world in general. We're as big of fans of Ghandi as the next girls, but we also don't find that quotes that belong on religious calendars do much to motivate most rowers. Masters women of a certain age and high school girls seem to like them. This kind of quote also seems to work well in the early morning, in the dark, and as the sun is rising. Go figure. We assume people are either too groggy to object or blinded by the beauty of nature and are in the right mind-set to hear them. If you can find a good one that everyone in your boat likes, by all means use it. But don't say we didn't warn you. Use them sparingly, and if you do use them a lot, be prepared to be laughed out of the boathouse.

E. What Really Motivates People?

Every single rower is motivated by something different. We're not above stereotypes, so here is what we've found motivates various types of crews in our experience. We're also providing tips on coxing each type of crew in races, long practice pieces, and erg pieces:

Junior Boys. Junior boys join rowing teams for a variety of reasons. Many are doing it because the school requires them to be part of a sport or because their parents thought rowing was a good idea. Some are doing it for the team camaraderie or their need for competition. Younger juniors will be flaky, and your job is to focus them. Juniors and seniors in high school, especially those on competitive high school teams, can be coxed much like college teams. Give them the data. Where you are in the race, time elapsed, time left, meters left, position relative to other crews, and location of moves. The younger they are, the less likely they are to be listening to you, and the more motivation they will need. Calling out individual rowers by their first names (not just by seat) is the most effective way to get them to pay attention to you. As junior boys get more experience and get faster, they're more like college crews, so cox accordingly.

Junior Girls. Junior girls join high school teams for a variety of levels, including being forced to do so by their parents and by requirements from the school that they participate in a sport. Most enjoy rowing for the sense of belonging, team camaraderie, and finding other girls they can be friends with. Shocking as it is, we've found this group to be the most responsive to the flowery variety of motivation. Go ahead and tape cute sparkly inspirational quotes inside the boat and send messages to them with the same. Pick a quote of the week. Make some t-shirts. Do tens for all the sappy inspirational things you can think of. The more serious of the bunch will still expect the data—where you are in the race, time elapsed, time left, meters left, position relative to other crews, and location of moves. As junior girls get more experience, they still like the notes with glitter, but they'll be getting more serious and need more data. You can cox experienced junior girls much like you would a college team. The last thing we will add is that this group is most likely to get their feelings hurt and their noses out of joint, so when it comes to motivation, consider that.

Novice Juniors. Who knows how they even ended up at the boathouse. If they are listening to you at all, it would be a miracle. Stay calm. Your chief role is babysitter for the equipment, which they may lose or drop at any moment. Explain what the basic rowing terms mean. Over and over again. Don't overwhelm them with words. Keep it simple. Remember that when you talk, they may stop rowing to listen to you. As far as racing goes, help them recover from crabs, let them know when they should start their sprint and when they cross the line.

College/Open Men and Women. People join college or open teams for a variety of reasons, but generally to row successfully at a competitive college or open level, people are motivated by competition, being part of a team, being with their friends, and finding their own identity in being a part of a larger group. Give them the data. Where you are in the race, time elapsed, time left, meters left, position relative to other crews, and location of moves. College crews may see the same crews week after week, and rankings are well known. Play to that. School spirit also plays well, as does reminding them of races from prior years or earlier in the season. Individual tens for specific inside jokes or specific rowers (especially the seniors in your boat) are typically well received. The more intellectual the school, the more you should strive to weave in imagery from the worlds of art, literature, war, and science, although if you're coxing at a place like that, it should come naturally to you, and even then it may fall on deaf ears. Aggressive phrases seem to work well for some crews, especially men. Mostly they want to hear words that connote power, going fast, and beating other crews from rival schools. Some crews respond to tens for specific pairs or people in the boat, their class years, specific technique, or other technique improvement images that make the crew go faster. Typically these crews have plenty of internal motivation and external stimulus, and races are generally close, so they don't need much, if anything, in the way of flowery motivational quotes from you. Many college and open women, like their high school counterparts, do still like glittery notes taped inside lockers and in the boat. (Just don't use the kind of tape that leaves residue or you will hear about it from the equipment manager!)

Masters Men. Masters men row for a few reasons—to stay in shape, to relive their glory days, to relieve stress, and to enjoy some male bonding on a basic level (though most would never admit to the latter). Mostly they just want to pull hard and tune the coxswain out. Many of them would probably be happiest with a cox who just shuts up, which we encourage. Don't get anywhere near coxing them on an erg unless they specifically ask—the screen gives them all they need. During races and long pieces, give them the data. Many masters men are completely and obsessively focused on data—this is your first job after steering. Where you are in the race, time elapsed, time left, meters left, position relative to other crews, and location of moves. Otherwise, shut the heck up. Seriously, they don't care about anything else, and you're just background noise. If they look like they are going to die, then feel free to add in a little motivational phrasing, but use restraint, and don't expect it will do much.

Masters Women. Masters women row for lots of reasons. Younger masters women row primarily to stay fit, relive the good memories of their high school or college rowing days, and work out their continued thirst for beating other people at races. You can cox that group the same way you'd cox for a college team. Older masters women by and large are far more complex. All of them are rowing to stay fit as they age. Many are enjoying a team sport or competitive sport for the first time in their lives. Many will tell you that after raising their kids, rowing is the first time in their lives they are doing something just for themselves. That group takes to rowing obsessively, not unlike junior or college rowers getting involved with rowing for the first time. Most older masters women have complicated relationships with other women on the team—friends and rivals both. A fair number will tell you they row to be out on the water, enjoy nature, find peace and solitude (those tend to be the scullers), and enjoy the 'flow' of rowing. Masters women are far more cerebral and far more likely to be control-freaks than other crews. God help you if you forget the countdown at the dock or fail to call the move at exactly the right point in the race—that is job number one. Some masters women's crews are motivated by flowery phrases and soothing tones, but not all. Some like the sort of 'we're all in this together' phrasing. This is the group to ask about what they want because they will have strong opinions, and they will not hesitate to share them with you. In races, you had better memorize that race plan like it's your mother's birthday and execute the race plan to perfection. You will hear about it for years if you don't. As with other crews, give them the data during practices and races—where you are in the race, time elapsed, time left, meters left, position relative to other crews, and location of moves. Many like the cox to talk about strength, the power of women (seriously!), swing, rhythm, tens for various techniques, and focus tens to clear their head space. For them, what the coxswain does and how the coxswain motivates them are extremely important. They want the coxswain to be on their side and be part of their team. The coxswains they like the best are the ones who listen to what they want and give them exactly what they want, but also think about what is best for the crew and occasionally come up with new ideas that benefit the boat.

CHAPTER 13
COXSWAIN CULTURE— ESTABLISHING YOUR AUTHORITY

A. Getting the Respect You Deserve from Your Coach and Your Rowers
B. It's OK to Be a Coxswain
C. Learning the Trade
D. Confidence Can't be Bought
E. Owning It—Developing Your Own Style
F. Etiquette in Practice
G. Working with Other Coxswains
H. Sportsmanship

A. Getting the Respect You Deserve from Your Coach and Your Rowers

One of the most common questions we get asked by coxswains is how to establish their authority with their rowers or get respect from their coaches. As the saying goes, respect is earned and not given. Earning respect does not come overnight. This will also come in time. Here are a few things you can do to speed that process along. Note that expertise of rowing is not on the list!

Be genuine and honest. Be who you are. That is not bad advice for life, by the way. If you are new, do not pretend to be an expert. Use what you have, wherever you are in your developmental stage. Never exaggerate your experience or pretend to know things you do not. It is fine to admit that you don't know something.

Confidence, not arrogance. Position yourself as a calm, in control, decision-maker. Avoid the ego.

Humility. Be open to learning. Do not act like you know more than you do. Admit your mistakes and learn from them. Again, leave your ego behind. Be gracious. When someone helps you or gives you feedback, thank them genuinely.

Commitment. Be on time and be prepared. Don't be the one who oversleeps or flakes out on practice. Know the workout, drills, and race plans. Encourage others in a positive way. Listen to your coach, and show him or her respect. Give the rowers respect yourself. In the off-season, learn to row yourself or work out with your team.

Patience. Know your development level. Give it time. You are not going to be an expert in a year. If Malcolm Gladwell is right and it takes 10,000 hours to become an expert at something, even if you coxed ten hours a week, it would take you almost 20 years to become an expert!

Hard work. Do the best job you can, and work hard to be a constant learner. Work to improve your skills each and every day.

Think like a team leader and problem solver. Avoid being the cox who the coach picks on—in other words, be in the right place at the right time, and help make sure your rowers are doing what they are supposed to be doing. Fix problems yourself instead of running to the coach. Know what makes your rowers tick. Be positive, and help others.

Embrace what it means to be a coxswain. It is OK to be a coxswain. In fact, it is pretty great. Do not for a moment feel inferior to your rowers. You are not above them either, but you are definitely special. It's OK to celebrate that. See more on that below.

B. It's OK to Be a Coxswain

Take it from us. There is nothing we hate more than hearing any self-loathing or insecurity from coxswains. A lot of people get a complex about being a coxswain. Sometimes rowers who get injured have to cox. Sometimes rowers who are too small or slow to row get 'stuck' coxing. Sometimes it is the general stupidity of the average non-rower who is shocked that you are spending an inordinate amount of time 'just sitting there' or that you're considered an 'athlete' by your athletic department but 'don't have to do anything athletic.' Now most coxswains have a surplus of confidence and a healthy ego, so they don't worry about what other people say. For the rest of you, all we can tell is you should not waste your time on people who don't get it and instead embrace the job. We say it is more than OK to be a coxswain.

C. Learning the Trade

You're reading this book, which is a good start. You are on your way to becoming a student of the sport. There are two parts to this. The first is building your knowledge of rowing technique and how to cox. This comes from reading technical coxing materials and watching technical videos, going to coxing clinics, talking with coaches about technique, reading kinesiology journals, and developing an understanding of exercise science. That kind of thing. The second, and not quite as important but still really important, is to learn about the culture of being a coxswain. Reading the rowing blogs, the rowing websites, scouring YouTube for videos, laughing at the coxswain problems memes, and enjoying being surrounded by a really cool world that most people know nothing about. The second part is the fun part. We encourage it, but don't let it overshadow the hard work and substantial effort you'll need to put in on the technical side. Studying your own tapes and video, using the notebooks to speed your progress, starting the positive feedback cycle, and reading everything you can will help you increase at the same pace as, or faster than, your rowers. That's your major goal as you progress—to get better as your rowers get better.

D. Confidence Can't be Bought

Natural coxswains are those who have a surplus of confidence. Enough for all nine people in the boat. Thinking back on our own coxing careers, we can't say we ever lacked for confidence. We'll confess that sometimes our own confidence is overwhelming. Lack of humility was more like it. For this we apologize to all of our former coaches. We were total pains in the you-know-what. With age comes the wisdom to realize this, although we haven't quite yet figured out how to control it. For those who struggle with confidence, here are a few tips:

Remind yourself that you can do this. You're not going to know anything at the beginning, and it is really hard to develop the skills, but once you've got it, coxing is not brain surgery. You just need to trick yourself into thinking that coxing is not that difficult. We're definitely not experts, but there seem to be vast selections of self-help books designed to boost self-confidence. Read one of them. Tell us how it was.

Remind yourself of prior successes. Pump yourself up on good things you've already accomplished in life, sporting or otherwise. Then read everything you can get your hands on, and become a student of the sport. That will lead to more successes, and, at least in theory, boost your confidence.

Don't express doubt. Avoid statements like, "Hmm, I'm not really sure which arch of the bridge I'm supposed to go through." If you're not sure what to do, make a decision, and stick with it. The crew doesn't need to know. Expressing doubt only causes everyone to look out of the boat.

Don't second-guess your decisions. Avoid second-guessing everything or saying things like, 'Oops, I shouldn't have cut so close to the channel marker; we might be in shallow water.' Don't make it an issue until it's really an issue. Odds are your crew will never notice.

Never apologize or dwell on your mistakes. A simple, 'Sorry; I'm learning; it won't happen again.' is the very most you should say. Move on from it. We have had coxswains who have apologized the entire practice for some minor mistake—this only frustrates your rowers and makes them think you are incompetent, which in turn makes you feel incompetent.

Don't beat yourself up or talk poorly about your abilities in front of your crew. Go home and cry in your pillow, but keep yourself together at practice. Talking about what a lousy cox you are only makes them nervous, which will make you more nervous and convinces them that you really are no good.

That said, we've got to be honest. Coxing may give you more confidence, but you're going to need it in spades to survive. Nervous types, apprehensive perfectionists, and depressive self-doubters will not do well as coxswains. The take charge, calm and under control, maybe-not-always-right-but-never-in-doubt types make the best coxswains. Making decisions and conveying the veneer of confidence and authority come naturally to these types of people, and coxing is a natural fit. If you don't have these qualities naturally, you're going to have to fake it until you get things under control. If not, coxing will not be a good fit for you.

E. Owning it—Developing Your Own Style

Developing individual style as a coxswain is much like developing individual fashion sense. It really depends on your personality. One thing all good coxswains have in common is that they use a style that comes naturally to them. If you're a super serious person in the rest of your life, you aren't going to be able to fake a laid-back style on the water. Nor should you. You've got to be who you are. Good advice for life, really.

F. Etiquette in Practice

Use good manners. Have your act together. Don't bad mouth the coach or the workouts—in fact, do the opposite. Never talk when your coach is talking. Don't complain to your coach or your rowers. Always raise your hand to acknowledge your coach any time he or she says something to you. Thank your coach for answering your questions. Follow the traffic pattern. Communicate nicely with other coxswains on your team during practices. As far as profanity goes, your authors have very divergent styles. One of us uses foul language and the other avoids it at all costs. Again, you need to know your audience—it unequivocally motivates some crews, but you need to be very careful, especially if your coach or bystanders are around.

G. Working with Other Coxswains

We talk a good deal in this book about working with other coxswains. Maybe it's due to the fact that this book was written by two coxswains, who, somehow, miraculously, worked together. It's natural for coxswains to view each other as competitors. We think that this is a big mistake. It may never be a total sisterhood or brotherhood on your team, but regardless of your position—top cox or newer—relying on each other makes the team better. (At least that's the selfless kind of nonsense people will tell you.) As a newer coxswain, you've likely got some more experienced coxswains on the team. Seek them out. As an experienced cox, help the new people out. You were once in their shoes. Coxswains who unite together can be a powerful force on any team.

H. Sportsmanship

Have you heard us talk about sportsmanship yet in this book? As the saying goes, you only have one chance to lose your reputation. (Take that to heart, especially from those of us who have lost our reputations on multiple occasions.) Sportsmanship is one of those areas where your standards need to be sterling.

Here are a few things to remember about being a good sport in practices:

Respect authority. The coach is always right, even when he or she is wrong. Never criticize.

Reward effort. If a rower on your team, in your boat or not, had a great practice, is making big strides, or put in a good effort, congratulate him or her.

Be gracious in defeat. If another coxswain beats you for a seat in the top boat, congratulate him or her from the heart, no matter how unfair you think it is. If another boat beats you fair and square in an intra-squad race, congratulate them. Be the bigger person. You can secretly hate them for as long as you want to, just keep it to yourself.

Respect boating decisions. Sympathize with the person who didn't get boated, but never question the coach's decision.

Be a good teammate. Be nice to everyone on your team, not just the people in the top boats. Treat everyone like equals, and don't talk badly about anyone on the team.

Avoid the garbage. If someone in your boat talks badly about another rower's technique or anything else, refer them to the coach and, change the subject.

Here is how to be on 'good sportsmanship' behavior at races:

Know the rules. Get familiar with them. Read the rules again before you cox a single race, and follow them to the letter. Go to the coxswain meeting before the race or look at the website for the regatta. Know the traffic pattern, the right of way rules, and, more than anything else, stay in your lane at sprint races and yield if you're being overtaken in head races. Period.

Stay out of the way of other crews. Talk to the other coxswains to tell them where you're going. Don't get dangerously close to other crews on warmups or in the marshalling area.

Watch your mouth. Never, ever, ever yell at or use profanities directed at another crew, or god forbid, the officials. You deserve more than a penalty if you're dumb enough to do that.

Remember, you're on a live mic. Never, ever, ever disparage individual rowers in other crews, particularly for their physical attributes, as least in a way they know you're talking about them, e.g., 'Power ten to pass that buck-toothed ginger with the bad acne in five seat.' If you're going to go down that road, do it in code, so that no one outside your boat has any idea what you're saying. Also avoid saying things that are deliberately mean or unsettling when you're blowing by a much slower crew, e.g. 'Five strokes to pull through a crew that's basically standing still.' or 'Wow, St. John's is terrible; it is going to take them an hour to finish the course.' Don't make their already terrible race experience that much worse. Let's also be real here—coxing is a head game. Inside jokes and code phrases have been a coxing tradition ever since boat speakers were invented. Surely you are creative to think of some, just do your best to keep it classy. We also don't need to remind you that you should leave the unflattering nicknames to other teams and schools, not people in other boats on your own team. That's just uncalled for, spiteful, mean, and officially makes you a bad person.

Treat the officials like they were your grandparents. Acknowledge the officials by raising your hand. Say please and thank you to them. If they tell you to do something, do it immediately.

At the end of the race, win or lose, congratulate the other crews. All you have to say is, 'good race [insert name of team]!' and leave it at that.

Be polite coming into the dock and launching. Raise your hand to acknowledge the dockmaster's commands to you, and don't cut in front of others unless you have a good reason to do so. If you're hotseating, let the dockmaster know, and ask other coxswains to let you cut in front. If they don't agree, wait your turn.

CHAPTER 14
AVOIDING THE GARBAGE AND BECOMING A TEAM LEADER

A. Leaving the Drama at the Dock
B. Keeping Your Ego in Check
C. Becoming a Team Leader
D. Sports Psychology Basics
E. Visualization

A. Leaving the Drama at the Dock

We've been party to some spectacular rowing club drama in our days. These include full-on screaming matches in public parking lots at regattas, caustic emails, mysteriously broken equipment, mutinies to oust coaches, juniors parents sabotaging each other's kids, coaches sneaking around with rowers, deliberate equipment theft at races, lightweight women throwing down over who ate a bagel with, get this, full-fat cream cheese, we've seen—and perpetrated—some bad behavior along the way.

It shouldn't be news to anybody that, much like anywhere else on the planet, rowing clubs and teams are notoriously rife with drama, cliques, and all around bad behavior. It doesn't matter if you're a 13-year old junior or a 75-year old senior masters rower. Maybe it's the Type-A personalities who are attracted to getting up three hours before normal people and punishing their bodies to the point where they occasionally vomit. Maybe it's due to the inherent juxtaposition of anything that dares to call itself 'the ultimate team sport' and then ranks its individual members so visibly. Erg scores are posted. Seat races happen, and everybody knows the identity of the ninth rower who didn't get boated.

Not only is there an outward ranking of every boat and team, but every boathouse also has a clear pecking order—the massive master's women's team who raises the most money to buy equipment that only fits them, or the heavyweight men who win all the races and have egos to match. Combine that with the fact that you're spending large amounts of time together, possibly starving yourself, and in the case of prep school or college rowers, often living together. Coxswains are definitely not immune. Gain a few pounds, hit one little bridge, or accidentally insult the alpha-male stroke, and suddenly you're demoted down to the third varsity boat.

So how does a coxswain avoid the fray?

Here is what we've learned, often by our own, often-repeated mistakes, over the years:

Shut your mouth. It goes without saying that you should not talk trash about anyone, coxswain, coach, rower, junior parent, athletic department administrator, or anybody else. Coxswains are notorious loud mouths and often on live mic or video, so turn that volume down when it comes to talking trash about other people. Better yet, zip it up. More than anything else, never complain about your coach's judgment or decisions to your rowers. We wish someone had reminded us of that early in our careers and slapped us a few times when we did it anyway.

Shut your Mouth Again. Don't be a mean girl (or guy). Don't repeat gossip. If someone tells you something, do not pass it along. Become the person who everyone trusts with secrets. Don't talk behind anyone's back. Don't backstab. Don't tolerate other people who do. As coxswain, you can set the example for your boat, and even if they're a bunch of lying, gossiping, backstabbing [insert your favorite non-flattering word here], make them better people by example.

Avoid the Relationship Drama. Yes, that means don't date, hook up with, or become otherwise romantically involved with anyone on your team, your coach, and especially not someone in your boat. Keep your nose out of other people's romantic lives when they do choose to make that mistake. You will probably do it anyway, but don't say we didn't warn you.

Never Put It In Writing. Do not send a nasty or potentially easy-to-be-misconstrued text, email, or message. Ever. If you don't put it in writing, it's your word against theirs. Come to think about it, this is good advice for life. Wow, we wish we could stop making this mistake over and over again.

Keep it in perspective. If all you're doing is eating, sleeping, breathing, and talking about rowing, let us be the first to tell you—stop being so boring. Even if you are spending what feels like every waking moment on rowing, you have got to get something else in your life. Hang out with your other friends, and do not mention rowing at all. It's only rowing, after all, which is like watching paint dry for normal people.

B. Keeping Your Ego in Check

Being a cox can be an ego trip. You've already got a few strikes against you. Strike one—give us another example of a situation where a 14-year old (or a 70-year old for that matter) gets a regular audience of eight of their peers who have to listen to them and do what they say for several hours straight, daily, all the while commanding tens of thousands of dollars of expensive equipment. Strike two—even worse, the sort of person who is attracted to coxing and excels at it is probably someone with a pretty healthy sense of self-confidence. Strike three—if you're short, particularly a short guy, you're already working with an, ahem, certain complex. So what do you do about it?

Know your ability level. If you have been coxing for less than a year, let us be the ones to clue you in—you don't know anything! If you have been coxing less than five years, well, maybe, but you are probably still obnoxious acting like an expert on all things rowing. Tone it down.

Find a sounding board. Find one friend, and one only, on the team who can give you a proverbial slap upside the head if you start getting out of hand. Ask for it, and be prepared for an honest answer.

Keep your mouth shut. If you're talking over or publically disagreeing with the coach, stop it. Even if you have been coxing for fifty years, and they have been coaching for a month, just stop it.

Be humble and keep a learner's mind at every practice. Hard for coxswains, but assume you can learn something new every day. You don't know it all, no matter how long you have been doing it. We sure don't.

C. Becoming a Team Leader

One of the most frequent questions we hear from coxswains is about how they can earn the respect of their rowers. Everybody wants respect, and everybody wants to be a team leader. The unfortunate reality is that not every coxswain will be respected or become a team leader. Getting there takes a lot of time and effort. If you're gunning for it, here are a few suggestions:

Toughen up. Again, as the saying goes, you don't get respect; you have to earn it. You are going to get beaten up and scapegoated a lot as a coxswain. Sometimes deservingly, sometimes not. Coxswains who get respect are the ones who are tough, resilient, and brush it off, vowing to do better next time, not the ones who complain, burst into tears, or freak out.

Set expectations and follow through. The best way to earn respect as a cox is by not letting rowers walk all over you. As a coxswain, you have the opportunity to enforce the rules every single day. Let your crew know what you expect and what the consequences will be if they do not meet expectations. Get your coach's backing on everything. If rowers do not follow your rules—e.g. they talk in the boat or while you are moving boats or second-guess your decision-making—you must consistently (and fairly) enforce a penalty for the entire boat. Making your rowers do extra jumpies or run the hill by the boathouse after practice will remind them that you are in charge. You should do the punishment with them. For high school or college rowers this is sometimes difficult because you are close friends with your rowers, but this is the best way to enforce your authority. If you open the door to letting rowers bully you or walk all over you, it will only escalate, and it is a very hard door to close once it is open.

Thirst for knowledge. The more you can demonstrate to your coaches and rowers that you're really interested in learning about rowing and working hard to improve your coxing, the more they will respect you. Nobody expects you to know it all when you start, but they will respect coxswains who try really hard to become students of the sport and are steadily improving.

Become your coach's favorite cox. It's really easy to be the favorite. Always do exactly what the coach says. Talk the coach up (honestly and sincerely, not in a sucking up sort of way). Be in the right place at the right time during practice with the workout in mind, and be able to translate what the coach is saying to the rowers. Don't hit things. Take care of the equipment like it is your own, and make others do the same. Be trustworthy. Become someone the rowers respect and look up to. Be warned, however. Coaches come and go. If you are aligned with the coach and the rowers rebel, you are part of the establishment.

Be fair. Treat all of the rowers on the team the same. Even if they are your friends. Even if they are the fastest on the team. Even if they are the slowest on the team. Never compare your rowers to one another or criticize anyone's technique off the water to other rowers.

Get it together. Rowers will respect the cox who is on time, has it together, knows the workout, and wrangles the rowers in a nice but authoritative way. It's the cox who has the wrench in the boat and spare athletic tape. At races it is the cox who knows all the lanes of the other crews at the race and exact start times, has the bow marker in his or her pocket, and gets the crew to the restroom, warmed up, and launched on time. Scatterbrains and flakes will not do well as coxswains, so if you have these tendencies, you'll have to do your best to hide them or compensate in other ways.

Create good buzz. Talk up your rowers, your coach, your team, and your program at every chance. Others will follow. If you say good things often enough, people will start believing them. That is good advice for life. You can thank us later. The following is a real example of good word of mouth. When a certain coxswain (whom may or may not be an author of this book) joined a masters women's team at a brand new club, she had never seen so much in-fighting, volatility, and lack of camaraderie. Although these women were in their 50s and 60s, they could have given middle school mean girls a run for their money. The team had been through four coaches in less than two years, one of which was ousted in a very public way. Members openly trash-talked one another. The entire club considered them the 'problem' team. Instead of living up to the reputation, we started talking up the team at every club board meeting and at every casual encounter at the boathouse about how great they were as people and how much fun the group was having. Things began to stabilize. Some of the bad eggs were killed with kindness, and the rest of the team began living up to their new positive reputation. Pretty soon everyone on the team was talking the team up. Eventually the rest of the club came to see them as a productive group who had fun. Moreover, they WERE having fun and behaving like a weird happy family.

Work hard, have fun. As a coxswain you've got a lot of power to influence the culture of your boat, your team, or your club. Think about ways to make things more fun. 10,000m erg pieces are miserable, slightly less so if you're wearing a crazy outfit or listening to 80s hair metal or Celine Dion. The challenge is to do things that are fun, but do not interfere with your coach's plans, the workout, or overall flow of practice. Something as lame as getting matching socks in obnoxious colors can brighten the mood on erg test day or a 5am practice when its 40 degrees and raining. Who doesn't love 16 lightweight men in skimpy florescent unis or singing a boat theme song on the van ride to the boathouse? You are the cox, so you can come up with this stuff, and you may be surprised at how quickly your rowers will follow. That's the kind of leadership that actually matters in the long run.

D. Sports Psychology Basics

Chances are you have probably heard people mention sports psychology. It's the concept of training your brain, not just your body, to perform at a higher level in sport. While it is generally associated with world-class athletes, it can work for everyone—even the slowest, most out-of-shape and un-athletic among your group. Being a coxswain lends itself naturally to encouraging this kind of thing, and if you want to become a team leader and just generally want to set a great tone for your club or your team, this is one sure-fire approach. Keep in mind that you might be taking a big leap in suggesting it if it is not already part of the culture at your boathouse, so take it slow, and expect resistance. The best way to silence the critics is by showing that it works, gradually, and over time. If you have the natural attributes that make a good coxswain, we know you will be able to sell this to your rowers. Remind everyone, at the very least, that it cannot hurt!

Here are a few basics:

Emphasize the positive. We've said this throughout this book, and we really mean it. As a coxswain you have a big impact on making people feel good about what they are doing, excited to be a part of the team, and ready to achieve high expectations.

Set big goals as a boat. With the assistance of your coach, get everyone to dream big, and make the commitment to put in the effort that it will take to reach those goals. Write them down and put them up where everyone can see them.

Visualize it. Create images of success for your rowers (and you!) to visualize off the water. Everyone on the team should regularly visualize the crew rowing at perfect pace, with great swing, crossing the line first at big regattas. See more on this below.

Emphasize the team component. Rowing requires individual effort to reach team goals. All for one and one for all. As a coxswain, one of your jobs is to build a support network where the best rowers are encouraging the slowest rowers to bring up the level for the collective team.

Talk and walk like winners. Build the winning culture and the winning attitude of your boat and your team. As a coxswain, you should be talking them up and then making sure they meet your high expectations. Despite what we say about controlling your own ego, having a little bit (or a lot) of boat swagger is to be encouraged.

Accept your human emotions. Encourage rowers to anticipate emotions like anxiety, nerves, and lack of focus, and plan for how they will calm down when those emotions arise. Use breathing strategies, trigger words, and visualization to calm rowers down and help rowers manage their nervousness and anxieties.

Create concentration triggers. Every rower loses focus at some point during practices and sometimes even during races. As a coxswain, it is your job to get it back. One of the best ways to do this is to plan for it! Agree as a boat on a phrase that will be used to get the focus and concentration back. It is fine to use "focus" or "concentration," but we like to use non-rowing related words with a clear image attached that everyone can picture, and that picture will help bring them back to good rowing. For example, let's say your trigger phrase is 'three green penguins.' First, have your rowers conjure up an image of what three green penguins look like, and then immediately conjure up a picture of themselves and the crew rowing well together. Have rowers mentally practice rowing a bad row, then hearing the trigger phrase, and then correcting the row by lengthening, slowing the slide, swinging together, etc… Hopefully then when you call the phrase in an actual practice or in a race, they will already know how to respond appropriately.

E. Visualization

Another way to really shine as a coxswain is to perfect the art of leading visualization exercises for your crews. One of the best-kept secret of sports is positive visualization. Most athletes who succeed at an elite level, particularly in endurance sports, employ various forms of mental conditioning in addition to the physical training. The good news is that it can help even the lowest level crews improve.

Earlier on in this book we mentioned how we were not huge fans of motivational quotes or generally sappy inspiration for our rowers. Likewise, we admit that we were skeptical when we first heard about visualization, passing it off as a bunch of New Age nonsense. Then we tried it. One of your authors' college coaches recommended purchasing a fantastic book called, <u>Preparation for Success: A Rower's Guide to Mental Training</u> by Sandra S. Dupcak. It is out of print, and unfortunately our last copy walked off with a former rower, but if you can find the author online and get your hands on a copy, we highly recommend it. We cannot recommend it enough. This book completely changed our opinion of visualization and on some level made us much better coxswains.

Again, when it comes to some of the more outside-of-the-box stuff like visualization, you might be fighting an uphill battle with your rowers, and maybe even with your coach, when you broach the idea. It sounds pretty wacky to the uninitiated, and we definitely recommend getting really good at it yourself before you float the idea to others. Then, when you do become proficient at it, offer up an initial session for your rowers to try it out. Done right, you will convert them. If they do not respond, practice more yourself until you are sure you can change some minds.

Here are the basics:

Practice practices. Especially when you are first starting out with visualization, before you go to sleep the night before, picture yourself coxing part of a great practice. Picture yourself taking the boat out of the boathouse and putting it in the water. Picture leaving the dock and running a perfect warm up. Picture doing a short piece, including the commands you will use, and how the rowers will respond. Picture yourself steering a perfect course and working well with the other coxswains on the team. Start small, just a few minutes, before you go to sleep at night until you get your comfort level up.

Practice racing in your head as much as you can. When you have practices down, you can then move up to visualizing coxing the perfect race in your head under all sorts of crazy situations. We like to get ourselves in a mostly dark room with a stopwatch and cox races in real time with our eyes closed for the most part. Or focus on the stopwatch for key parts of the race. It seems crazy the first few times you do it, but we promise that if you do it regularly, you will be completely hooked. In order to make it interesting, picture different scenarios—passing other crews, being in the lead, coming up from the back, responding to someone catching a crab, etc… By the time you get to races, you will be prepared to execute.

Do group visualization sessions. After you perfect coxing imaginary races in your head, it is time to make it a group effort with your crew. During racing season, we like to do it once before every race, especially the night before, but if you really want your rowers to get good at it, you need to start during the off-season while you are in winter training. Again, get into a dark room, have everyone close their eyes, and picture themselves rowing in the Grand Final of the championships at the end of the season—you cox the race (out loud), IN REAL TIME, and they picture themselves rowing. Your coach can join you after these become routine. Again, it will seem crazy and incredibly intimidating at first. Get over yourself because when you learn to do it right, the rowers practically have a religious experience. While we mostly did this in college, we have done it for our crews over the years with great response. Done well, the rowers absolutely think that you walk on water. After you've done a few of these with your rowers, they can start doing their own visualization themselves on their own time.

CHAPTER 15

WHAT COXSWAINS WISH THEY COULD SAY TO COACHES

A. The Short and Snarky Coxing Manifesto
B. Notes to Coaches on Coaching Coxswains

A. The Short and Snarky Coxing Manifesto

We have been meaning to write a coxing manifesto for years. This is for our rowers and coaches, past, present, and future:

First, coxing well is much harder than it looks. Rowing is simple. You just pull the same stroke over and over again. Rowing might be pain, but it is still simple. We, on the other hand, might 'just be sitting there' but are in charge of a thousand things that you will never see. We are watching where we are going with eight people blocking our view, driving an unruly and unresponsive craft, calling drills, remembering workouts, correcting technique, looking at the Cox-Box, trying to record our calls, dealing with ornery rowers, and it is probably dark half the time we do it. Also, has anyone ever mentioned to you that it is ridiculously hard to see when you're wedged in a hole six inches below eight hulking individuals or even twelve-year-old lightweight girls? As is so often analogized, it is like driving a car with eight people standing on the hood. Also, a word on rowing shells—even the most expensive, brand-spanking new boat is not a high-performance Ferrari. These things steer like driving a team of sled dogs, and they are as long as a bus. Give us a little time to figure it out.

For our coaches, keep in mind that we are basically doing the same kind of job you do but steering with eight people blocking our view and watching rowing at an unfavorable angle. Steering a launch and viewing from the side doesn't even come close. Also, coaches, can we just request something small? Please learn our names. On the first day. That should be easy given that there are not that many of us. Yelling 'coxswain' at us all the time is like giving us the middle finger. Plus, we are never sure which coxswain you are talking to.

That pales in comparison to our biggest gripe with coaches. It is saying things like, "Get your point," or "Watch your course'. Those are completely unhelpful, frustrating, and pointless. Saying "Steer straight" is just a bold-faced lie. Anyone who has ever been to a lake or a river, or for that matter looked at a map of any body of water on the planet, can tell that there is nothing straight about watercourses. When you say things like, 'Steer straight' or 'Find your point,' what you probably actually mean is to hold a line off the side of the lake or river or follow the traffic pattern. If you want to help us, you can instead say things like, "Keep the V1 and V2 crews 20 feet apart," or "I'm bringing up the launch on your starboard side; please move over to port," or "Make sure you're exactly ten feet off the riverbank," or if we're close to a big landmark, you can tell us to actually find a specific point, such as saying, "Aim for the right side of the second arch of the Congress Avenue bridge". Those things make sense to us. We can tell you from real world experience that ANY coxswain who needs to be told to "Find your point" ad nauseam is in no way experienced enough to be using a point to steer. Period. Teaching coxswains to follow a line instead of following a point in the early days makes far more sense.

Oh, and rowers, here are a few things for you. Keep your trap shut in the boat. When you critique someone else's technique or point out the shortcomings of others, it only makes you look bad. Not to mention pointing out the obvious. We probably already know six seat rushes; you probably do not need to point it out for the fifteenth time. We are working on it while we make sure the crew doesn't crash into the container ship, get broadsided by wake from a powerboat, or ram the coaching launch. Also, please, please stop ganging up on us. There are eight of you and only one of us. Keep those odds in mind. If you have a problem with us, come talk to us individually, after practice, in a discreet manner. Not in the boat and not in a large group unless you want us to quit and never come back. Then you will have to find a new coxswain, who will be even worse than you think we are.

We will get off our soapboxes now. Drop mic.

B. Notes to Coaches on Coaching Coxswains

We know you were a rower growing up, and you don't really know what to say to a coxswain. Perhaps out of uncertainty about coxing, or probably because it takes extra time 'away from' practice, you probably mostly talk to the coxswains when they are in the wrong place, saying the wrong thing, or not following your instructions. This is a big mistake. A little time and effort spent growing your coxswain squad will make your team significantly better in the long run. You can make your coxswains better with a few simple steps:

Don't recruit flakes. Remember that while most of coxing can be learned, you should only take on people who have the right temperament for coxing. We would take a fat coxswain with the right attitude and personality traits over a tiny one with the personality of a wet dishrag. Keep that in perspective. You should be looking for smart, responsible, confident decision-makers, especially people who are hard-working, positive, funny, and interesting. Everything else can, and should, be taught. It is really hard, on the other hand, to teach someone to think on their feet or have a good work ethic, especially a teenager. If someone is not cut out for coxing based on personality or temperament, let him or her know nicely and immediately. Do not punish them by letting them hang around or bully them into quitting. You might think that you are testing for tenacity, or avoiding confrontation, but you are only making people feel bad about themselves. Just be honest and upfront, and do not let them stay on the team if they have little chance for success.

Ride alongs. Require all new coxswains to ride in the launch at least twice before they cox their first practice. Give all new coxswains a map of the place where you row to look at while they are in the launch. Let them know that they will be quizzed about all of the information presented and that they are expected to write everything down. During that ride along, point out all of the major landmarks on the waterway, and talk about steering (steering a line, NOT steering a point, as we talk more about in Chapter 5). Point out where you typically start your practices, what obstacles are common on the place where you row, typical hazards like powerboat traffic, shipping traffic, or tides, and any other things they should be watching for. Talk about the traffic pattern. Frequently point out where you are on the map and quiz them. Stop in the middle of the lake at different points, and ask questions to verify that they understand what you are telling them. (They will never admit they have no idea what you are talking about, so you need to check to see if they understand.) Ask them what they should head towards as a point or how they would steer a line from where your launch is located. Ask them if they are in the right spot according to traffic pattern. Ask them where they would go if they were being overtaken by a faster crew or if they were overtaking a slower one. Ask them collectively how they would steer multiple boats at this point in the lake. Require them to bring a notebook, and encourage them to take notes and draw pictures. Give them enough time to write down things you say. All experienced coxswains should also be required to do a ride-along each season as a brush up. Quiz them, too. You would be shocked at how much they still don't know and are afraid to ask at this point. You may think that this is a waste of time, but it will save you countless hours over the course of a season if your coxswains are properly oriented. Then take them out again, and make sure they really get it! Those who fail to prove they understand should be given individual tutorials.

Boathouse tours. Require all new coxswains to get a tour of the boathouse and facilities from one of the coaches. Require them to bring a notebook, and tell them they will be expected to write down information and will be quizzed later. Show them how boats, oars, and Cox-Boxes are stored, and walk them through the proper procedures for taking equipment out of the boathouse and bringing it back in. Show them common obstacles that they will need to maneuver boats around, and discuss any quirks of moving boats in and out of the house. In addition to learning how things work, really have them look at the equipment. Tell them how much each piece of equipment costs and how your program is funded. Share the budget, repair times, and common breakage issues. Stress the importance of taking care of the equipment and not hitting things because of the high cost of equipment and loss of time associated. People are much more motivated not to crash an eight when they know it costs as much as a car.

Find an expert. Have your experienced coxswains spend an entire practice (two or so hours) talking about steering with your new coxswains before they cox a single practice. This should be done at the boathouse, playing with the steering apparatus on an actual boat, not in a classroom. You should not attend this session. Have the rowers erg or do something else while this is going on. They will talk about you and how hard the job is, and it is important that they get the opportunity to do so. Plus, your experienced coxswains know how to steer way better than you do, even if you think they are terrible. It encourages coxswain bonding and positions the experienced coxswains as a resource for the new coxswains.

Define expectations. Think hard about what you expect of your coxswains, both novice and experienced, and let them know what those expectations are. Use our list as a guide. Evaluate them on each standard periodically with routine check-ins, and require them to self-evaluate. Again, this might seem like a lot of time and effort, but it will save you countless hours over the course of a season and contribute to making your crews faster. The Coxswain Evaluation Form at the back of this book is a good start.

Take time for your coxswains at the beginning of every practice. You should make time, at least two minutes at the beginning of every practice, for a quick coxswain briefing on land before anyone gets hands on boats. During this time you should give your coxswains the lineups, the workout, the drills, and focus of the practice. Let them know logistically what you envision. Give them time to write things down, and make it an expectation that they have a mini-notebook to write things down at every practice. This seems like a lot of work, but will save you countless time on the water, encourages your coxswains to work together, and helps establish your coxswains in a position of authority for the rowers. Little things like this can go a LONG way in helping your coxswains do their jobs.

Make self-analysis a regular thing. Make it an expectation that all coxswains record practices at least once a week and keep a notebook. Get in the habit of making time in practices for your coxswains to set up recording or video equipment between pieces. It only takes a second, and will pay itself back in time. For juniors, require them to show you their notebooks periodically. We recommend that they follow Chapter 7, but ultimately it does not really matter what they write. It is the act of chronicling their progress that is important.

Lines versus points. Do yourself a huge favor and teach your new coxswains, or anyone who has been coxing for less than a year, how to cox using a line rather than the concept of a point. If we had a dollar for every coach that said, "Just line up an object on the horizon over the left shoulder of your stroke and go towards it," we could wallpaper the Weeks Footbridge and have money left to burn. Even if this were easy, if your coxswains did this, they would probably not be headed where you want them to go. Read our section on holding a line versus holding a point, and don't even mention using a point to steer until a cox has at least a few months of coxing under his or her belt. Once they get to that point, illustrating the differences between holding a line and steering a point using real world maps from your home water way will be incredibly helpful to all of your coxswains.

Be patient. Steering takes a long time to learn. Do you really need to start the drill at the exact point in the lake you intended? Stop yelling, "COXSWAIN, GET YOUR POINT!" under the guise of getting your coxswains into good steering habits. Sure there is something to that, but on many bodies of water there is not really much else around to hit. (For those of us on narrow, urban, heavily traveled waters, yes, it is a great idea to instill a healthy sense of fear in crossing out of the traffic pattern!) Unless there is a major safety issue or it significantly slows the practice down, have a little flexibility and let them figure things out.

Foster independence from day one. As a coach, it is incredibly hard to give your coxswains enough latitude and control to work things out on their own. However, if you do, it will pay itself back in spades. We recommend setting expectations and then letting your coxswains run the warm up independently from the beginning and get themselves lined up and ready to start the practice. Make sure they know the warm up and can do it, but put the expectation on them that the warm up is their time to run that part of the practice, and it is the responsibility of all coxswains on the team to collectively get themselves pointed and organized. This will demonstrate to the rowers that YOU trust the coxswains and will help the rowers learn to trust the coxswains as well. It will also force coxswains on a team to work together and communicate with one another.

Reward the good. Give your coxswains positive feedback when they do things right. Something as simple as "You stopped in exactly the right place" or "You are steering a nice course today—this is where I want you for every warm up" is just what they need to hear. If you are constantly critical of them and only talk about the negatives, they will never know when they are doing the right things. It will also make the rowers think that their coxswains are terrible. Or they will quit. Then you will have to find new coxswains, who will be even worse at steering.

CHAPTER 16

COXING STRAIGHT TALK: STUFF NOBODY ELSE WILL TELL YOU

A. How to Earn the Top Spot at 1V Coxswain
B. How to Get Into a (Better) College by Coxing (Maybe)
C. How to Make Yourself More Interesting, Awesome and Entertain an Audience
D. How to Snag Additional Coxing Opportunities—Camps, Clinics, Races
E. How to Cox Masters When You're Much Younger
F. How to Navigate the Politics of a Masters Rowing Club
G. How to Deal When Your Boat Absolutely Sucks
H. How to Deal with Mean Girl Drama of the Coxing Variety
I. How to Keep Healthy
J. How to Get Your Coach to Like You Better
K. How to Deal with the Weight Issue
L. How to Deal with a Disorganized Coach or Flaky Rowers
M. Damage Control in the Wake of Totally Blowing It
N. How to Cox for Rowers of the Opposite Sex
O. When to Hang Up Your Cox-Box Mic for Good

When we told you at the beginning this book was not going to be like other rowing books we meant it. This chapter is the 'straight talk' part of the book. The sections in this book come straight from our rowing clinics and contain the unvarnished truth—at least our experiences with all of these.

A. How to Earn the Top Spot at 1V Coxswain

One of your authors managed to snag and hang on to the top 1V spot throughout many consecutive college seasons. Some people might say that there was not a whole lot of competition and that the other coxswains on the team were flakes, drama-starters, or anorexic head-cases. Or that all the good coxswains had graduated by that point. We disagree. (Well, in part anyway.) Here is how to do it:

Be at exactly the right weight. Whatever it is for your category, be right at it all the time. Make it a non-issue for your crew and your coach. Internally you can sweat it all you want, diet, and stress about it, but don't tell a soul. As far as they know, you were 110 pounds when you were born, and you'll be 110 pounds the day you die, without any work or effort on your part.

Gain the confidence of your crew by total competence. Again, stress like crazy to soak up as much as you can about fixing technique and rowing in general, but play it off nonchalantly like it just comes naturally to you. Never open up about your own coxing insecurities, not with the other coxswains, your rowers, or your coaches. In other words, project confidence but not arrogance.

Put yourself in the coach's shoes. Spend a lot of time thinking about things from the coach's point of view and perfecting the art of anticipating what the coach wants. Then do that.

Be coachable. Listen to what limited direction your coach is giving you, and really work hard to anticipate the other things he or she is seeing. If your rowers give you feedback, take it to heart. Make the changes.

Put in the face time. Beyond just attending practices, be around for meetings, volunteer for repair projects around the club, stop by the coach's office during office hours, just generally get your face in front of the coach. Don't do it in an annoying or obnoxious way, but as the expression goes, 80% of success is just showing up. Again, be mindful of your coach's time.

Show integrity. This means no lying, no cheating, and no cutting corners. If you say you will do something, do it, and do it better than people expect.

Never let them see you sweat. Be calm at all times. Don't second-guess yourself. Don't apologize or take blame unnecessarily. Don't paint yourself as the victim. Project your image as a confident, competent cox.

Be positive. Say only positive things about the coach and your rowers. Enough said.

Have fun with your crew. Think about ways to have fun in the boat, ways to entertain them, and how your own style can benefit the crew. If the crew and the coach have to choose between two equally qualified coxswains, they're going to pick the one who entertains them and has fun every single time.

Become close friends with the best rowers on the team. Really. It works especially well if at the start of your first year you befriend the best rowers in your class/year in school and those one year ahead. As you move through the ranks, you will move into the varsity boats together. If your best friends are the best rowers on the team, they are probably going to want you as their coxswain. Plus you will have a good time rowing with your friends. This one works better than just about anything because it is subtle—your coach sees you coming to his office together, coming to practice together, having lunch together, sharing inside jokes off the water—it will put it in the coach's mind that you belong with those rowers.

Keep your distance from other coxswains on the team. Seriously. Don't become close friends with them because it is much harder to compete with your friends. Don't talk about them behind their backs, and never project any insecurities about your position in the coxswain pecking order. Keep it a business-like relationship where you communicate, but you're not close to one another. For those coxswains who haven't had a real job yet, this is great practice for your future workplace.

Don't stir up trouble. Leave all of the drama, baggage, and ego at the dock. Don't bring drama upon yourself, and do not perpetuate the drama of other people. Hold yourself to the highest possible standards, refusing to talk about other people on the team behind their backs, spread gossip, or bash the rowing technique of other people. If you live by the rule that you should never say anything about anyone that you wouldn't say to their face, then you should be good. Never get romantically involved with anyone on the team.

Never put it in writing. We've sent many a misdirected or misinterpreted missive in our day. Then there was that one teensy all-club email sent in pure, unadulterated fury. If you've got a bone to pick with someone or take issue with something, say it in person. That way it's your word against theirs, and they are far less likely to misinterpret what you say in person. Text, email, social media, or voicemail is a terrible idea. Trust us on this one; we have learned this lesson the hard way.

Be awesome. Here is something that should be obvious, but nobody will ever come straight out and say to you. Being the top coxswain at your club or on your team is, at least in large part, a popularity contest. If two coxswains are equally qualified—have the same steering, the same weight, the same commands—the coach (and the rowers) will always want the one they like better. If you're well liked, sometimes you can get the top boat even if you're far less qualified than someone else. You might do this by being exceptionally charming, entertaining, sympathetic, or buying extravagant gifts. This, however, isn't a book about how to be well liked. We're not the ones to ask. (Just ask some of our former coaches and rowers). Consider it in your game plan. Relationships make the world go around, and the sooner you realize that, the better your life will turn out.

B. How to Get Into a (Better) College by Coxing (Maybe)

We hate to break it to you, but you're probably not going to get into an Ivy League university just by being a good prep school coxswain. Even at bigger state universities with large rowing programs, very few, if any, admissions offices hold slots open for coxswains, but your coxing experience might help you get into a better school. Talk to your high school coach early on about the college recruiting process and registration with the NCAA. The recruiting process for coxswains is different from rowers, and even if you are recruited, you are not guaranteed a spot. There are also a number of companies that advise high school rowers and coxswains navigating the college admissions process. We are not involved with any of these, so we can say objectively that, like a lot of other things associated with college admissions—SAT prep courses, paid college counseling services, and the like—if your parents can afford it, it certainly cannot hurt, and will probably help, although an enterprising young person can certainly do it all independently.

The biggest thing you'll need in the recruiting process is phenomenal, well-edited coxing recordings. You should only send your very best, and most high school coaches will be willing to help you select really good segments to send off to college programs. See Chapter 7 for more information on recording your practices and races. Top finishes at big regattas are a sure-fire way to get potential college programs to notice you, but we'll also say that even if your crew doesn't win a lot of gold medals, you can polish your coxing 'resume' with camps, clinics, and coxing for local open or masters competitive teams in the summers, in addition to your normal high school or club team.

C. How to Make Yourself More Interesting, Awesome and Entertain an Audience

It's often said that being a coxswain is like having your own radio show. Sometimes people are listening, but most of the time it's on in the background. The question is whether your show is going to be like local talk radio that everyone tunes out or something a bit more interesting. If you're rowing morning practices, think about what is on the radio at that time. If you're going to have your own radio show, it is critical that you understand your audience.

It is almost certain that most, although not all, senior masters rowers do not appreciate fart jokes, prank phone calls, and news about celebrity nip-slips at 5am or any other time of the day. Many high school and college rowers do not either. However, that doesn't mean that they want to be bored either. Here are a few ways to spice up practices.

Interesting stories. Reserve these for long pieces, especially long erg pieces. The 10k days, or at least the 20-minute pieces. Think about these stories beforehand, and perfect the art of storytelling. If you're going to do it, really make it count, and make it a good story, otherwise you're just talking for no reason. This is not the time to vent your stress about your upcoming organic chemistry exam; this is the time to share self-deprecating stories, good uplifting stories, or funny stories. Save the downers, and if you're going the self-deprecating route, definitely make sure it has nothing to do with your overall competence or things that impact your coxing ability (like mishaps while driving a car)! Whatever you do, don't let this interfere with the flow of practice, but instead contribute to it.

Motivational quotes. Yeah, we really hate these, but some crews like them. Just don't go overboard, or you'll turn into the kind of person everybody secretly laughs at.

Jokes. Really, everybody should be able to tell a good joke even if it is a just a knock-knock joke. Even if it's a bad joke, bad pun, whatever, it can break the drudgery of a long practice or get the boat back to listening to you during a bad practice.

Theme days. This can be a rowing technique theme or another kind of theme. Yes, we once convinced 35 senior masters (age 60+) rowers to don metallic 80s prom dresses for rowing practice. Don't even ask. Check with your coach first, and don't overdo it—save the theme days for special occasions.

I like-itis. Tell your crew what you like about what they're doing. Be specific. "I like Lauren's quick hands out of bow because it helps us set the boat on the lower ratings pieces." Or try, "I like it when William wears his pink spandex long-sleeve because I can see his shoulder angle even in the dark." Compliment your crew, and they'll like you better. Trust us, but use this sparingly, or you become a brown-noser or captain obvious.

The real world around you. One of your authors is guilty of completely abusing this, but who doesn't want to know if there is a moose swimming across the river or an eagle grabbing a fish right next to the boat? Who doesn't want to see the hippies treating your private stretch of river as a skinny-dipping spot or the bikini shoot underway on a nearby dock? We believe it is completely worth mentioning the massive police chase for an escaped fugitive underway along the levee next to the river or the fact that the reindeer farm across the road clearly has a hole in its fence because there are reindeer everywhere. (Yes, all of these things have really happened during rowing practices, and you had better believe we pointed them out to our crews!) We think that if you're going to get up at the crack of dawn, it is worth reminding your crew to turn around for a five second glance of the amazing sunrise behind them, so long as its between pieces. If you can't enjoy the place you're rowing, you officially have no soul and should instead erg in a windowless basement.

Countdowns. You'd be shocked at how much you can find out about your rowers with interesting countdowns. Every crew has to count down off the dock. Instead of their seat numbers, why not make it more interesting? These shouldn't be thinkers, they should be funny, quick, and take no more time than yelling a simple number. Asking your crew to count down with their favorite movie quote of all time or favorite type of sushi doesn't take any more time than counting down with their seat numbers. The big thing is not to waste time getting off the dock, or your coach will nix this in no time.

D. How to Snag Additional Coxing Opportunities—Camps, Clinics, and Races

There are spots available every year for coxswains at camps, clinics, and the bigger races. Camps and clinics allow you to work with different kinds of coaches, different kinds of rowers, and learn more about rowing technique. They may also provide some compensation, allow you to travel, meet people at other rowing clubs, and see new racing venues. These generally fall into the following categories:

For-profit companies that hold summer rowing camps for juniors. These programs are typically held at prep schools or universities, and coxswains generally have to pay to attend. Participants stay in the dorms and have several coached practices each day. Some of these companies offer coxswain-specific instruction. These camps are a great opportunity to get exposure to top junior and college coaches, meet rowers from other places, and delve deeply into rowing technique in a new environment. You might also consider signing up for a camp as a ROWER, so you can learn or improve your own technique.

University rowing programs that host a camp or two every year for juniors or college level athletes. These programs vary. Some are by invitation to certain experienced coxswains; others are open enrollment, and coxswain spots go to the first ones who sign up. Participants pay to attend and stay in the dorms while attending several coached daily practices. Generally coxswains have to pay to participate, although some programs allow coxswains to come for free or pay local coxswains to help out.

Local rowing club programs that offer more intensive camp programs during the summers for either juniors or masters or both. This depends on the club, but typically with the masters programs, coxswains are paid or participate for free or nominal fees. Generally practices are longer and more involved than a normal summer program and may include several practices a day. For the juniors programs, generally the coxswains either pay to participate or participate for free. You might also consider signing up as a ROWER to learn or improve your own technique and better be able to relate to your rowers.

For-profit companies that hold rowing camps for masters. These camps are held throughout the year, typically in the summer, as well as a few week-long programs in warmer climates in the winter. These may take place at a host club, university, or other 'summer camp' type location. Masters rowers pay to participate and attend several coached practices a day. These programs generally pay coxswains or allow coxswains to participate for free.

For-profit companies that organize race entries for masters. Many of these companies that hold masters camps also organize crews for bigger races throughout the year (Head of the Charles, US Rowing Masters Nationals, Canadian Henley, San Diego Crew Classic), where masters participants pay to participate in races. Coxswains are generally compensated for travel, expenses, and often given a stipend to cox for these crews. Similarly, club programs, 'rolodex crews,' and alumni crews who participate in these races may also be looking for coxswains from time to time and may pay for coxswain travel expenses or look for local coxswains near the rowing venues to steer for the race.

Invitation-only national team identification camps at all levels. These are typically held in the summer and are organized at a variety of levels (junior, pre-elite, U23, etc…). More information is available through national rowing governing bodies such as USRowing and Rowing Canada. In many cases, participants pay to participate, and these programs are identification camps for national teams of all levels. Getting asked to be a part of any of the invitation-only camps is based on a combination of factors—generally you have to cox for a nationally-recognized juniors/prep school or college program, have great recommendations from coaches, or have some sort of connection to the coaches running the camps. If you find yourself in this category, congratulations. Otherwise, it will be up to you to make opportunities happen, and they are few and far between.

Generally speaking, opportunities to cox for camps and races will fall into your lap, and you will be asked to cox for them based on your reputation and experience. If you are interested in coxing for camps and races, have an honest conversation with your regular coach about whether or not you're ready, and ask him or her to help identify opportunities and open doors. If you are a junior and your parents are willing to pay for it, attending a juniors rowing camp as a paying participant can be an extremely valuable experience. Getting to know the coaches who put on these camps is an essential step. If your club is hosting any of these camps, you might consider volunteering to cox for free, which may lead to other paid opportunities. (Keep in mind that all juniors who are serious about coxing in college will want to have a long conversation with their coaches related to how these opportunities could impact their college rowing careers.)

E. How to Cox Masters When You're Much Younger

Many of us will find ourselves in situations when we're coxing people older than our parents. Older than our grandparents even. Here are a few things to keep in mind when you're a younger cox coxing for older people:

Ask them what they want. Masters, especially masters women, will have a very clear idea of exactly what they want their cox to say and do. Write those things down, and do not stray from the script.

Keep it enjoyable. Remember that they have limited free time, and that rowing is their outlet from their hectic lives. Don't add to their stress levels.

Show some respect. Respect them because they're older, even if they haven't been rowing as long as you have. You may know more, but you've got to be deferential.

Do not patronize them. Your role at races, during race travel, and during practices is not the same as with your peers. Adults can take care of themselves. You do not need to remind them to go to bed early, eat healthy, or not miss the flight. Trust us, they know the time of the race, the lane of every single other team, the blade colors of the other teams, and probably even all the names of the other rowers on the other teams. They have mentally catalogued the exact pitch they want their rigger at, brought their own wrench, brought their own backup wrench, and can tell you the exact length of the race course, past year's records, and the names of all the officials. They know exactly how many minutes before their race; they will consume their specific flavor of energy bar, how many swigs of water they will need, and the location of their extra socks. They know the exact time the coxswain weigh in starts, the latitude and longitude of where the trailer is parked, and the times of each and every race, whether they are racing in them or not. Attention to detail doesn't even begin to describe it. You can only complicate things by getting involved with any of this.

Don't make age an issue. Don't call attention to them being old. ("Wow, you're doing great for a bunch of old guys." Or "Seriously, class of '97? I wasn't even born yet!").

Learn the pre-practice ritual. Be warned that masters rowers have to go to the bathroom ALL of the time. Especially old men. It is crazy how often. Give them enough time before practices and races.

F. How to Navigate the Politics of a Masters Rowing Club

One of the starkest and most surprising things about growing up is realizing that adults are just as immature and petty as kids are. Rowing clubs are not immune, and, in fact, are full of drama, backstabbing, rivalries, and factions. Here are some rules to live by:

Get the lay of the land. If you are new to a club, ask for a sit down with the club's president when you first arrive. You are ostensibly there to learn about how the club works, but your real goal should be to casually inquire about the hot heads, huge egos, who hates whom, and any political battles that are currently brewing. Keep it light, make notes, and you should buy the coffee. If the club president is not forthcoming, find others who are, but don't obsess too much about this. You will learn these things in time.

Understand the pecking order. There is a clear pecking order at any boathouse. Learn it. Avoid the jerks, and keep those at the top on your good side.

Go to the board meetings. This is the best way to find out what is really going on with the club. All of the dirty laundry will be aired at this point. Sit in the corner and say nothing.

Listen. Keep your ears open and your mouth closed whenever gossip flies around.

Volunteer for club projects. It is never a bad idea to learn how to fix basic boat breakage, swing a hammer, or pick up trash around your rowing venue, and you'll meet a cross-section of club members at these events. Building alliances across teams, between scullers and sweep rowers, and across genders and ages will go miles in the future if you ever need something in a pinch (equipment, trailer space, substitute coaching, etc…). Plus, you'll get to know people across the club, contribute to the wellbeing of the club, and build bridges among the factions.

Contribute. Be willing to share your coxing expertise for the greater good of the club. Consider volunteering to cox for your club's learn to row program, give coxing clinics to new coxswains, cox for camps, or find another way that you can contribute. Offer to write content related to coxing for your club's website. You can also help put together coxing equipment kits, help maintain the Cox-Boxes, or contribute to discussions of safety from a coxswain's point of view.

G. How to Deal When Your Boat Absolutely Sucks and Will Be DFL at Every Race

This is one of the absolutely worst situations a coxswain can be in. It generally means that either your whole team is terrible, or you are in one of the worst boats on the team. Regardless of how good you are as a coxswain, your crew has no realistic hope of doing well, in any race, no matter how weak the competition. Here is how to deal:

Accept the situation personally. Acknowledge to yourself that this is your boat, and you are going to make the most of it. Forget the ego, and banish the thoughts that you deserve better.

Believe in yourself. Your crew is terrible, but that does not mean you are a terrible coxswain. Do not let their shortcomings as rowers hurt your confidence or ability to improve as a coxswain. Continue to focus on improving your own coxing abilities.

Make room for improvement. Try to make your boat the best rowers they can be. Instead of seeing the situation as futile, look for areas of potential improvement. Any crew can get better than they currently are.

Row against yourselves. If your crew lost last week by three boat lengths of open water, try to cut it to two and a half this week. If you rowed last year's head race at the slowest time in course history, see if you can go a second faster this year.

Put in full effort. Commit to these rowers like they were on the National Team. Cox them like they are in the grand final at the big championship. Avoid phoning it in just because you can.

When in doubt, have fun. That is the whole point of coxing for a bad crew. If you are not having fun, turn the season around. It is never too late.

H. How to Deal with Mean Girl Drama of the Coxing Variety

We are adding this section because infighting is so common on rowing teams, and coxswains are often the center of the controversy. Let's face it—most coxswains are young and female, and whenever you add young women to any mix, you will have some sort of mean girl drama. Typically it happens when a coxswain is new and was put into a position of power and either oversteps or feels like her rowers don't listen to her or respect her. Because there are far more rowers than there are coxswains, the rowers can easily gang up. The other part of the problem is that while the rowers' abilities can be measured by erg pieces or seat races, coxing skills are way less tangible, making coxswains feel insecure. Coaches can also add to the pressure because they don't understand how to help coxswains improve or are constantly pointing out the mistakes that the coxswains are making. On women's high school and college teams, there is also the additional normal mean girl drama of young women on any sports team or school environment.

We are adults now, so what we are saying comes from that perspective. These things will seem like a big deal, and they are a big deal, but in the grand scheme of life, they are minor issues to overcome that will make you a better person. Suffice to say, when you are in the middle of it, nothing feels more overwhelming.

Here are the most common situations and how to deal:

No respect. You feel like your rowers don't respect you (or like you). They don't listen to you, and they might even talk smack about your coxing skills, either behind your back or to your face under the guise of "helping" you. You feel like they've ganged up against you.

They all hate you. Maybe you have a bad attitude; maybe you slept with someone's boyfriend; maybe you did something specific that they didn't like; maybe they just don't like you for no good reason.

They always compare you to other coxswains. You will never be as good as the old coxswain who graduated last year. She walked on water, and they make you feel like you are the sorry replacement.

The above three situations require a similar response. We recommend the following:

- **Be honest.** Have an honest, but very short and one-sided, conversation with them immediately. It's not really a conversation, it is just you telling them from the heart how you feel and asking them to give you a break. ("I know that I'm new to the varsity team, but everyone trying to tell me what to do when we are in the boat in the middle of pieces makes me feel disrespected. I appreciate everyone's input, but I need time to get better on my own, and I'm doing a lot off the water to work on it including reviewing my recordings, reading about rowing calls, and working on my counting. I'm asking you guys to give me a break for the next few weeks, and we can see how it goes. I'm counting on you to do your jobs and pull hard while I figure out my job of coxing.") If you are making changes in response to certain situations, let them know what those changes will be and the consequences if they do not follow the new rules. (e.g. "You guys know that we have had a lot of talking in the boat lately. It compromises my ability to do my job, and it ends today. If it happens again, coach will make sure we are all going to run 50 stadiums after practice as a crew.") Do it before practice, and finish by saying, "Now, let's get hands on and have a good row." If anyone tries to respond, repeat your command to get hands on. This will force them to think about it for two hours and keep them from talking with anyone else about it. Be glad you are not on a soccer team.

- **Take charge of your crew.** Everything you say and do both on and off the water should be confident, in charge, and in control.

- **Make friends.** Genuinely try to get to know everyone off the water. It is hard to hate someone when you are friends. Well, maybe not, but it's slightly harder.

- **Commit to getting better.** Don't give them anything to dislike about your coxing. Commit to improving in your problem areas.

- **Be cautious about getting the coach involved.** Your coach can sometimes be your strongest ally in resolving a very difficult situation without a clear path forward, but there is nothing coaches hate more than getting sucked in to mean girl drama. If your rowers love the coach, you could potentially use the coach as an ally or mediator, but this too can backfire. First of all, it might make your coach blame you for the entire thing or just generally annoy the coach. Tread lightly. If your rowers do not like the coach, you should definitely avoid getting the coach on your side in the drama. If it becomes a 'rowers against the coach' situation, you are going to come down on the wrong side no matter what.

Not getting boated. You didn't make the boat with all of your friends, and your feelings are hurt because you don't know why the coach didn't put you in that boat. Maybe you had the top boat last season, and now the coach picked a younger coxswain instead of you for that seat. The rowers want you back as a coxswain for their boat and don't like the new coxswain, or they like the new coxswain better than you, and that hurts your feelings. Here is what we recommend that you do:

- **Meet with the coach.** Ask for feedback. Find out what you need to be doing differently. Stress your commitment to improvement and the fact that you are competitive and want that top boat. Let the coach know what you are doing off the water to improve. It is fine to say that you are disappointed, but avoid comparing yourself to the coxswain who got the spot or talking trash about the abilities of other coxswains. Continue to follow up.

- **Ask your old rowers for backup.** This one is controversial, but it can work, especially if it is done immediately and unanimously following the switch. If all of the rowers in the old boat go to the coach and ask for their old coxswain back, the coach just may listen. The coach might also say things to the rowers that he or she would not say to the coxswain directly, which can clue you in as to why the switch really happened. This can also make the coach furious, so beware.

- **Get over yourself.** Perhaps it was your ego that was the problem. Perhaps you have some things to work on (don't we all!). Whatever it is, you are not perfect. It is fine to be disappointed, but let it motivate you to work harder.

- **Commit to your new boat.** Have fun with them. Make it a great time, and do such a good job that it gets back to the coach and your old rowers. Remember, this is what a coach is looking for when he or she is thinking about which coxswain is going to get the top spot.

- **Continue to be friends with your old rowers.** Make the effort even if it seems like they like the new coxswain better. Have fun off the water, and act like it does not matter. When they bring up rowing, just change the subject. If they ask, tell them how much fun you are having with your new boat. You can go cry at home later.

Infighting. The rowers in your boat are fighting, and you don't want to take sides, but you feel caught in the middle. With this type of situation, you need to do your best to stay out of it. Here is what we recommend you do:

- **Keep your mouth shut.**

- **Don't get pulled in.** When one rower complains about another, just tell him or her you are not interested in hearing about it, and change the subject or walk away. Try to be Switzerland. Easier said than done, we know.

Rank insecurity. You might feel like you are in a better boat than you deserve to be coxing, or you feel like the other coxswains (or some of the rowers) think you don't deserve to be in the boat you are in. You know they think they are better coxswains and aren't afraid to say things behind your back or even to your face.

- **Fake it 'til ya make it.** Really. The best thing you can do is act like you are super confident in your seat. Not that you deserve it, not that you are entitled to it, but that you are confident in it.

- **Work twice as hard to get better.** Never let anyone see how hard you are trying, but try as hard as you can off the water.

- **Have fun.** Your coach must see something in your abilities. The best way to win the rowers over is to have fun with them. This should be a big focus for you, in addition to making them work hard.

I. How to Keep Healthy

Coxing can wreak absolute havoc on your eyes, your back, your neck, and your voice. Even if you are 13, you need to protect yourself, so your body won't be trashed later in life. Trust us on this one.

Eyes. High-quality, polarized sunglasses are a must. See Appendix A for information on eyewear. One of your authors has permanent eye damage from a misspent youth that included lots of coxing without proper eyewear. Get one of those ridiculous looking straps that goes around your neck, so you don't lose them in the lake. If we see you with one of those cheap $8 pairs, we will drop them in the river for you. Those are probably worse than no sunglasses at all.

Voice. As far as keeping your voice healthy, it is really critical to choose your words and your tone of voice wisely. Practice speaking deeply, from the diaphragm. Never scream or speak in a really high pitched voice—coxswains who do may develop vocal nodules, which are painful, make your voice sound permanently raspy, and can require surgery to fix. We also don't like to yell off the water when trying to round up athletes. Leave that to your coach, or buy a small, lightweight megaphone. We like the small coxswain-sized ones. If your rowers make fun of you for using a megaphone, you can send them our way, and we will scare them straight. Old-fashioned remedies like hot tea with lemon and honey are great, but probably the single best thing you can do is to drink lots of water and don't abuse your vocal chords.

Back and neck. You should be sitting forward enough that your back is not being slammed into the back of the coxswain seat. Don't be afraid to buy all manner of seat pads and foam to protect your back, and by all means use the strap at the back of the coxswain seat if you have one available. In bowloaders, bring whatever you need to make yourself comfortable. Only lie down completely in a bowloader during a race. In practices with a bowloader you should be sitting up. Some coaches do boneheaded things like make their coxswains lie down in bowloaders during seat racing or practices to gage race performance or measure boat speed. This is because the coach does not realize how much of a toll it takes on their coxswains. If they ask you do this more than occasionally, feel free to show them this section.

J. How to Get Your Coach to Like You Better

Maybe we are not the ones to ask about this. We've had conflict with a lot of our coaches over the years, and we think it's probably us, not them. We have managed to make coaches consistently mad by second-guessing their decisions, especially in front of rowers. That seems to be the number one thing coaches hate, so the best thing we can tell you is that you should keep your opinions to yourself. Also watch your attitude—remember that sometimes confidence is synonymous with arrogance. Curbing a coxswain with attitude is no easy task for any coach and can lead to a multitude of problems. The other big problem is that after you have been coxing for a long time, you might know as much, or even more, than some of your coaches, or there is a battle of egos that the coxswain can never really win. The best thing we can tell you is to show respect for your coaches, regardless of their ability level, follow their instructions to the letter even when you disagree, never bad mouth them or their decisions to your rowers, and compliment them relentlessly without seeming insincere. If you figure out how to do that effectively, please let us know.

K. How to Deal with the Weight Issue

We have heard from a surprising number of high school and college coxswains who feel like their rowers are constantly hounding them to lose weight, joking about their weight, watching everything that goes in their mouth, or pointing out how tall they've gotten or how heavy they are. Conversely, the coxswains who are under weight are constantly subject to jokes and inquiries about eating disorders. This is not an easy situation. Young women especially have enough pressure from society to be thin, but coxswains, especially those who are still growing, often feel it worse. All we can say is that if anyone brings it up, you can either brush it off and change the subject or confront it directly. If it is a consistent problem, tell your rowers directly that it's a non-issue for them to worry about, and you do not appreciate it being brought up ever again. Talk to your coach about it if it is a problem. The last thing you and your coach want is for you to develop an eating disorder. Heavier coxswains can consider moving to a men's team where the weight limits are slightly higher, but if you really have a growth spurt and can't maintain good health and a coxing weight at the same time, the sad reality is that this is probably your last season of coxing. Which is OK because it means you can row now! If rowing isn't your forte, see if your coach or another team would be willing to take you on as volunteer assistant coach. This is how many coaches get started.

At the same time, we're not going to lie to you and tell you we haven't done dumb things to lose weight, including not eating for days and getting exercise obsessed. We've had teammates (coxswains and rowers both) that threw up regularly, dropped weight doing all sorts of crazy supplements, taking serious amounts of Ex-Lax, drinking gallons of 'dieter's tea,' or combined Adderall (when they didn't need it) and high amounts of caffeine. But now that we're older, what we will tell you is that we've seen enough girls break ribs from vomiting, end up in the hospital for months on end with serious eating disorders, end up with serious long-term health problems like losing teeth and serious heart problems, and just look a lot older than they really are by the time they are in their 20s and 30s. It might seem like a good idea at the time and no big deal, but the long-term toll it can take on your body is not worth it. Trust us on this one.

L. How To Deal with a Disorganized Coach or Flaky Rowers

Most rowing coaches are models of good organization, although we've known a few who have been just the opposite, or maybe its just you--some people live in a world where no one else takes life as seriously as they do. Some of the personalities that are attracted to coxing fall into this category. No matter what your coach does, he or she will not have thought about things as much as you have, have planned sufficiently, or have put in what you feel is sufficient effort. Perhaps your rowers do not take rowing very seriously—they come to practice tired, hung over, or skip altogether—or maybe they don't put in the effort you think they could if they want to do well during race season.

Keep your role in perspective. You are not anyone's mother or babysitter. If you try to take on this role, everyone will hate you.

Do the best job you can. It might be frustrating to put in lots of effort when you feel like nobody around you cares. Keep at it. Your work will pay off in the long run. There may be another team or group of rowers who can use your skills, and you want to be ready for that opportunity when the time comes.

Have an honest conversation with your coach. Perhaps there are ways you could help the situation. Keep it solution-oriented, respectful, and productive. Do not cast blame on the coach, your rowers, or anyone else.

M. Damage Control in the Wake of Totally Blowing It

Oh, we have some good stories. We've been disinvited to cox for camps, never been paid for coxing, and had huge blowups with coaches, rowers, other coxswains, parents, and other rowing people. One of us can distinctly remember the senior banquet where the coach 'forgot' to acknowledge her as one of the graduating seniors after a particularly eventful regatta travel fiasco. You name it. You might say that the chapter on developing a sparkling personality and keeping our egos in check contains lessons we have not yet learned. Even though we've learned many lessons the hard way, we anticipate more spectacular flameouts to come. In light of the fact that we have screwed up in some spectacular ways, we can share some personal experience on what to do after the unfortunate event happens.

You coxed a terrible race. Maybe you lost control of your crew (literally or figuratively); maybe you steered a terrible course; maybe you failed to follow the race plan; maybe you just plain called bad calls and failed to motivate the crew.

- **This is not the end of the world.** Really, it isn't.
- **Talk to your rowers.** Acknowledge that this wasn't your finest moment, and vow to do better. Then outline the specific things you'll be working on.
- **Talk to your coach.** Acknowledge what happened and vow to improve. Talk about all of the specific steps you are taking to improve yourself to prevent this sort of thing from happening again.
- **Move on.** Don't rehash the race over and over again, even in your head. If anyone brings it up, simply say, "It was a bad race, but it's making me work harder." Leave it at that.
- **Work hard to get better.** Work on being the best coxswain that you can be for the next few months, and show what a hard worker you can be.

You screwed up and lost your spot in the boat you were in. Maybe you got lazy; maybe you got sloppy, or maybe you made someone mad. We're talking about losing your spot due to a specific incident that was totally your fault. You are still on the team now, but in a different, and likely not as good, boat. What do you do?

- **Talk to your coach.** Acknowledge what happened and vow to never do it again. Talk about all of the specific steps you are taking to improve yourself to prevent this sort of thing from happening again. Do not assume that this was the only reason you were demoted—it may have just been the last straw. Take a more holistic approach to improvement, and demonstrate that to the coach.

- **Keep your mouth shut.** Don't complain about it with the rowers or the coxswain who got your spot. If anyone brings it up, simply say, "Sure I'm disappointed, but it's making me work harder." Leave it at that.

- **Work hard to get better.** Work on being the best coxswain that you can be for the next few months, and show what a hard worker you can be with your new boat. Work on endearing yourself to your new group of rowers.

Your personality got you into trouble. Coxswains are notoriously opinionated loudmouths. Maybe you swore up a storm at the Sunday school teacher in stroke seat. Maybe you blatantly trashed your coach's decision-making. Maybe you got into it with the coach directly. Perhaps you turned your entire boat against you by being too honest about their technique problems in a less-than-tactful way. Perhaps you sent a particularly nasty email out to the entire team questioning their work ethic. Now what?

- **Apologize.** Face to face as soon as possible.

- **Vow to never do it again.**

- **Move on.** Do not dwell on it. People will probably never forget about it, but with time it will seem like less of a big deal.

You really hit something hard and damaged equipment. We remember the junior cox who crashed a masters men's 4+ during a head race in such spectacular fashion that she ripped the entire side of the boat off upon impact with a recreational dragonboat right in front of the entire audience of spectators watching the finish. Nobody was hurt, but the damage was in the thousands of dollars. She never coxed again. What do you do when you really damage equipment?

- **Apologize.** To everyone involved, face to face and as soon as possible.

- **Offer to help with repairs.** It is never a bad idea to learn how to repair boats. If it requires off-site repair, offer to help organize a fundraising effort to pay for it. If your offer to help is turned down, move on, and do not bring it up again.

- **Vow to learn from your mistakes.** Identify why the crash happened and what you could have done differently.

- **Move on.** Do not dwell on it or start to question your competency as a coxswain.

- **Never bring it up again with rowing people.** It won't be a funny story for at least 20 years. Then it will be hysterical when you take a stroll down memory lane recounting how boats used to be made of carbon-fiber.

You got a penalty in a big race. This is not a big deal. It is unfortunate, but it is not a big deal. It happens. It has never happened to either of your authors, but we know plenty of decent coxswains who have received them. Most were for missing buoys, some for failure to yield, and one memorable one for unsportsmanlike conduct. Trust us, using four letter words around referees is like playing with fire.

- **Acknowledge it to your rowers, post race.** You can apologize for letting them down and share your own disappointment, but do not belabor it.

- **Vow to never get another one again.**
- **Don't let it shake you.** Do not bring it up every again or let it question your own confidence in your coxing abilities.

You had a panic attack while coxing. We distinctly remember rowing in bow seat of an 8+ that crashed into a very old masters sculler. He was pretty shaken up and banged up, but he was ultimately OK. The cox's reaction was not OK. She had a massive panic attack and freaked out. She completely froze and refused to cox more. She went on a rant and expressed every coxing insecurity in the book. The coach pulled her out of the coxswain's seat, and one of your authors climbed over everyone and coxed the boat back to the dock.

- **Evaluate what happened and why.** At your core, are you uncomfortable coxing? Do you have problems responding to emergencies? Did the sight of an old man bleeding out of his head set you off? Do you lack the personality to handle stress or bad situations?
- **Talk to your coach about what happened.**
- **Acknowledge what happened to your rowers, give a brief explanation, and move on.** Do not spend more than a minute on it.

You got 'fired' or 'cut' from the team, but you want to keep coxing. We know coxswains who have not been asked back or cut from teams. It might not have been any specific incident, just that they were not a good fit for the team. Most of the time they lacked the personality or temperament to handle coxing or just could not maintain the appropriate weight. If you fall into one of those categories, find something else productive to do with your time, and do not look back. If there is another reason, try to get to the bottom of it.

- **Get feedback.** Ask for real, honest feedback as to why it happened. Ask the coach to be honest and provide real reasons, not sugarcoat it.
- **Get specific suggestions.** If you have a genuine interest and think you can improve, ask for suggestions on improvement.
- **Work hard to get your seat back.** If you can put the time and effort in and demonstrate that to the coach, perhaps they will be willing to invite you back to try again the next season.

You were part of a serious accident or emergency. Rowing accidents resulting in injury and drowning are very real. This one hits really close to home for us. We had a tragedy on our lake where one of our coaches drowned. A group of junior rowers attempted to make the rescue, but unfortunately were too late. One of us was involved in another situation years ago while sculling in a 2x with a senior masters rower who started having signs of a heart attack several miles away from the boathouse. We know of other situations where boats have collided, and rowers have drowned or been seriously injured. It is a scary situation. How do you handle it if you are involved?

- **Expect everyone to deal in their own way.** Acknowledge that everyone will have different emotions about the situation.
- **Evaluate what happened and why.** Was it avoidable? What could have been done differently?
- **Talk to your coach about what happened.** Make a plan to move forward.

N. How to Cox for Rowers of the Opposite Sex

Call us old-fashioned, both of your authors are female, and we have primarily coxed for women's crews over our coxing careers. However, we have coxed enough men's crews to know that coxing for men's and women's crews are slightly different. We also know male coxswains who cox for women's crews and approach that differently than they would a men's crew. It is generally going to be one of three situations:

- You are a high school/college coxswain, and you are coxing for your peers on your high school/college's team of the opposite gender.
- You are a masters woman who is coxing for masters men or vice versa.
- You are a juniors or younger masters coxswain who is coxing for masters rowers of the opposite gender.

In the first two situations the coxswain and the rowers have a peer relationship. In the third scenario you as a coxswain are much younger and are coxing for a master's team which is comprised of rowers who are probably older than your parents or even your grandparents. If you find yourself in category three, regardless of gender, treat them as you would your grandparents—be polite, respectful, do not swear unless they tell you it is fine, and turn the Cox-Box volume all the way up!

Overall, don't spend too much time dwelling on your gender. Playing the 'I'm just a cute girl' role with the men's team or trying to exert your alpha male fantasies on a women's crew might be work for a little while, but it will quickly wear thin. Just as you would in the workplace, spending a lot of time emphasizing gender differences is not going to get you very far. You have a job to do regardless of whether you are male or female. Just do it. We've also said it before, but it is worth repeating—never get romantically involved with anyone in your boat, regardless of your gender. It is the fastest way to screw up a great season and complicate the interpersonal relationships of everyone in the boat. Just don't do it.

Then again, we are not above stereotypes. Here are a few things we have observed about coxing crews of different genders over the years:

- You can be more aggressive with your language when coxing men's crews.
- You should shut up more with men's crews and talk more with women's crews.
- Men's crews care less about what you say and more about your steering. Women's crews care about both.
- Men's crews may seem to be less Type-A than women's crews, but they are just as serious about their rowing. Most rowers are extremely Type-A.
- Men can get their feelings hurt just as easily as women, so avoid bullying or picking on certain rowers just as you would with women's crews.

If you stand up to them and command authority, they will respect you. If you fail to do this, they will walk all over you regardless of gender.

O. When to Hang Up Your Cox-Box Mic for Good

Most people age out of coxing at natural times in their lives—graduation from high school or college. Here are a few other signs that it might be the end of your coxing career (We like to think of it as the start of your coaching career!):

- You can't maintain coxing weight.
- You can't get excited about racing because of all of the headaches associated with regatta travel.
- You want a normal life that does not require waking up at 5am.
- The idea of hanging around in spandex for 18 hours to race for seven minutes has lost its appeal.
- You know more about rowing than the coaches.

APPENDIX A
BIG LIST OF COSXWAIN STUFF

This list is reflective of our own personal preferences. We aren't sponsored nor have we accepted any compensation from any of these companies to promote the products listed below. This is the just the list of brands we like and recommend. That does not mean that there aren't other brands out there that are better or just as good.

Coxing Tool Kit

Your team or club may have coxing tool kits, but if you're serious about coxing, make your own. Label everything with your name and phone number. Use colored tape to mark your wrenches. We recommend sticking all of your items in a large-mouthed clear plastic water bottle. It is waterproof, theoretically floats in the lake if you drop it in, and keeps everything from being crushed. Even better, you can stick it in the waistband of your shorts like your rowers do. Keep in mind that even if you only weigh 90 pounds, you don't have a lot of extra space in the coxswain's seat to carry around bulky equipment, clothing, or extra junk in the boat anyway. This list is all you need and nothing you don't.

- 7/16 inch wrench
- Adjustable 'spanner' wrench
- Vespoli Coxswain tool (available at www.vespoli.com) or similar. This multi-function tool removes spacers, works like a wrench, and is all-around handy in the boat. If you have one of these, you don't really need a wrench.
- Extra spacers that actually fit the boat you're rowing that day
- Ziploc bag with band-aids, white athletic tape, neosporin spray/gel
- Sunscreen
- Medical supplies as needed by your crew (e.g. inhalers, glucose, epi-pen)
- Mini-notebook and pen (We like waterproof www.riteintherain.com.)
- Water bottle as the container (We like www.nalgene.com.)

You're also going to want:
- Cox-Box
- Mobile phone with rowing apps in flexible waterproof case ideally with a strap that goes around your neck
- Stroke Coach if you don't have rowing apps on your phone

You might also consider:

- Mini-sized megaphone for corralling your crew on land (We like www.toaelectronics.com.)
- A big brown sponge, the kind used for washing cars (or boats!). This can be used to bail out the boat in the rain, particularly for races in inclement weather.
- An industrial strength whistle if you row in an area prone to fog
- A small backpack with zippers, or, less desirably, a drawstring style backpack to hold all of your gear. Fanny packs are big with the masters set.

Practice Wear

The truth is you could probably wear anything to cox in, from an evening gown to a sleeping bag, as long as it's comfortable enough to sit in in a confined space for hours on end and would not be responsible for your drowning if you fell out of the boat. Custom and tradition dictate what coxswains actually wear in the real world. For hot weather, the rule of thumb is that you should dress like your rowers. That means spandex shorts, running shorts, or cheerleading-type cotton shorts on the bottom for women, spandex or basketball type shorts for men, t-shirts and tanks on top. Avoid cutoffs, denim, overly nice clothes, or anything dressy. Jewelry is a no-go unless you're OK accidentally dropping it in the lake. For cold weather you need to wear a lot more clothing than your rowers. Yoga or fleece pants with rain pants over on the bottom, long-sleeve JL racing shirts, and a turtleshell or fleece jacket topped by a waterproof jacket are most common. Cold or rainy climates may demand a survival suit. A hat that fits tightly on your head and high quality polarized sunglasses are a must regardless of climate. Trust us, you'll be glad you did when you're 30. As far as footwear goes, in the summer it's flip-flops, sneakers/running shoes in the spring and fall, and in the winter in cold places it should be wool socks and something warm like fleece-lined boots. In California they wear Uggs all year, and the Brits favor wellies, but we won't hold that against them.

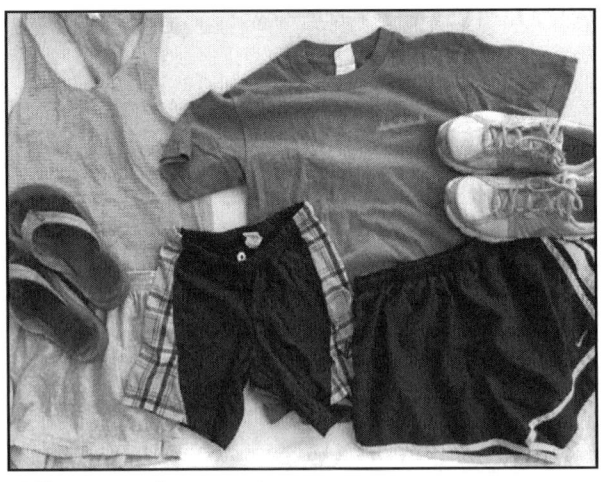

Warm weather practice wear

Warm weather race wear

Race Wear

You don't have a lot of choice when it comes to team uniforms. You'll likely be issued or asked to buy a unisuit, team 'splash' jacket, and long-sleeved racing shirt at a minimum. Sure unisuits, better known as unis, border the sexy-horrifyingly unattractive line like nothing except maybe those 'so-ugly-it's-cute' pet contests won by hairless dogs. In addition to highlighting certain anatomical features and fueling female body image issues, wearing a uni requires several additional steps when you need to use the bathroom. If you're going to be involved

Cold weather race wear

in rowing, you'll have to get over it. JL Racing is the most popular brand for unis as of late (www.jlracing.com). We love us some JL. In addition to unis, JL makes a great turtleshell for cold days, long trou, form fitting racing shirts, and other stretchy clothes necessary for rowing. Boathouse Sports (www.boathouse.com), RegattaSport (www.regattasport.com), and SewSporty (www.sewsporty.com) are other popular options for unis and other rowing gear.

Survival Suits

More and more clubs and teams in cold climates are requiring their coxswains to wear survival suits (a.k.a. Mustang suits). Even if you can't convince your club to invest in these pricey pieces, you might consider buying one yourself. They could save your life in freezing water and also do a good job of keeping you toasty warm on freezing cold days. www.mustangsurvival.com

Cold weather top layers (long sleeve tech shirt, fleece vest, splash jacket, waterproof shell)

Stadium Seats

Believe it or not, there are many kinds of microwaveable seats designed for outdoor sporting events, ice fishing, and other cold weather activities that promise to keep your rear end hot for hours. We are big fans of the brand called Lavabuns although it looks like the trademark was recently sold, and they may or may not still be manufactured. The good news is that there are several other companies that sell a similar product. You want a version that fits up on bottom and the sides of the coxswain seat without much extra bulk. We very much enjoyed this device for several spring seasons in northern New England until the fateful day when we discovered the sad fact that Lavabuns don't float (www.lavabuns.com).

Cold weather bottom layers (running tights, fleece pants, rain pants)

Polarized Sunglasses

Coxswains of a certain age will tell you about the long-term eye damage they got while wearing cheap sunglasses on the water in their teens. Some premium brands include Smith (www.smithoptics.com), Oakley (www.oakley.com), Costa del Mar (www.costadelmar.com), and Ray-Ban (www.ray-ban.com). It makes us cringe to see high school and college coxswains still wearing $6 sunglasses. If you're a parent of a junior coxswain, the single best thing you can buy for your kid is good quality polarized sunglasses. It's almost certain that a few pairs will end up at the bottom of a river. It's still money well spent. You can rock those stupid-looking sunglasses straps from Croakies (www.croakies.com).

Cold weather accessories (fleece mittens and waterproof liners, Bean boots, Wellies, wool socks, fleece-lined wool hat)

APPENDIX B
BIG LIST OF ROWING TERMS

We will preface this list by saying that we have included a list of rowing terms commonly used in North America. Many of these are not used in the UK and elsewhere, where they have different, and far more charming, words for these things. You will have to forgive us for taking the lazy way out here, and just including the words we use commonly.

Backsplash – Desired splash when blades are moving slightly backward as they come into the water. Not to be confused with the crashing around at the catch perfected by novices.

Backstay – Part of the rigger that runs between the boat and the oarlock to the rear of the oarlock.

Backstops – A rubber or plastic bumper affixed to the end of the slide/track that stops the seat from rolling any further toward the bow of the boat.

Blade – The painted part of the oar that actually goes into the water. Also what you would like to hit a coxswain from an opposing team in the head with after they cut you off in a race.

Boat – The thing you row in, also known as a 'shell' or 'rowing shell.' While the coaching launch is also technically a boat, when it comes to rowing, it is always called a launch.

Boat Strap – A woven canvas strap generally with a metal buckle that cinches the strap at the end of it. Used to secure boats on trailers and onto boathouse racks. Also what your rowers will forget to appropriately tighten or crank down so hard they weaken the hull of your rowing shell.

Body Angle – This refers to bend forward of the rower's back from the hips. Generally rowers are reminded to make sure they are achieving the correct body angle before compressing their legs on the recovery and holding that body angle as they come into the catch.

Bow – (a) The front part of the boat; the furthest part of the boat from the coxswain; where the bow ball is attached; what you want to get across the line first; and (b) the rower seated nearest to the bow of the boat (aka 'bow seat').

Bow Ball – The rubber ball attached to the bow. Designed to keep the bow of your boat from impaling someone or damaging the dock and the boat when you crash one into the other. Protects the bow of the boat from damage inflicted upon it by being steered by inexperienced coxswains into other boats, docks, buoys, bridges, and miscellaneous fixed objects.

Bow Number – A plastic card with a number printed on it used to identify lanes in sprint races or racing order in head races. Only used in racing. Affixed to the bow deck of the boat by a small plastic holder, sometimes called a 'bow number holder' or by duct tape/sheer force of will after the bow number holder breaks off.

Bow Seat – The rower closest to the bow of the boat. Ideally a smaller rower with strong technical precision. Commonly the place where the coach hides one of the worst/most inconsistent rowers in the novice crew.

Bowloader – A 4+ where the coxswain seat is in the bow. The coxswain lies down inside of the bow deck with only his or her head sticking out. Far more aerodynamic than a 'stern coxed' boat and easier for the coxswain to see what is up ahead, but a nightmare for watching technique in practice or seeing what is approaching from the back.

Bowman/Bowwoman – The rower sitting in the bow seat of the boat. Most commonly used to refer to the bow seat rower in sculling boats (2x or 4x) or straight fours (4-), although the term can also apply to the bow seat rowers in 4+ or 8+ boats. In sculling boats or straight fours, the bowman/bowwoman functions as a coxswain, calling the race, and steering the course.

Catch – The point at which the rowers' oars enter the water, and rowers are at full compression.

Check – (a) Motion resulting from rowers incorrectly moving in the opposite directions, especially felt by the coxswain; (b) to 'check it down' is when rowers square their blades and put them into the water to help stop or turn the boat.

Clam – A piece of plastic that clips onto the oar between the collar of the oar and the oarlock; it adjusts the load on the oar; acronym for "Clip on Load Adjusting Mechanism" manufactured by Concept 2.

Crab – An unpleasant experience, not unlike being bitten by its namesake crustacean, whereby the rower loses control of the oar handle, sucking the oar underwater, and occasionally ejecting the rower from the boat; also 'to catch a crab.'

Collar – The plastic part of the oar that goes around the sleeve; it holds the oar against the oarlock. Also known as a 'button.'

Concept2 – Manufacturer of ergometers and oars.

Cox-Box – a voice amplification system used by the coxswain. Cox-Boxes also provide data including stroke rate, time, and speed. Cox-Box is a trademark of Nielsen-Kellerman. Other voice amplification systems include the Australian brand Cox-Mate.

Coxswain or Cox or Coxie – The small person who steers the rowing shell. Also the person who rowers have nightmares about and coaches spend their days figuring out how to manage.

Coxswain Toss – The tradition in rowing is for rowers to toss their coxswain into the river after a major victory. We cannot say why, but it's a great tradition. It should also be reserved for big wins at big races. Save it for big deal races like championships or beating your big rival school for the first time in four years. Otherwise you just look foolish. If you get tossed after every scrimmage your rowers are just trying to punish you. For tips on your mid-air form search "coxswain toss" on YouTube.

Deck – Flat parts that form the 'top' of the bow and the stern of the boat; part of the compartment that traps air in the bow and stern should the boat flip over.

DFL – Stands for 'Dead F****** Last'; this colorful rowing term contains an expletive, but we had to include it because it is so commonly used in the sport. Generally refers to a crew who loses a sprint race by open water or a crew who finishes last in a head race by a minute or more. Also used as a verb, as in, "St. John's is really slow this season. They DFL-ed their last three races."

Eight (8+) – Boat with eight rowers and one coxswain. Each rower has one oar. The coxswain has one Cox-Box and a big mouth.

Engine Room – Refers to the four rowers in the middle of the boat (seats 3,4,5, and 6) in an 8+. Generally the strongest rowers are put in those seats, hence the reference to power generation.

Ergometer or Erg – Training tool used on land to simulate rowing. Also considered a rower's worst nightmare. Concept2 is the most popular manufacturer.

Feather – (a) when the flat part of the blade is perpendicular to the water on the recovery; (b) 'feathering' is the act of flattening your blade while on the recovery; (c) 'on the feather' means rowing by feathering blades.

Finish – The end of the rowing stroke where the blade exits the water; when rowers are at the end of the stroke with full layback position and hands by the bodies.

Footplate – The part of the hull where rowers place their feet to step into the boat; similar to the deck but under the seats.

Footstretcher – The apparatus that rowers attach their feet to in the boat; comprised of a piece of wood, composite, or plastic that is screwed into the bottom of the boat and can be unscrewed and moved up and down a track; shoes are typically affixed to the footstretchers.

Four (4+ or 4-) – A boat with four rowers. A 4+ has four rowers and a coxswain. A 4- or 'straight four' has four rowers and no coxswain. Each rower has one oar.

Frontstops – The front of the tracks; a rubber or plastic bumper affixed to the front of the slide/track that stops the seat from rolling any further to the stern of the boat.

Full Pressure – When rowers are rowing as hard as they can.

Gate – The metal bar that screws down and locks the oar in the oarlock.

Grand Final – The top race in any sprint race; generally comprised of winners of the heats competing for the top 1-6 positions.

Gunwales (pronounced 'gun-els') – The sides of the boat.

Half Pressure – When rowers are rowing but only applying 50% of their maximum power.

Handicap – Amount of time subtracted from raw time in a masters race. Masters rowers are awarded a 'handicap' based on age – the older they are, the bigger the handicap, and the more time subtracted from the raw time. As they often say in masters rowing, it is better to be old than better at rowing fast.

Hands Away – The act of pushing the oar handle away from the body and out of bow to start the recovery; sitting stationary at a position of legs down, lay back, and hands extended straight away from the body.

Handle – The plastic, composite or wooden end of the oar; where rowers grip the oar.

Hatch/Hatch Cover – Plastic porthole type disks that screw and unscrew from the boat; located on the bow and stern decks and sometimes under seats; when closed they hold air in; when open they let water out. Also known as 'vents' or 'vent covers.'

Head Race – A race of 5,000-6,000m or approximately 3 miles; crews start in staggered intervals and attempt to catch and pass one another.

Heat – Initial round of rowing in a sprint race regatta. Winners of the heats advance to the finals.

Heavyweight – Also called 'open weight'; heavy weight crews do not have a weight limit and can be as fat or as giant as they can make themselves.

Hot Seat – To switch boat and oars with another group of rowers at a regatta on the dock or in the water, generally with a fast turn around time between races.

Hull – The outside of the boat; easily scratched, dented, and punctured by careless coxswains.

Inside Arm – The rowers' arm closest to the rigger; with ports, inside arm will be the right arm, and with starbords, the inside arm is the left arm. 'Inside Arm Only' rowing is a drill done with only the inside hands on the oar. Rowers place their outside hands behind their backs.

Inside Hand – The rowers' hand closest to the rigger; with ports, inside hand will be the right hand, and with starbords, the inside hand is the left hand.

Junior – Typically a rower under 18 or still in high school.

Keel – The centerpoint, lengthwise, on any boat. Rowers should row with their body weights over the keel of the boat.

Launch – The term 'launch' refers to the motored boat driven by a rowing coach. We were about to tell you that we had no idea why it was called a launch. Then we wised up. Thanks to our good friends at Wikipedia, we can tell you with no authority whatsoever that the word 'launch' is derived from the Portuguese word 'lancha' which is translated as 'barge,' and during the 1700s the British called boats used to set anchors 'launches,' which then led to the British Navy using the term to refer to military support ships during World War II. Somehow this trickled down to modern day rowing, but Wikipedia left that part out. There you go. As we always like to say, if it's on the Internet, it must be true.

Layback – The position at the end of the stroke when the bodies swing back toward the bow.

Leg Drive – The part of the drive where pressure is applied on the legs by pushing off the footstretchers.

Lightweight – Rowers who weigh less than a certain weight limit and row in a separate category. You can always tell who the lightweights are because they will be walking around the regatta with hungry looks on their faces.

Masters – Post-university level adult rowing designation. Generally used to refer to rowers in their late 20s or older.

Masters Age Category – Some masters events have age categories which are designated with letters. For example, Masters A category may include rowers between the ages of 27 and 35; Masters B category would include rowers between the ages of 36 and 42, and so on. Masters categories are an average of the ages of all of the rowers in the boat except the coxswain. Masters Age Categories replace handicaps in some races under the theory that all the boats in a given event will have a similar handicap.

Missing Water – Rowing mistake in which the rower's blade fails to enter the water at the appropriate time.

Novice – Rower in his or her first year of rowing in high school or in college; a masters rower who has rowed for less than one year. A rower who has rowed in high school may still compete as a college novice. Masters novice rowers may not have rowed for more than one year.

Oar – The thing that goes in the water.

Oarlock – The U-shaped thing attached to the rigger that holds the oar; has a gate to lock the oar in place.

Outside Arm – The rowers' arm on the opposite side from the rigger; with ports, outside arm will be the left hand, and with starboards, the outside hand is the right hand. 'Outside Arm Only' rowing is a drill done on the square with only the outside hands on the oar. Rowers place their inside hands behind their backs.

Outside Hand – The rowers' hands closest to the rigger; with ports, outside hand will be the left hand, and with starboards, the outside hand is the right hand.

Over Square – A mistake where the rower's blade is not at a 90 degree angle to the water but is instead over-rotated forward.

Paddle/Paddle Pressure – When rowers are rowing at very light pressure, about 25% of maximum power or less.

Pair (2-) – A sweep boat with two rowers and no coxswain. Each rower has one oar.

Pause – A hesitation, either on purpose or accidental, at some point during the stroke.

Pause Drill – A drill where the rowers deliberately hesitate at a certain point during the stroke; pause drills are intended to exaggerate and/or segregate certain components of the drive or the recovery.

Petite Final – A second level final in a larger sprint regatta. Generally comprised of the third and forth place finishers from the heats vying for places 7-13 overall.

Piece – A rowing workout of a specific length of time (e.g. ten minute piece).

Poagies – Mitten-like garment worn over the hands and the oar on cold weather days.

Port – Rowers on the port side of the boat; from the coxswain's seat, when facing the bow, ports are on the left hand side.

Puddles – The indentations in the water made by the blades catching the water.

Pull Through – The second and third portion of the drive when the backs are swung into the boat and oar handles are pulled toward the rowers' bodies.

Rating/Rate – The number of strokes a crew takes per minute.

Ratio – A shortened expression that means the ratio of time spent on the drive to time spent on the recovery. Generally a crew strives for a 2:1 ratio, when the recovery takes twice as long as the drive. A crew with 'reverse ratio' is incorrectly rowing slowly on the drive and rushing on the recovery.

Recovery – The second part of the stroke where the rowers are moving toward the stern of the boat, and the oars are out of the water. The recovery begins at the finish with hands coming away, followed by bodies coming forward, and then lastly the legs compress as rowers come back up to the catch to take another stroke.

Regatta – A rowing race, generally with multiple teams competing. Races between only two teams are generally called 'races' or 'duals' and are not referred to as 'regattas.'

Release – The point at which the blade exits the water; the finish.

Repechage – A 'second chance' race at a larger sprint regatta; generally rowed by crews that finish in the 2nd, 3rd, or 4th place in the heats; the top finishers in the repechage will advance to a spot in the Grand Finals and will compete for the top spots overall.

Rigger – (a) The triangular metal or composite piece that attaches to the boat and holds the oar in place; (b) an employee of the boat club or team who rigs the boats before races and generally helps maintain the equipment.

Roll Up/Rolling Up – Also called 'Squaring Up'; the act of rotating the blade to a square position, or 90-degree angle, from the water.

Rudder – The steering mechanism portion of the boat; generally the rudder is a small flat piece within the skeg that moves from side to side when manipulated by the coxswain via the steering cords and the tiller.

Run – The motion of the boat forward.

Rush/Rushing the Slide – When rowers mistakenly move too quickly forward into the stern on the recovery.

Quad (4x) – A sculling boat rowed by four rowers. Each rower has two oars. Generally 'quads' do not have coxswains although some quads are equipped with coxswain seats and coxswain steering.

Sculler – Someone who rows in a boat with two oars per person. Scullers row in singles (1x), doubles (2x), or quads (4x).

Set – The balance of the boat.

Seat – (a) Part of the boat with wheels that slides up and down the tracks; rowers sit on it; (b) 'seat' is also a shortened version of saying 'seat number,' as in 'Rob always rows in three seat.'

Seat Number – Each rower is assigned a number that corresponds to his or her seat position in the boat; bow seat is seat one, the next seat back is 'two seat' and so on; often 'seat number' is shortened to 'seat.'

Seat Race – A race between two boats on the same team as a means for the coach to determine which rowing lineup is the fastest. Rowers are swapped out and raced against each other over a set distance; during seat races, coxswains stay silent and steer in straight lines.

Settle/Settle Stroke – The strongest stroke of the race; follows the start sequence, and is the first stroke where the rowers 'calm down' to race pace.

Shaft – The long, skinny part of the oar between the blade and the handle.

Shell – The boat itself; short for 'rowing shell.'

Shooting Your Slide/Shooting Your Tail – Mistake by newer rowers involving pushing the butt backward well ahead of the shoulders on the drive.

Single (1x) – A sculling boat with one rower and two oars.

Skeg – The triangular piece on the bottom of the boat; serves to stabilize the boat and contains the rudder; commonly ripped off by novice coxswains.

Skying/Skying Your Blade – Mistake by rowers that involves inappropriately dropping the hands too low when approaching the catch. This hand drop forces the blade to pop up skyward into the air.

Sleeve – Piece of plastic that wraps around the shaft of the oar and has the collar (or 'button') located around it.

Slides – Also known as 'tracks'; the metal or composite sliders that the seat moves up and back on.

Slings – Metal frames with canvas pieces that hold a boat temporarily while on land, generally used at regattas and when moving boats between the boathouse and the water.

Spacer – Plastic C-shaped disk that fits onto the oarlock and adjusts the height of the oarlock. Generally easily movable on the water.

Spacing – Difference between each rower's arc of the oar through the water; ideally spacing is identical for all rowers.

Speed Coach – An electronic device made by Neilsen-Kellerman that measures speed, rating, and strokes per minute. Used by coxswains, coaches, and scullers. Gradually being replaced by mobile apps.

Split/Split Time – Amount of time it takes the crew to cover 500m. For example, a split of 1:45, means that the crew would take one minute and forty-five seconds to cover a distance of 500m.

Sprint – The final portion of any race where a crew is rowing as hard as possible; also short form of 'sprint race.'

Sprint Race – A shorter, high-intensity race covering 1,000m, 1,500m or 2,000m with crews lined up over multiple lanes and racing simultaneously.

Square – When the blade is at a 90-degree angle from the water; 'squaring up' is the act of rotating the hands to bring the blade to the 90-degree angle; 'on the square' is rowing with the blade at a 90-degree angle to the water throughout the stroke, both on the drive and on the recovery.

Squaring Up – Also called 'Rolling Up'; the act of rotating the blade to a square position, or 90-degree angle, from the water.

Stakeboat – A boat or platform that holds crews at the start of a sprint race; stakeboats are anchored or attached at a fixed position.

Sweep – Any rowing where rowers have one oar per person; sweep rowing is done in pairs (2+, 2-), fours (4+, 4-) or eights (8+); different than sculling where rowers have two oars per person.

Starboard – Rowers on the starboard side of the boat; from the coxswain's seat, facing the bow, starboards are on the right hand side.

Starboard Rigged – A somewhat unorthodox rigging configuration where stroke seat is a starboard rower, and bow is a port rower. Infrequently used in North America, more commonly seen elsewhere.

Start – (a) The beginning of the race; (b) the first few strokes of the race, generally when rowers row using a combination of partial strokes.

Steering – The coxswain's main job of navigating the crew.

Steering Cords – The cords in the coxswain seat attached to the tiller and the rudder, which controls the boat's direction.

Stern – The back of the boat, generally where the coxswain seat is located.

Stern Deck – The flat part that forms the 'top' of the stern of the boat located directly behind the coxswain in a stern-loaded boat; part of the compartment that traps air in the stern should the boat flip over.

Stroke – (a) the motion of placing the blade in the water and pulling it through; (b) the rower in the eighth seat who sets the pace and rhythm for the crew (short for 'stroke seat').

Stroke Rating – The number of strokes taken by the crew in a single minute.

Stroke Seat – The rower in the eighth seat who sets the pace and rhythm for the crew; often shortened to 'stroke.'

Swing – (a) The act of rowers opening their backs up and laying back toward the bow; (b) the mythical zen state of rowing when all rowers are swinging back simultaneously and the boat is running out under them making everyone feel fantastic about the row.

Tiller – The metal bar, generally located behind the coxswain seat, that attaches to the rudder; part of the boat's steering and functions at the intermediary between the steering cords and the rudder.

Three-quarter Pressure – When rowers are rowing at 75% of their maximum power.

Toe-Steered – A steering mechanism in sculling boats that is controlled by a rower's foot. Literally the rower moves his or her toe from one side to another to steer the boat.

Top Nut – The nut at the top of the pin that holds the oarlock onto the boat. Loose or missing top nuts are one of the most frequent causes of on-the-water equipment problems and are prone to pop off at inopportune times. Coxswains frequently remind rowers to 'check your top nuts,' meaning that they should be tightened down before a row. There is also a 'bottom nut' at the bottom of the pin in some oarlocks, but that one does not get nearly the same amount of attention as the top nut.

Tracks – Also known as 'slides'; the metal or composite sliders that the seat moves up and back on.

Trailer – The vehicle that transports boats from the boathouse to a regatta. Generally towed behind a large truck.

Wake – The 'dirty water' spit out by a motored boat, often the coaching launch, that wreaks havoc on rowing shells by sending waves into the inside of the hull; what coxswains need to avoid.

Walking – Moving on another crew in a race. Generally refers to rowers pushing hard with the legs to 'walk' on a competitor.

Washing Out – Incorrectly moving the blade out of the water in a feathered position; the effect is that the blade slides out without generating full, effective pressure at the finish.

(+) – In rowing the plus symbol '+' means a boat with a coxswain. 2+ is called a 'pair with,' 4+ is a four, and 8+ is an eight. Eights always have coxswains for safety reasons, so the '+' is a bit redundant, but it is still used. We like to think of the '+' as in plus a coxswain.

(x) – In rowing an 'x' means a sculling boat – 1x is a single; 2x is a double; 4x is a quad. None of these boats have coxswains. The rowers do all of the steering, which is why these boats tend to crash into things more frequently. We like to think of the 'x' as in crossing out the coxswain, but that's just our interpretation.

(-) – the minus symbol '-' indicates a sweep boat with no coxswain, also known as a 'straight' boat. 2- is a pair; 4- is a straight four. A pair is never called a 'straight pair' just a pair. Don't ask us why. We like to think of the minus as in minus a coxswain.

APPENDIX C
BIG LIST OF ROWING COMMANDS AND PHRASES

Again we will remind our readers that these are rowing commands and phrases commonly used in North America. Some of these are not used in the UK and elsewhere, where they have different, and far more endearing, turns of phrase for these very same things. Forgive us for our provincial ways. Here are some of the commands and rowing phrases we encounter the most frequently:

Add in – When rowing with pairs sitting out, a coxswain will use 'add in' when he or she is ready for a certain pair of rowers to start rowing again; often combined with asking another pair to sit out (e.g. 'in two strokes, five and six out, three and four add in, 1-2-add in').

Back It – When the coxswain needs the crew to move the entire boat toward stern or backward, he or she will ask the rowers to 'back it.' Rowers turn their blades over to square with the concave portion forward and push the blades away from the bodies (e.g. 'stern pair back it for three strokes.')

Blades Down – (Also called 'Let Fall') Used to tell the rowers to let their blades drop back down to the water in a resounding slap after they have finished a piece and let the boat run out while blades are balanced off the water.

Check it/Check it Down – (Also called 'Hold' or 'Holding' or 'Holding Water') When the coxswain needs to stop the boat or turn the boat quickly to one side when the boat is still moving, this command can be used to get the rowers to square their blades and jam them into the water (e.g. 'ports check it' or 'all eight, check it down').

Count Down – When the crew is leaving the dock or getting ready to start a new piece, the coxswain will ask rowers to 'count down when ready' when they are ready to go. Rowers will start with the bow seat, will yell 'bow', two seat will yell 'two,' three seat will yell 'three,' and so on.

Down on Port/Down on Starboard – This means that the boat is 'down' or lower on either port or starboard indicating that the balance is off. A coxswain should never point out that the boat is down on port or down on starboard and then do nothing about it unless he or she wants to make all his or her rowers grouchy.

Ease Up on Port/Ease Up on Starboard – The command when you want rowers on a certain side to apply less pressure; used to turn the boat slightly without using the rudder (e.g. "last two strokes at full pressure- 1-2-paddle it out").

Even Pressure – The command when you want rowers on both sides of the boat to pull with the same power. This is typically used after asking for more pressure from one side (e.g. "Heavy on starboard for three strokes-1-2-3, OK, now back to even pressure").

Hands On – The command when you want the rowers to grab onto the boat off the water; used when moving boats. Also known as the code for "Everybody stop talking and pay attention because we are ready to start practice, so let's get this boat on the water".

Hit It – When the crew is stopped and the coxswain is trying to get a point, this command tells a specific rower to take a few strokes to get the boat into the right place (e.g. 'bow seat, hit it for two strokes').

Heavy on Port/Heavy on Starboard – The command when you want rowers on a certain side to apply more pressure; used to turn the boat slightly without using the rudder (e.g. 'Heavy on starboard for three strokes-1-2-3-now even pressure').

Hold for Cox – Command given at the dock when you want your rowers to hold onto the boat so that you can get into it. Typically used immediately after the count down on the dock, the cox will call 'hold for cox' and then get into the boat and then call for the rowers to get 'one foot in…and down.' A variation on this is allowing the rowers to get into the boat first while you stay on the dock and then calling 'hold for cox' when you want them to hold onto the dock while you get into the boat.

Hold/Hold Water – (Also called 'Check it' or 'Check it Down') When the coxswain needs to stop the boat or turn the boat quickly to one side when the boat is still moving, this command can be used to get the rowers to square their blades and put them into the water (e.g. 'ports hold' or 'all eight, hold water').

Hold Water Hard – The loudest thing a coxswain ever says; when the coxswain needs to stop the boat immediately, he or she will yell 'HOLD WATER HARD!' until rowers square their blades and jam them into the water to stop the boat fast; should be reserved for emergencies only.

Let Fall – (Also called 'Blades Down') Used to tell the rowers to let their blades drop back down to the water in a resounding slap after they have finished a piece and let the boat run out while blades are balanced off the water.

Let it Run – At the end of the piece when your rowers are finished rowing and you want them to balance the boat with the oars off the water, you can use this command (e.g. 'Last two strokes-1-2-weigh enough, let it run').

One Foot In…and Down – The command given at the dock at the beginning of practice, when you want the rowers to get into the boat; rowers put one foot into the boat, and then sit down. There should be a considerable pause between the two parts of the command (e.g. 'one foot in…[pause, and wait for all of your rowers to do it] and down').

One Foot Up…and Out – The command given at the dock at the end of practice when you want rowers to exit the boat; rowers put one foot up on the dock and then get out. There should be considerable pause between the two parts of the command (e.g. 'one foot up…[pause and wait for your rowers to do it]…and out').

Paddle/Paddle it Out – When you want the crew to row very lightly, typically immediately following a full-pressure piece (e.g. 'last two strokes-1-2, paddle it out'). You never want to stop your rowers immediately after a full-pressure piece, so paddling is a nice downshift before you stop the crew.

Power 10 – When you want the crew to row as hard as possible (harder even than maximum sustained race pace pressure) for ten strokes; should be used very infrequently. Power tens should be special and saved for times when the crew really needs one. We do not recommend more than one per practice. Coxswains who overuse power tens will be summarily ignored and will fail to get the response from the crew when they give this command.

Race Pace – The maximum pressure or rating that a crew can sustain over the duration of the race.

Ready Row/Ready All Row – The starting command for any piece or workout. When you want the rowers to start rowing, you say 'ready…row' or 'ready all…row.'

Run the Blades Out – Command given on the dock when you want the rowers to ship their oars into the oarlocks (e.g. 'starboards run the blades out').

Touch It – When the crew is stopped and you are trying to get a point, this command tells a specific rower to take one light stroke, generally with arms and backs only, to get the boat into the right place (e.g. 'bow seat, touch it').

Weigh Enough – Pronounced 'weigh 'nuf'; the stop command when you want to get rowers to stop rowing (e.g. 'last two strokes, 1-2-weigh enough').

APPENDIX D
SAMPLE RACE PLANS–1000M Race

1,000M Race							
Meters	Pre-Start	0-100	100-200	200-400	400-500	500-700	700-900	900-1000
Tactics		START 1	START 2	TRANSITION 1	TRANSITION 2	MIDDLE	KICK 1	KICK 2
		HIGH 5	HIGH 20	LENGTHEN	MOVE	UP 2	UP 2	LAST 15!
Coxswain Mindset	Automatic	Automatic	Automatic	Analytical	Analytical/Data Driven	Data Driven	Emotional	Emotional
PURPOSE	Keep nerves under control	Get Boat Moving	Get Boat to MAX speed; 20 strokes to accelerate at high rating	Settle into Race Pace and Rhythm; Settle stroke as the STRONGEST of the race	Aerobic Shift; Embrace the transition	Consolidate Length & Swing to lock in race position	Increase Boat Speed	MAX Boat Speed; Accelerate across the finish line
FOCUS	Breathe, relax the shoulders	Pry and Send	Leg Drive; Lock on and pry; focus on feet; getting the rating up	Sustainable speed; lower rating; anaerobic treshold	20 strong strokes; sitting up tall; motivatioal calls for POWER!	Scan for positions of other crews; give data; technique Postive reminders of what makes them row more proficiently (e.g. 10s for posture, length, hanging on the oars, kicking with the legs)	Increase rating by 2s (e.g. 30 to 32, 32 to 34, 34 to 36)	MAX speed across the line; finishing strong; rowing together
CUE WORDS	Affirmations				Power and Technique		Emotionally charged words that motivate and drive the crew	Final power phrases; last few strokes of the race
ISSUES	Anxiety	Bad Start; Late to the Start; General Nerves	Timing, missing water	Rushing the slide; timing, missing water				Not knowing how many meters are left

APPENDIX D
SAMPLE RACE PLANS–2000M Race

2,000M Race								
Meters	Pre-Start	0-100	100-200	200-400	400-600	600-1600	1600-1850	1850-2000
Tactics		START 1	START 2	TRANSITION 1	TRANSITION 2	MIDDLE	KICK 1	KICK 2
		HIGH 5	HIGH 20	LENGTHEN	MOVE	UP 2	UP 2	LAST 20!
Coxswain Mindset	Automatic	Automatic	Automatic	Analytical	Analytical/Data Driven	Data Driven	Emotional	Emotional
PURPOSE	Keep nerves under control	Get Boat Moving	Get Boat to MAX speed; 20 strokes to accellerate at high rating	Settle into Race Pace and Rhythm; Settle stroke as the STRONGEST! of the race	Aerobic Shift; Embrace the transition	Consolidate Length & Swing to lock in race position	Increase Boat Speed	MAX Boat Speed; Accelerate across the finish line
FOCUS	Breathe, relax the shoulders	Pry and Send	Leg Drive; Lock on and pry; focus on feet; getting the rating up	Sustainable speed; lower rating; anarobic treshold	30 strong strokes; sitting up tall; motivatioal calls for POWER!	Scan for positions of other crews; give data; technique	Increase rating by 2s (e.g. 30 to 32, 32 to 34, 34 to 36)	MAX speed across the line; finishing strong; rowing together
CUE WORDS	Affirmations				Power and Technique	Postive reminders of what makes them row more proficiently (e.g. 10s for posture, length, hanging on the oars, kicking with the legs); unique to what makes YOUR crew tick	Emotionally charged words that motivate and drive the crew	Final power phrases; last few strokes of the race
ISSUES	Anxiety	Bad Start; Late to the Start; General Nerves	Timing, missing water	Rushing the slide; timing, missing water			Crew "hitting the wall" exhausted	Crew distracted-not knowing how many meters are left, loss of trust in coxswain or looking out of boat

APPENDIX D
SAMPLE RACE PLANS–5000M Head Race

5,000M Head Race

	Pre-Start	0-250	250-1,000	1,000-2,000	2,000-3,000	3,000-4,000	4,000-4,750	4750-5000
Meters		START	TRANSITION	MAINTAIN	MAINTAIN	MAINTAIN	SUSTAIN	KICK
Tactics	Timing of start-hang back or jump start	At full pressure across the line; Focus on jump start or hanging back; settling into race page	Settle in a race pace	LENGTHEN	MOVE	MOTIVATE	ALL OR NOTHING!	LAST 30!
Coxswain Mindset	Strategic	Strategic	Strategic/Data Driven	Competitive	Competitive	Motivation Driven	Data Driven/Emotional	Emotional
PURPOSE	Timing the start effectively to maximize advantage	Get Boat Moving	Get Boat to MAX speed; Settle in at race pace	Good Steering-Shortest Course possible; Settle into Race Pace and Rhythm; focus on maintaining length and power; making moves on other crews	Good Steering-Shortest Course possible!; Give lots of data on position relative to other crews; focus on maintaining length and focus on Race Pace and Rhythm; power; making moves on other crews	Steer a great course; Focus on calls for Length & Swing; motivational 10s to keep the crew going; making moves on other crews	Start giving data about meters left; Calls to sustain Boat Speed; Hold off Other Crews	MAX Boat Speed; Accelerate across the finish line
FOCUS	Communication of strategy to crew	Pry and Send	Leg Drive; Lock on and pry; focus on feet; getting the rating to race pace	Sustainable speed; Keeping rating under control; keeping crew focused on speed and where other crews are	Scan for positions of other crews; give data; give calls for technique; sitting up tall; motivatioal calls for POWER!	Scan for positions of other crews; give data; give calls for technique; sitting up tall; motivatioal calls for POWER!	Increase rating by 2s (e.g. 30 to 32, 32 to 34, 34 to 36)	MAX speed across the line; finishing strong; rowing together
CUE WORDS		Pry and Send	Ratings; calls for good technique	Postive reminders of what makes them row more proficiently (e.g. 10s for posture, length, hanging on the oars, kicking with the legs); unique to what makes YOUR crew tick	Postive reminders of what makes them row more proficiently (e.g. 10s for posture, length, hanging on the oars, kicking with the legs); unique to what makes YOUR crew tick	Postive reminders of what makes them row more proficiently (e.g. 10s for posture, length, hanging on the oars, kicking with the legs); unique to what makes YOUR crew tick	Emotionally charged words that motivate and drive the crew; Calls for specific people in the boat–seniors, bow pair, stroke, rival schools, emotional connections and inside jokes in the boat	Final power phrases; last few strokes of the race; EMPTY THE TANK!
ISSUES	General nerves	Going out too high, rush, not settling in at race pace	Timing, trouble getting into a rhythm, or maintaining focus when other crews are around	Rushing the slide; timing, missing water; getting distracted by other crews around	Getting really tired; demoralized due to being passed; getting distracted by other crews around	Crew really tired; demoralized due to being passed; crew getting distracted by other crews around	Crew exhausted; not knowing how much time or meters they have left in the race; demoralized due to being passed; distracted by other crews around	Not knowing how much time/meters left; crew distracted, loss of trust in coxswain or looking out of boat

APPENDIX E
NOVICE/INTERMEDIATE COXSWAIN EVALUATION FORMS

Basic Boat Handling on Land	
Score (1-5) 1=Needs improvement/5=Full Mastery	
	Makes LOUD, clear, and concise calls when moving boats on land
	Has the attention of all rowers before moving boats
	Understands where to stand and walk when moving boats
	Follows boathouse procedures (moving boats, signing boats out, strapping boats down, etc...)
	Stands and walks in the appropriate place while moving boats on land
	Does not hit riggers when moving boats
	Has not broken equipment or injured people on land while moving boats

Docking/Launching	
Score (1-5) 1=Needs improvement/5=Full Mastery	
	Understands appropriate club docking/launching procedures
	Stands by the skeg when putting boats in and taking them out
	Follows appropriate club docking/launching procedures
	Understands where to stop before bringing boats into the dock
	Stops with two boat lengths of distance before brining boats into the dock
	Has not broken equipment on the dock while docking/launching

Equipment	
Score (1-5) 1=Needs improvement/5=Full Mastery	
	Takes the Cox-Box, tools, first aid kit, and other equipment in the boat for every practice
	Brings mini-notebook in the boat
	Understands how to connect the Cox-Box in the boat, adjust the volume on the Cox-Box, charge the Cox-Box, and proper care and storage of the mic and Cox-Box.

Safety

Score (1-5) 1=Needs improvement/5=Full Mastery	Understands that safety is top priority
	Understands the typical hazards and weather conditions on the home watercourse (boat traffic, tides, wakes, etc...)
	Understands the locations of physical hazards on the home watercourse (bouys, docks, rocks, mud flats, etc...)
	Understands the basics of using rowers to hold a course
	Understands the traffic pattern
	Follows the traffic pattern
	Understands that safety is top priority

Steering

Score (1-5) 1=Needs improvement/5=Full Mastery	
	Understands how to adjust for weather conditions, wakes, and obstacles up ahead
	Understands how to stop and turn boats quickly and safely
	Maintains appropriate spacing with other crews during practice
	Understands the basic differences between steering a line and steering a point
	Can steer a line
	Understands how to steer with the coaching launch
	Does not impede the courses of other boats
	Knows distances between major landmarks on the home course, and can convey that information to the crew

Running an Effective Practice—Part I

Score (1-5) 1=Needs improvement/5=Full Mastery	
	Writes down what the workouts are for every practice
	Understands the technical skills that the coach is focusing on for the practice, and can communicate those to the crew; keeps the crew focused on those skills
	Understands how to add pairs in and out
	Understands how to use the data on the Cox-Box
	Routinely gives the crew data from the Cox-Box at the appropriate times
	Is focused and has it 'together'; always knows exactly what is going on; seeks clarity from the coach if not

Running an Effective Practice—Part II

Score (1-5) 1=Needs improvement/5=Full Mastery	

	Is alert and aware of what is around in a 360-degree area
	Understands the warm up, the pieces, and drills
	Does not talk over the coach
	Raises his or her hand to acknowledge instructions from the coach
	Is in the right place at the right time
	Stays calm when things go wrong

Technical

Score (1-5) 1=Needs improvement/5=Full Mastery	
	Understands the basic mechanics of the stroke
	Watches for common technical errors
	Makes corrections for common technical errors
	Notices and attempts to fix basic set issues
	Repeats the coach's instructions and technical corrections to specific rowers
	Regularly records practices, keeps a notebook, and self-evaluates
	Counts crisply and accurately, at the right place at the catch
	Gives crews advance warning of conditions (e.g. wakes, steering, etc…)

Giving Commands

Score (1-5) 1=Needs improvement/5=Full Mastery	
	Commands are direct, clear, concise
	Makes decisions quickly and effectively
	Does not apologize
	Voice is deep and powerful, not screaming or whining

Interpersonal Relations

Score (1-5) 1=Needs improvement/5=Full Mastery	
	Easy to talk to; listens
	Patient
	Communicative, asks when he or she doesn't know something
	Does not talk over the coach
	Takes rower personalities, style, and ability level into consideration

Intangibles

Score (1-5) 1=Needs improvement/5=Full	

Mastery	
	Confident but not arrogant
	Self-starter; takes initiative
	Responsible
	Rowers trust the cox
	Rowers like the cox
	Rowers respect the cox
	Makes the crew go faster

APPENDIX E
EXPERIENCED COXSWAIN EVALUATION FORMS

Boat Handling on Land/Docking and Launching	
Score (1-5) 1=Needs improvement/5=Full Mastery	
	Follows appropriate procedures for taking boats in and out of the boathouse and into the water—does not take risks or cut corners
	Evaluates equipment for stress and breakage
	Helps keep equipment in good working error

Safety and Steering	
Score (1-5) 1=Needs improvement/5=Full Mastery	
	Keeps safety as number one priority; keeps a 360-degree perspective on other things around the boat
	Thinks about steering before it happens; is in the habit of seeing the best course forward with an advanced level of forethought

Steering	
Score (1-5) 1=Needs improvement/5=Full Mastery	
	Steers a course that helps the coaching launch, and other crews, maintain their positions
	Makes minor adjustments when steering
	Adjusts steering to account for wind and weather conditions
	Adept at steering for sprint and head races
	Has mastered steering a point
	Lets crews know when steering will be used
	Understands how to accurately gage distance, and conveys that information to the crew

Technical Input	
Score (1-5) 1=Needs improvement/5=Full Mastery	
	Understands the specific crew's issues and works to correct technical errors as they arise at each part of the stroke

	Can identify technical problems and fix them
	Can single out individual rower technique problems without making them feel bad or picked on
	Makes the crew better technically
	Gears technique input to the day's workout and coach's focus
	Regularly records practices and self-evaluates

Running an Effective Practice

Score (1-5) 1=Needs improvement/5=Full Mastery	
	Is focused and has it 'together'; always knows exactly what is going on; seeks clarity from the coach if not
	Takes direction from the coach; is not 'competing' with the coach for the crew's instructions or attention
	Focuses on the same technical aspects that the coach is stressing for the practice
	Works well with the coach, translating his or her instructions to the rowers
	Anticipates where the coach wants the rowing shells; is in the right place at the right time and helps other crews get there as well
	Calm under pressure; helps other crews and the coach in emergencies

Giving Commands

Score (1-5) 1=Needs improvement/5=Full Mastery	
	Commands in the boat are direct, clear, concise
	Adjusts tone and rhythm to fit the situation
	Calls are not repetitive
	Calls are creative, interesting, diverse, and motivating, depending on the situation and what works for each group of rowers
	Calls translate the coach's instructions and say the same things in different ways

Interpersonal Relations

Score (1-5) 1=Needs improvement/5=Full Mastery	
	Easy to talk to; listens
	Patient
	Communicative, asks when he or she doesn't know something
	Respects the coach's authority
	Takes rower personalities, style, and ability level into consideration

Intangibles	
Score (1-5) 1=Needs improvement/5=Full Mastery	
	Confident but not arrogant
	Takes initiative; makes things happen
	Rowers trust the cox
	Rowers like the cox
	Rowers respect the cox
	Makes the crew go faster

APPENDIX F
BIG LIST OF ROWING DRILLS

Big List of Rowing Drills

Rowing Sequence Drills

Drill	How to Run the Drill	Purpose of the Drill
Pic Drill	Done by 4. Standard warm up. Arms, Arms and Backs, 1/2 Slide, Full Slide. Do 10-20 strokes at each position.	Works on different parts of the stroke, isolating movements. Especially good for body preparation out of bow; eliminates 'diving' at the catch.
Reverse Pic Drill	Reverse order of Pic Drill. Do by 4s. Full Slide, 1/2 Slide, Arms and Backs, Arms.	Isolates the parts of the stroke just as the Pic Drill does. Challenge for advanced crews who 'check out' during regular warmups.
Straight Arm Rowing	Done by 6 (or by all 8 with experienced crews) at full pressure. Start at the catch with blades square and buried. Rowers pull through the drive with the legs and then open the back up, but do not break the elbows. Arms will remain straight the entire drill. As soon as rowers complete the layback, they will tap down, bring the body back over, and come back up to the catch. Can be done one stroke at a time or continuous rowing. Repeat with different combinations of 6. Remind rowers to focus on pushing with the legs, and hanging on the oar with their arms.	This drill prevents the arms from breaking early, and forces rowers to drive the legs first, and then open the back up, emphasizing proper rowing sequence. This is a great drill for novice crews.

Acceleration Drills

Drill	How to Run the Drill	Purpose of the Drill
Add a Pair	From a dead stop, your first pair starts rowing. It can be done at full slide or using the Pic Drill sequence. After 15-20 strokes, the next pair comes in, then the next, until all 8 are rowing. Stop. Then start with a different pair. Continue until each pair has had a turn 'starting' the drill.	Accelleration. Each pair will feel what it is like to push their legs down. Especially good for novice crews to feel their personal contribution to boat speed. Good in novice crews for general timing as well, and practice adding pairs in.
4-Stroke Speed Drill	Done by 4 or 6. On the first stroke, from a dead stop, sit at the finish with blades square and buried. Cox will call 'row' and rowers will come up to the catch together and drop the blades in. Stop. Take blades out of the water and go back to the finish. On the second stroke, the cox calls 'row' and rowers come up, drop blades in, and pull through with no power whatsoever. Stop. Go back to the finish. On the third stroke, cox calls 'row' and rowers come up, drop blade in, and pull full pressure through the first half of the drive. No pressure as blade continues through the rest of the drive to the finish. Stop. Sit at the finish. On the fourth stroke, pull through at full pressure. Repeat with other combinations of 4 or 6.	Accelleration, catch timing, general catch connection to the water. Helps rowers feel their contribution to boat speed. This is a good drill for all levels, but especially good for introducing novice crews to adding pressure.
Stairsteps	Row by all 8 at paddle pressure for 20 strokes. Then add 3/4 pressure for the first half of the drive, paddle pressure for the second half of the drive for 20 strokes. Then go full pressure for the first half of the drive, and paddle pressure for the second half of the drive for another 20 strokes. Finally, go to full pressure for 20 strokes throughout the entire drive. Repeat. Maintain a consistent rating throughout.	Great for accelleration, for each rower 'feeling' his or her own contribution to boat speed, isolating their own different levels of power. Good for novice crews learning about accelleration, using the legs to push on the first part of the drive.
Five and Glides	Done at full pressure, rowing by all 8. From a dead stop, take anywhere from 5-20 strokes at low rating. Then the cox indicates the last stroke, and rowers gunnel the oars and let the boat run. Try to see how much run you can get without falling off to one side or the other. Five and glides are done with five strokes, ten and glides with ten strokes, etc...	Good for 'feeling the boat,' great for introducing new rowers to the concept of 'run' and how their balance impacts the accelleration of the boat.
Five and Glides at Super Low Rating	Done at full pressure by all 8. Same as five and glides, but do the drill at a much lower rating, under 16 or lower.	Great for accelleration, timing, and ratio. This drill forces the rowers to slow down the slides and helps isolate pressure from rating, while still maintaining good balance.
4-Stroke Sequences for Pressure	Done by all 8. Paddle one stroke, go 1/2 pressure one stroke, 3/4 pressure one stroke, and full pressure one stroke. Repeat, keeping the rating consistent throughout.	Accelleration, separates increase in power with increase in rating. Also good for timing, following the stroke's rhythm, and not rushing the stroke.
Stand Up-Sit Downs	Done by 4 or 6 (or all 8 in experienced crews). From a dead stop, go one stroke at a time, stopping in between. Rowers start at the catch, focusing on prying the blade through the water. The idea is to stand up on your footstretchers, elevating the body off of the seat, without burying the blade too deep. Focus on lateral, front-to-back motion of the drive, instead of going deep with the blade. Make sure rowers do not go crazy trying to jump off the seat, but instead seeing how much connection they can get with the leg drive. Repeat with other combinations of 4 or 6.	Good for 'feeling the boat,' 'standing' on the footstretchers, emphasizing pushing on the legs, and feeling how each rower is contributing to overall accelleration of the boat. Great for introducing the concept of 'hang' to newer rowers. Also good if you have rowers who tend to bury their blades too deep. This drill is suitable for all levels, but with experienced crews, see if you can run the drill continuously for a few strokes, gradually going back to 'regular' rowing, without stopping.

Balance Drills

Drill	How to Run the Drill	Purpose of the Drill
Eyes Closed Rowing	Done by all 8. Row with eyes closed. The coxswain should keep their eyes open, of course!	Great for balance, and 'feeling the boat.'
Square Blades	Done by all 8 with square blades (or by 6 with less experienced crews).	Good for balance and general timing.
Flyers (a.k.a. Skyers, a.k.a. Flying Dragons)	Done by all 8. Start rowing at half pressure to build boat speed. After about ten strokes, cox calls for Bow 4 to gunwale their oars while Stern 4 keeps rowing. Continue with bow oars gunwaled and Stern 4 rowing for about ten strokes, then add Bow 4 back in. Row another ten strokes by all 8 and then have Stern 4 gunwale their oars while Bow 4 continues rowing. Remind rowers about the importance of getting their finish turns together and keeping handle heights even and consistent.	This drill should be done with experienced crews ONLY! This drill emphasizes balance throughout the stroke. It is very difficult to balance the boat while four oars are skyed in the air.
Air Rows	Row by all 8 at 3/4 pressure normally. Every few strokes, rowers will take an 'air stroke' keeping blades in the air. Remind rowers to keep handle heights level.	This drill should be done with experienced crews ONLY! This drill emphasizes balance throughout the stroke. The air stroke reminds rowers to follow stroke and maintain good handle heights.
Feet Out Rowing	Done by all 8, if possible (or by 6 with less experienced crews). Rowers take feet out of shoes and row.	Good for balance, testing the limits of layback, getting rowers to engage with their core muscles.

General Technique/Bladework

Drill	How to Run the Drill	Purpose of the Drill
Inside-Outsides a.k.a. 'Juggling'	Done by all 8 (or by 6 with less experienced crews). Drive with the outside hand only, recover with the inside arm only. Switch hands as/when at the feather. Work on keeping the wrists flat, with no hesitation during the transition.	This drill is good for feeling separation between hands, good for bladework. Forces rowers to concentrate, and is great for fixing problems related to bent wrists, super tight grips, or weird angled or bent elbows.
Inside Arm Only Rowing	Done by all 8 (or by 6 with less experienced crews), on the feather. Put the outside hand behind the back, and row with inside arm only. Focus on clean releases, and keeping the wrist flat.	This drill works the feather, and focuses on clean releases.
Outside Arm Only Rowing	Done by all 8 (or by 6 with less experienced crews), on the square. Put the inside hand behind the back, and row with outside arm only. Be sure rowers keep the shoulders relaxed and catch only by unweighting the outside arm, letting the blade fall into the water. Focus on using the outside arm as a level, and keeping the blades all going into the water together.	Good for oar height, catch connection, and general blade control at the catch and finish. This drill works especially well for novice crews learning about 'lock on' or 'catch connection.''
Pause at the Release on the Square	Done by 4 or 6 (or all 8 in very experienced crews). Row on the square, pausing every stroke at the release. Focus on square blades coming out of the water together, with a clean release by all blades simultaneously. Repeat with other combinations of 4 or 6.	Good for clean releases and finish timing.
Wide Grip Rowing	Done by 4 or 6. Rowers take their inside hand off the handle, and hold down onto the shaft of the oar. Rowers row at full slide, normally. Repeat with other combinations of 4 or 6.	This drill keeps the outside shoulder higher than the inside shoulder. Good for rotation around the rigger. This drill forces rowers to sit up on the recovery, and is good for body preparation because it requires rowers to sit up and get the body over to avoid flopping into the catch. This drill is also good for general flexibility. Use it sparingly with older masters rowers because it seems to be hard on their backs.
Narrow Grip Rowing	Done by 4 or 6 (or all 8 in experienced crews) at half pressure. Rowers put hands close together at the end of the handle and row normally. The rowers will not get as much extension at the catch as they would normally. Continue, repeating by combinations of 4 or 6, and then switch to rowing by 8 normally.	This drill is designed to improve blade control because the narrow grip will give the rowers less control. Note that this drill is difficult to do on oars with separated handles.
Square Finishes	Done by 4 or 6. Rowers row normally, but remove the blade square at the finish and keep it square until the arms are fully extended, then feather. Rowers re-square the blade as they would normally, between the knees and ankles. Repeat with other combinations of 4 or 6.	This drill helps prevent 'feathering under' (feathering while the blade is still finishing the stroke). This drill is good for general timing and coordination.
Alternate Square and Feather Rowing	Done by all 8 (or by 6 with less experienced crews). This drill can either be done by rowing for 20 strokes on the feather and then 20 on the square, or rowing square-feather-square-feather, etc...	This drill is great for blade control and balance.
Extra Layback	Done by all 8 at half pressure. Start rowing at a low rate, adding extra layback to the point where rowers feel the engagement in their core muscles. Remind rowers to swing from the hips into bow and get their bodies over together after the hands come away. Gradually decrease the layback until you get back to normal.	This drill is great for emphasizing body swing, particularly for rowers who have minimal laybacks, or fail to swing their bodies forward, or have problems following other rowers in front of them, especially coming out of bow.

Drill	How to Run the Drill	Purpose of the Drill
One Finger Rowing	Done by 4 or 6 at half pressure with square blades. Start at the catch with one finger of each hand on the oar. Row a few strokes, and then add one more finger on the oar on each hand and row a few more strokes. Continue to add more fingers until rowers have full grip on the oar.	This drill is designed to force the rowers to keep a light grip on the oar and prevents rowers from 'throwing' with the backs, instead doing all of the work with the legs.
Italian Feathering	Done by 4 or 6. Row normally, but remove the blade square and feather the blade only slightly (10% feathered or 90% square). Rowers re-square the blade as they would normally, between the knees and ankles. Repeat with other combinations of 4 or 6.	This drill is great for blade control.

Timing Drills

Drill	How to Run the Drill	Purpose of the Drill
Pause Arms Away	Done by all 8 at half pressure. Take five strokes to build boat speed. Cox will then call the pause. Rowers pause at arms away. Cox then calls 'row' and rowers come forward to complete the rest of the stroke. Pauses can be added every stroke, every other strokes, or every few strokes. Remind rowers to get their bodies over after the pause, coming out of bow, as opposed to 'diving' at the catch.	This drill is good for timing, especially body preparation. Reminds rowers to get the hands away quick, eliminating the pause at the finish.
Two-Part Pause @ Arms Away and @ Body Over	Done by all 8 at half pressure. Take five strokes to build boat speed. Cox will then cause the pause. Rowers pause at arms away. Cox calls 'row' and rowers move to body over position and pause. Cox calls 'row' and rowers move up to the catch normally. Pauses can be done continuously, every other stroke, or every few strokes. Remind rowers to focus on swinging the body over early in the recovery, and holding the body for the rest of the recovery. Also remind rowers to focus on controlling the slide after the second pause.	This drill is good for timing, body preparation and ratio.
How Low Can You Go?	Done by all 8 at half pressure. Start rowing at an 18, and try to drop the rating as low as possible. Focus on keeping the drive quick and strong, and the recovery super slow. Remind rowers to follow the stroke.	This drill helps crews work on ratio, acceleration on the drive, timing, and learning to follow the stroke.
Pause 1/2 Slide	Done by all 8 at half pressure. Take five strokes to build boat speed. Cox will then call the pause. Rowers will pause at half slide. Remind rowers to focus on squaring up together and slowing down on the second half of the recovery.	This drill is good for general timing, ratio, and slowing down the rush on the second half of the slide.
4-Stroke Sequences for Rate	Done by all 8 at half pressure. Take five strokes to build up to a 22. Take one stroke at a 22, one stroke at a 24, one stroke at a 28. Repeat as needed.	This drill is for advanced crews only, and requires an experienced stroke. It is good for general timing, getting crews to isolate ratings. This drill also helps crews focus on following their stroke, not rushing the stroke, and keeping the recovery slow and consistent while the drive gets quicker.
Russians	Done by all 8 at half pressure. Rowers take one stroke with arms only, one stroke at arms and body, one stroke at 1/2 slide, one stroke at full slide. Repeat.	This drills is good for concentration and timing. It forces the rowers to think and follow their stroke. Add at the end of practice when rowers tend to 'check out.'
Cut the Cake	Done by 4 or 6 (or all 8 in experienced crews) at half pressure. Rowers row at half pressure for a few strokes to build boat speed, then from the finish, push arms away, bring arms back to the finish, then push arms away, and then complete the stroke as normal. Can be done every stroke or every few strokes. Remind rowers to bring hands in and out at the same speed, keeping hands quick out of bow. Repeat with other combinations of 4 or 6.	This drill is good for timing and blade control. It helps rowers think about setting the boat at the finish, keeping hands quick and together at the finish.
SUPER Fast Drive, Super Slow Recovery	Done by all 8 at half pressure. Similar to 'How Low Can You Go?' where the rowers start out rowing at a low rating ~18. As you go, start pushing the drive faster, while holding the recovery consistent. The cox should keep an eye on ratings. Continue until rowers have a 3-1 ratio.	This drill is good for ratio, keeping the drives quick, and not rushing the slide. It also forces the rowers to follow the stroke.
1/4 Slide/Full Slide Drill	Done by all 8 (or by 6 with less experienced crews) at half pressure. Alternate rowing one stroke at 1/4 slide and then one stroke at full slide. Remind rowers to keep slides under control, and decelerate as they approach the catch.	This drill is good for following stroke, and for crews that tend to rush because it requires concentration to keep the slides under control on both the 1/4 and the full slide strokes.
Slaps	Done by 6 (or all 8 in experienced crews) at half pressure. Take a few strokes to build the boat speed. Rowers will row continuously, but instead of squaring up and catching, they will leave the blade feathered. At the normal catch spot, they will slap the blade onto the water. Then, instead of putting the blade in the water, they will slide the blade on the top of the water. Rowers will pick the blade up off the water as they normally would on the recovery. You can also do this drill one stroke at a time.	This drill forces rowers to think about catch timing, balance, and getting the blades up off of the water on the recovery. The slap provides an audible cue to the cox and the rowers as to which rowers are 'off' and which rowers are together. This drill is great for timing generally, and is suitable for more experienced crews.

Catch Drills

Drill	How to Run the Drill	Purpose of the Drill
1/4 Slide Rowing	Done by 6 at half pressure. Rowers start at the catch, pull through 1/4 of the drive, and come back up to the catch. Focus on timing, quick catches. Can be done one stroke at a time, or continuous rowing. Repeat with different combinations of 6.	This drill is done for timing and quick catches. It is suitable for intermediate and advanced crews.
1/2 Slide Rowing	Done by 6 at half pressure. Rowers start at the catch, pull through 1/2 of the drive, and come back up to the catch. Focus on timing, quick catches. Can be done one stroke at a time, or continuous rowing. Repeat with different combinations of 6.	This drill is done for timing and quick catches. It is suitable for intermediate and advanced crews.
Double or Triple Speed Catches	Done by 6 (or by all 8 with experienced crews) at half pressure. Rowers row normally, but accellerate the top 1/8 of the slide and the catch. Remind rowers to square early and lock on together. Try to get faster and faster as you go.	This drill is good for timing, catching together, and following stroke. It forces rowers to square up early and catch together.
Double Catches	Done by all 8 at half pressure. Row normally to build up boat speed. On cox's command, rowers will begin a double catch, essentially levering and unlevering the blade, making a small chop at the catch on the first 'catch', and catching and pulling through on the second 'catch.'	This is good for relaxing the hands, and the idea of using the arm hinging off the shoulder as the level to put the blade into the water.
Whistle Catches	Done by 4 or 6, rowing on the square continuously. Cox blows a whistle or says 'catch' at random points in the stroke. The rowers must react, dropping the blade in immediately.	This drill is fantastic for improving timing, anticipation of the catch, and following stroke. It is best suited for more experienced crews, but novice crews can use it as well. This drill is great for crews that are burned out with workouts or rowers that tend to 'check out' during practices. It forces crews to listen to (and trust) the coxswain and follow the stroke.
Chops	Done by all 8 (or by 6 with less experienced crews) from a dead stop. Rowers sit at the catch with oars square and buried. On cox's call, rowers push the hands down, forcing the blades out of the water, and then letting the blades fall back in, making small chops. The idea is to get the chops perfectly together, with all 8 blades hitting at the same time. The cox should let rowers do this without talking, forcing the rowers to listen to the sound of the chops. It should be apparent to the rowers who is off.	This drill is done for catch timing, and helping rowers listen to the sound of all the blades entering the water simultaneously.
Stationary Double Catches	Done by all 8 (or by 6 with less experienced crews) from a dead stop. Rowers sit at the finish, and on cox's command come up to the catch, making a small chop at the catch on the first 'catch', and catching and pulling through on the second 'catch.' Rowers pull through to the finish and stop. Repeat as necessary.	This is good for relaxing the hands, and the idea of using the arm hinging off the shoulder as the level to put the blade into the water.
Finish to Catch	Done by 4 or 6 (or all 8 in experienced crews) from a dead stop. Rowers sit at the finish with hands by the body with the blade in the water square and buried. Cox will call 'row' and rowers will tap the oar handles down, feather the blades out, continue on the recovery as they would normally, squaring at the normal point, and drop the blades in together. Then stop. Go back to the finish with hands by the body with the blades in the water square and buried. Repeat as needed, one stroke at a time. Remind rowers about getting the tap down together, hands quick out of bow, and get the bodies over together.	This drill works on catch timing and catch placement. It reinforces the idea that body preparationout of the finish is key to good catch placement.
Catch Placement Drill	Done by 4 or 6 (or all 8 in experienced crews) from a dead stop. Rowers sit at 3/4 slide with blades feathered and flat on the water. On cox's call, rowers will lower their hands, square their blades, and come forward to the catch, dropping in the blades at the catch. Stop. Go back to 3/4 slide and repeat.	This drill helps rowers think about squaring up together, moving hands forward at consistent handle heights, and catching together.
Karate Chops	Done by all 8 at half pressure. Rowers will pull through the drive as normal, but will place their hands on the top of the oar handle in a karate chop position. At the catch, let the blade drop into the water, and grip the oar normally.	This drill relaxes the upper body, which allows for good catches.
Underwater Back Downs	Done by all 8. From a dead stop, rowers will sit at 1/2 slide with the blades square and buried. Rowers come forward to full compression, moving the blades underwater, until they get to the catch. At the catch, rowers pause, and then pull through a regular drive, finishing, and pausing at hands away. Stop. Repeat, going one stroke at a time.	This drill is designed to help rowers feel consistent pressure with all 8 blades at the catch.

Drill	How to Run the Drill	Purpose of the Drill
Gunwale Taps	Done by 4 or 6 (or all 8 in experienced crews) at half pressure. Rowers row normally to build boat speed. On the cox's call, as rowers come up to about 3/4 slide, they square the blades, and push the hands straight down to the gunwales, carrying the hands along the gunwales up to the catch, and then lifting at the last minute to drop the blades into the water together. Remind rowers to hinge the arms from the shoulder to drop the blades in together. Note that this can cause pinches fingers, so remind rowers to be careful not to put fingers between the oar and the boat.	This drill is great for correcting late roll up and poor catch timing, although it is best suited for more experienced crews.

Finish Drills

Drill	How to Run the Drill	Purpose of the Drill
Double or Triple Speed Hands Away	Done by all 8. Rowers row normally, but will accellerate the hands away from the body at two or three times their normal speed. Focus on trying to get the hands away together consistently. Gradually slow down back to normal speed, still focusing on tapping down and away together, keeping the hands away quick to help set the boat.	This drill helps rowers understand the importance of moving the hands away consistently at the finish, tapping down and away together to help the set of the boat.
Down and Outs (a.k.a. Bobbing, a.k.a. Finish Chops)	Done by all 8 (or by 6 with less experienced crews) from a dead stop. Rowers sit at the finish withhands by the body and with blades square the buried. Cox will call 'row' and rowers will push their oar handles down together, bringing the blade out of the water, then letting the blade fall back in, making small chops on cox's count. Do one stroke at a time initially, then do successive chops continuously. The idea is to balance when the blades are out of the water.	This drill helps with tapping down and getting the hands away consistently. Good for helping set the boat up at the finish.

Printed in Great Britain
by Amazon